BACKROADS & BYWAYS
OF
MICHIGAN

BACKROADS & BYWAYS OF MICHIGAN

Drives, Daytrips & Weekend Excursions

Matt Forster

SECOND EDITION

THE COUNTRYMAN PRESS
WOODSTOCK, VERMONT

We welcome your comments and suggestions. Please contact
   Editor
   The Countryman Press
   P.O. Box 748
   Woodstock VT 05091
   or e-mail countrymanpress@wwnorton.com

Backroads & Byways of Michigan
Second Edition
ISBN 978-1-58157-198-1

Interior photographs by the author unless otherwise specified
Maps by Michael Borop, siteatlas.com, © The Countryman Press
Book design by S. E. Livingston
Composition by Chelsea Cloeter

Published by The Countryman Press,
P.O. Box 748, Woodstock, VT 05091

Distributed by W. W. Norton & Company, Inc.,
500 Fifth Avenue, New York, NY 10110

Printed in the United States of America

10 9 8 7 6 5 4 3 2 1

THIS BOOK IS DEDICATED TO ALL THOSE
WHO HAVE ROAMED BEFORE ME
AND TAUGHT ME TO LOVE TIME ON THE ROAD.

A sandy trail leads to the waterfront on Beaver Island.

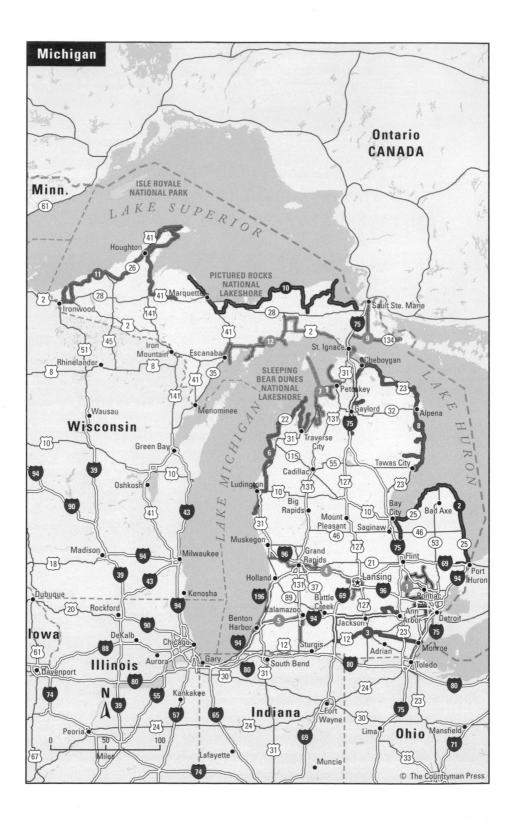

CONTENTS

Introduction 9

1. An Adventure through Car Country...................... 17
   Detroit, Dearborn, Redford, Northville, Farmington, Milford,
   Holly, Oxford & Metamora, Stony Creek, and Rochester

2. Blue Water and a Green Thumb 37
   Port Huron, Lexington, Port Austin, Caseville, Bay City,
   and Frankenmuth

3. Forgotten Highways: The River Raisin and the
   Chicago and Territorial Roads 53
   Monroe & Dundee, Tecumseh, the Irish Hills, Allen,
   Coldwater, Marshall, Chelsea, Dexter, and Ann Arbor

4. Through the Heart of Michigan:
   Following the Grand River 75
   Eaton Rapids, Lansing, Grand Ledge, Lowell,
   Grand Rapids, Rockford, and Grand Haven

5. The Grape Coast: Michigan's Wine Country 93
   Three Rivers, Kalamazoo, Paw Paw, Coloma, Harbor Country,
   St. Joseph, South Haven, Fennville, and Saugatuck

6. The Cherry Coast...................................... 115
   Silver Lake, Ludington, Sleeping Bear Dunes,
   the Leelanau Peninsula, and Old Mission Point

7. The Great Northwest 135
   Elk Rapids, the Chain of Lakes, Charlevoix, Beaver Island,
   Petoskey, and Bay View

8. The Sunrise Coast: Old Lumber Towns and Lazy Rivers ... 155
   Tawas City, Au Sable & Oscoda, Harrisville, Alpena, Presque
   Isle, Rogers City, Cheboygan, and Pigeon River Country

9. **Where Great Lakes Meet: The Straits of Mackinac and the St. Mary's River** 171
Mackinaw City, Mackinac Island, Hessel & Cedarville, the islands of the St. Mary's, and Sault Ste. Marie

10. **Superior's Scenic Shoreline** 191
Point Iroquois, Whitefish Point, Newberry, Grand Marais, Munising & Au Train, and Marquette

11. **Waterfalls & Big Snow, Iron & Copper: The Porkies to the Keweenaw Peninsula** 211
Ironwood & Bessemer, the Porcupine Mountains, Houghton-Hancock, Lac La Belle, Copper Harbor, Eagle River, Calumet & Laurium, L'Anse, and Michigamme

12. **Lake Michigan's Other Coast** 233
Curtis & the Manistique Lakes, Blaney Park, Manistique, and Escanaba

Index 244

INTRODUCTION

Si quaeris peninsulam amoenam circumspice
(If you seek a pleasant peninsula, look about you)

—Michigan's state motto

Michigan is best known for two things—the automobile industry and the Great Lakes. While making cars and trucks has traditionally driven the state's economy, it's the lakes that inspire visitors. Throughout the region's history, water has been the big attraction. Even the state's natural resources, lumber and copper and iron ore, were all the more valuable because they could be transported by water.

Michiganders live with the understanding that they are at all times surrounded by water on three sides. In fact, no matter where you are in the state, you are never farther than 85 miles from a Great Lake. And while millions of travelers make their way here to lay out on Lake Michigan's sandy beaches or see Superior's Picture Rocks, they also come for the 11,000 inland lakes and to enjoy fishing, paddling, and swimming on 36,000 miles of rivers and streams.

All of the state's large urban centers are found in the southern half of the Lower Peninsula. North of Flint, the only interstate is I-75, which makes a beeline north for

The Round Island Lighthouse greets visitors to Mackinac Island.

Stacked rocks on Grand Traverse Bay *Kim Forster*

the Mackinac Bridge and then northeast to Sault Ste. Marie. Michigan is the largest state east of the Mississippi, and with most of the population concentrated in the south, this leaves much of the state's 58,000 square miles inaccessible by the interstate highway system. It turns out then that back roads and byways are the best way to explore Michigan. With a few exceptions, travelers who stick close to the multilane highways will miss out on nearly all the beauty and adventure Michigan has to offer.

This guide is the result of a lifetime of exploring the state. I like to get off the highway and seek alternate routes. If the highway is the shortcut, I am inclined to find the longcut. Over the years, I am still surprised at the number of charming small towns and villages that lay right off the beaten path. Even in the cities, there is so much off the beaten path that is missed by the day-to-day commuters.

Each of these towns tells a story about a different time in Michigan's history. Interestingly, the first Europeans to find their way into the Great Lakes did not linger in the Lower Peninsula; the French missionaries and trappers made their way to Native American settlements farther north. The land was home to several Native American tribes, like the Ojibwa and the Menominee, who used the waterways as transportation and fished the area's rivers. One of the region's most important meeting places was near Sault Ste. Marie, where fish were plentiful on the St. Mary's River.

Missionaries set up small chapels, and trappers took advantage of the meeting places for trading furs for goods and supplies. The fur trade soon became a significant industry, and trappers traded their furs at the Sault or near the Straits of Mackinac before heading back into the wilderness. Their furs were shipped eventually to Europe, beginning their journey on the St. Lawrence Seaway.

Later, lumber and mining would become the main drivers of the region's economy. When the Upper Peninsula's vast mineral resources were

discovered in the early 1800s, mining was begun, and immigrants soon arrived to tackle the hard job of getting iron ore and copper to the surface. They came from all over Europe, but primarily from Norway, Finland, Italy, and England. They and their descendants have profoundly shaped the Upper Peninsula's unique culture. It is said that the pasties (meat pies) you find at every restaurant were brought over by English miners from Cornwall.

The Upper Peninsula (U.P.) is unlike any place you've visited before. Some have said that anywhere you go in the U.P. is off the beaten path. That's true. This region is known for its rugged wilderness and natural beauty. Surrounded by three of the largest freshwater lakes in the world, the U.P. hosts two mountain ranges, over 150 waterfalls, and 4,300 inland lakes. It is custom-made for hiking, biking, paddling, and fishing.

Cities in the Lower Peninsula took advantage of the state's natural resources. Early on, Michigan's lumber was being used to make furniture in Grand Rapids. The industry grew to the point that it was known as Furniture City, the furniture-making capital of the world. Though the material is different, Steelcase continues the industry's legacy with the manufacturing of heavy-duty office furniture.

In 1903, a Detroit inventor named Henry Ford incorporated the Ford Motor Company. By 1908, his little outfit was

A sheltered inlet on Lake Michigan
Kim Forster

A waterfront view of Hancock from Houghton

producing Model Ts, soon at a pace that revolutionized industry. The automobile industry attracted thousands of laborers from around the country. Many came up from the South, which was still struggling to transition from an economy based on agriculture to one based on industry. By 1914, Ford was paying factory workers five dollars a day, and there was plenty of work for all. The role of the auto industry in the growth and development of Detroit cannot be underestimated.

By the 1960s, Detroit fell on hard times. The first blow was essentially cosmetic. Once known for its hundreds of thousands of stately elm trees, Dutch elm disease first hit Detroit in the '50s. By the '70s, the elms were all but completely decimated. The biggest change, however, came in 1967, when racial tensions were at an all-time high. The Detroit Riots lasted for five days and seemed to spur wealthier white residents to move away to the suburbs. The city is still trying to recover from the effects of this demographic change. In fact, it's not hard to see how the loss of population led to the city's recent decision to declare bankruptcy.

There is good news, however. Downtown Detroit is experiencing a revival. The new Comerica Park is filled all summer with screaming Tigers fans, and Ford Field has brought the Detroit Lions in from the suburbs. Though casinos have cost the city some of its character, they have brought thousands of people into town. Culture continues to thrive with the Detroit Opera House, the Fox Theatre, and the Detroit Symphony Orchestra at the Fischer Music Center. Recently, the Detroit Institute of Arts completed a

Ring-necked ducks in the Seney Preserve

The view of Detroit from Belle Isle *Kim Forster*

six-year, $25-million renovation and across the street the Michigan History Museum has been completely redone.

As more tourists find their way to Detroit, they are discovering that this metro area has some back roads of its own. Not only are there numerous hidden gems in the city, away from the popular Greektown area, but the suburbs have some attractions as well.

With all the shoreline in Michigan, you would think there would be plenty of big towns along the way. In fact, many of the towns and villages you will find around the Thumb of Michigan's mitten, up the Lake Huron shoreline, and even along Lake Michigan are not huge tourist towns. They are little burgs that sleep in the winter,

A beaver dam in the UP's Seney National Wildlife Refuge

and in the summer open with seasonal restaurants and art galleries—and even then, they are pretty low-key.

Whether you travel in summer or winter, you will find that the sun seems to have its own schedule. Because most of the state is so far north (we are dissected by the 45th parallel after all), the changes of the seasons are more dramatic. And because of the quirky way in which the time zones were drawn, Michigan finds itself in the Eastern time zone. You may not think much of this until one July you are up north and find it is 9:30 at night and the sun has yet to set. This is just part of life in Michigan—short days in winter, and in the summer, days that never end.

The weather here is pretty typical of the Midwest: Summers are warm and humid; spring and fall receive a good dowsing of rain; and in the winter, snowfall can be significant. This is especially true in the Upper Peninsula and along the west side of the Lower Peninsula. The U.P. stays cooler in the summer than the rest of the state, and its summer season is shorter. In early and midsummer, the U.P. is notorious for black flies and mosquitoes. If you are planning on hiking north of the Mackinac Bridge during the bug season, it's always recommended that you wear pants and long-sleeved shirts. Bug spray has little effect with the flies, and I've seen hikers don netted headgear and light gloves.

Summer is the high tourist season, but fall pulls in a close second. When the colors begin to change, the rolling woodlands can seem ablaze. In the winter, many folks will head north to the ski hills or hit the hundreds of miles of trails open to snowmobiles. More and more, it seems, are discovering the pleasant exercise of cross-country skiing and snowshoeing.

This book will guide you as you stray from the beaten path and find the hidden beauty and adventure of Michigan. There are plenty of guidebooks for seeing Detroit, or Traverse City, or Mackinac Island. Here I will show you the most scenic driving itineraries, where you can explore the state's quieter attractions. You will get a better feel for both the state and the people who live here.

One of the places where you can learn about Detroit's car-making history is the recently opened Piquette Plant.

1 An Adventure through Car Country
DETROIT, DEARBORN, REDFORD, NORTHVILLE, FARMINGTON, MILFORD, HOLLY, OXFORD & METAMORA, STONY CREEK, AND ROCHESTER

Estimated length: 135 miles
Estimated time: 4 hours

Getting there: The trip begins in downtown Detroit. Following Michigan Avenue west to Dearborn, the trip then heads northwest with stops at Redford, Northville, and Farmington on the way to Milford Taking Milford Road north to Holly, continue east on Grange Hall, traveling MI 15 south to Seymour Lake Road east. In Oxford, continue south on MI 24 to Lake Orion. Turn southeast on Orion Road. A short side trip takes you over to the Stony Creek Metropark; then the route ends in Rochester and Auburn Hills north of Detroit.

Highlights: This trip begins in Detroit, where you will check out the restaurants of Mexicantown and Greektown, tour the country's largest farmer's market at the Eastern Market, explore ceramics at Pewabic Pottery, and browse through hundreds of thousands of books at John K. King Books. An introduction to automobile history begins at the Ford Piquette Plant, where Henry cranked out the first 12,000 Model Ts. In nearby Dearborn, the education continues with a day at Greenfield Village and the Henry Ford Museum, or a field trip to see production in action at the Ford River Rouge Complex. The next two stops—Redford and Northville—have some interesting sites including an old movie theater, a family-run Scottish bakery, and the historic Mill Race Village. Before heading to more remote locales, there's a stop at Marvin's Marvelous Mechanical Museum in Farmington Hills. Throughout the Detroit suburbs, thousands of acres of park beckon. On the way to the little town of Holly in north Oakland County, stop by the Kensington Metro Park near Milford for a picnic or pontoon boat tour of the lake. In Holly, visit the downtown antiques shops and eat at the Historic Holly Hotel. Heading east, there's swimming, hiking,

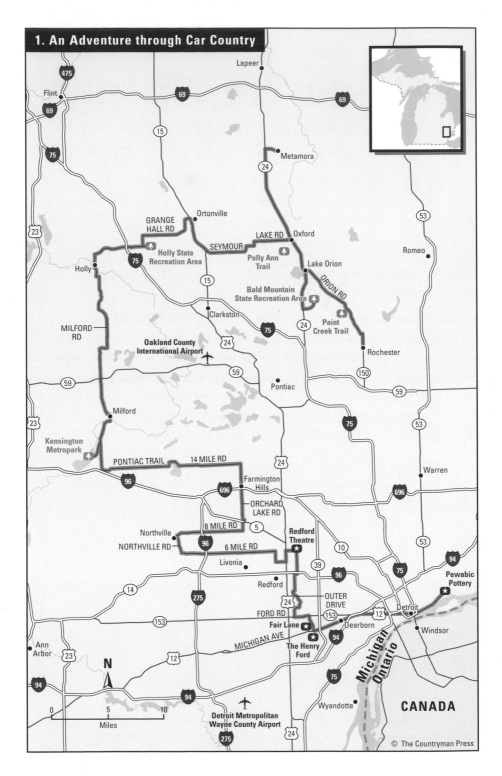

1. An Adventure through Car Country

and mountain biking at the Holly State Recreation Area. When you reach Oxford on MI 24, consider the side trip north to the Historic White Horse Inn in Metamora. From Oxford, we head south back toward the suburbs of Detroit. The Paint Creek Trail connects Rochester with Lake Orion (and Bald Mountain State Recreation Area), roughly following Orion Road. In Rochester, grab a bite at Red Knapp's Dairy Bar and stop at the Yates Cider Mill. Coming full circle back to automobiles, tour the Meadow Brook Hall in Rochester, the home of Matilda Dodge Wilson (John Dodge's widow).

The home of Ford, General Motors, and Chrysler, Detroit has become synonymous with the automobile industry. Not only has car manufacturing dominated the local economy for nearly a hundred years, but the manufacturers have had a direct impact on the community. This is most certainly a car town, from the preponderance of American-made vehicles on the roads, to Labor Day festivities that celebrate the UAW (United Auto Workers), to street parties like the **Woodward Dream Cruise** and countless ad hoc car meets that gather in area parking lots like those of local A&W restaurants.

That Detroit is the Motor City has almost become a cliché, but still a true one. Over the years, however, Detroit has picked up a number of nicknames aside from Motor City and Motown. For Red Wings fans, this is Hockeytown. For classic rock fans, Detroit will always be Detroit Rock City. Less known are those nicknames from earlier in the city's history. Before Dutch elm disease wiped out the city's trees, Detroit was the City of Trees. During World War II, when Michigan manufacturing joined the war effort, it was called the Arsenal of Democracy, and during the Gilded Era of mansions and great promise, the Paris of the Midwest.

Begun as a fort on the Straits of Lake Erie, Detroit was for some time the capital of Michigan. With a constant flow of natural resources following the currents of the Great Lakes to its front door, Detroit was positioned to play a part in the industrial revolution. Before cars, the city was home to five companies making iron stoves. (Even as late as 1922, after car manufacturing took hold, stove manufacturers made 400,000 stoves in one year.) In 1908, however, the writing was on the wall. That was the year Henry Ford began production on his Model T. In 1927, when the last of that model rolled off the line, Ford had produced 15 million Model Ts.

In the mid-20th century, the city of Detroit went through a dramatic transformation. Many factors are cited for why the heart of the city began to erode. The new highway system, for example, made it easier for people to move farther from town. The migration of whites to the suburbs was spurred on by the Twelfth Street Riot of 1967, which led to the burning of two thousand buildings. That, combined with the already massive loss of trees to Dutch elm disease, left the city looking like a

Comerica Park is where the Tigers come to play.

war zone. Abandoned buildings still are a signature feature of Detroit. By 1985, it was labeled the murder capital of the United States.

For years, countless efforts have been made to revitalize the old downtown. In the 1970s, the Renaissance Center was built on Detroit's waterfront. Trapper's Alley in Greektown was promoted as a center of retail. In the late '80s, the Detroit People Mover—an elevated train making a 3-mile loop through town—was opened to passengers. These and other projects have met with minimal success, but there is still a lot happening in Detroit, and there's still a lot to be hopeful for.

In recent years, the number of people visiting Detroit has increased with the establishment of the Greektown Casino and the MGM Grand Detroit; the new Ford Field, the home of the Detroit Lions; and Comerica Park, the ballpark for the Detroit Tigers. All of these are close to long-standing institutions like the Fox Theatre, Detroit Symphony Orchestra, and the Detroit Opera House. A few miles away are the Detroit Institute of Arts, the newly re-done Detroit Historical Museum, and the Detroit Public Library.

The city's official flag, which was adopted in 1948, has two mottos that aptly sum up the future promise of Detroit. The Latin *Speramus Meliora* and *Resurget Cineribus* translate to "We hope for better things" and "It will rise from the ashes."

The Arts and Crafts movement in America reached its peak around the turn of the 20th century. Various handicrafts were rediscovered and celebrated in England and in the States—papermaking, bookbinding, cabinetry, leatherwork and metalwork, and (in Detroit) pottery. In 1903 Mary Chase Perry Stratton and her partner, Horace Caulkins, rented an empty horse barn on Alfred Street. Caulkins had developed

CONEY ISLAND—IN DETROIT?

C hicago has its deep-dish pizza and Chicago-style hot dogs. Philadelphia has the Philly cheesesteak. New Orleans has Cajun jambalaya; Massachusetts, baked beans; and Maine, lobster. And every region has its own brand of BBQ. Detroit's contribution to the American culinary melting pot is the Coney dog—traditionally a beef hot dog (with natural casing) smothered in a beanless chili with mustard and diced onions. (In Flint, the chili has a tomato base, and up that way you have to ask for your Coney "Flint" or "Detroit" when you order.)

You can get this delicacy at almost any diner around, but they are properly served at Coney Island restaurants. The concept of the Coney Island restaurant—a diner serving the all-American Coney dog and Greek combos like a gyro and fries—began in Detroit. The first was American Coney Island downtown, founded by Constantine "Gust" Keros in 1917. His chili-covered hot dogs were so popular that his brother opened Lafayette Coney Island just one door down the street. Over generations a rivalry has developed, and people are more than happy to take sides.

Coney Island restaurants have since become a dining phenomenon in southeast Michigan. There are big Coney Island chains like National Coney, Kerby's Koney, and Leo's Coney, as well as dozens of mom-and-pop joints scattered across the metro area with names like Genie's Wienies and Joe's Top Dog Coney Island.

a unique kiln, and Stratton was an artist with a passion for glazes. In 1907 **Pewabic Pottery** was moved to its present location on East Jefferson. (*Pewabic* is an Ojibwa word that means "clay the color of copper.") The Tudor revival building was designed by William Buck Stratton and is an example of how architecture was influenced by the Arts and Crafts movement. Mary Stratton became known for her iridescent glazes, and the Pottery produced tiles, jewelry, and things for the home.

Today the Pottery is a National Historic Landmark, and the work begun by Mary Stratton continues. The studio has both a museum store and galleries that display the work of ceramic artists from around the country. And the studio's larger installations can be seen all over metro Detroit—at the Cranbrook Institute, along the People Mover, and at several important public buildings like the Detroit Public Library and the Detroit Institute of Arts.

On the other side of town, inside the old Advance Glove factory on Lafayette, is a bibliophile's paradise. It's the home of **John K. King Books,** a four-storied tribute to the love of the hunt. With somewhere around a million books in stock, and no computer database to keep track of them, anything's possible. The Rare Book Room is a gem, however, and the people here really know books, so you won't be stumbling across pages from one of Gutenberg's Bibles among the regular stacks. Instead, you will find rows and rows of shelves, each as well organized as a library.

John King began humbly enough, selling books at antiques fairs while still in high school. In 1971 he opened his first used-book store in Dearborn. His stock of books soon outgrew that location, as it did his next storefront in the Michigan Theatre Building in downtown Detroit. So in 1983 King bought the glove factory. Today there are two other bookstores beside this one, the Big Bookstore on Cass Avenue in Detroit and John K. King Books North on Woodward in Ferndale.

North of the Wayne State campus there's an important stop on the automotive history tour. Henry Ford's Piquette Plant (officially now the **Model T Automotive Heritage Complex**) saw the Ford Motor Company develop from one of many companies trying to jump-start an industry to a world leader in automotive production. The company produced a number of different models on Piquette Avenue—the Model N, the Model C, the Model F, etc.—but these were all just steps on the way to developing the Model T. A runaway seller, 12,000 Model Ts were built here before production was moved to the new Highland plant in 1910.

The Tin Lizzie, as it's affectionately called, is considered the world's first affordable car. It was built for the common man, so to speak, and Henry Ford would go on to see more than 15 million of them roll off the line before production ended in 1927. This history is on display at the Piquette Plant. (Be sure to check the website for hours before you show up to tour the museum. There is some seasonal variability.)

While you're in town, be sure to stop by the **Eastern Market**, the largest farmer's market in the country. Detroit's Farmer's Market was opened in Cadillac Square back in 1841. It was moved

At Detroit's Piquette Plant

in 1891 to its current location between Gratiot and Mack and renamed the Eastern Market. Tuesday through Saturday, upward of eight hundred farmers can be found selling their produce from the market's open-air stalls, the area called "the sheds." The market has its seasons, from the spring's hothouse rhubarb to the apples and pumpkins of the fall. Even in the winter, when business has moved into the enclosed sheds, root vegetables are offered.

In addition to farm-fresh produce, the market is surrounded by brick-and-mortar shops—fish markets, butcher shops, and small groceries selling imported ethnic foods. Many of these stores date to the late 19th century. The R. Hirt Jr. Company, for example, was founded in 1887. In 2012, the shop became **DeVries & Co.** (still in the same family). The store carries over three hundred varieties of cheese, and regulars line up at the old wood cheese counter to discuss options with the store's knowledgeable staff. They also carry a wide selection of specialty groceries—imported olive oils, aged vinegars, tea, and coffee. The third floor of the building is dedicated to wicker items and other home-decorating pieces, many made in Michigan.

If you find yourself at the Eastern Market around meal time, be sure to stop into the **Supino Pizzeria.** Quite a few Detroiters will tell you this is the best pizza in the city, and there are not a lot of people lining up to argue the point. The restaurant serves up excellent thin crust pizza. A favorite with regulars is the Bismark, which is topped with mozzarella, prosciutto, and egg. For something altogether different, try one of their no-sauce "white" pizzas.

Open every day but Sunday, the Eastern Market draws shoppers from all over the state, even the country. To get to the Eastern Market, take I-75 to Mack Avenue (exit 52), head east two blocks to Russell Street, and turn right. There is a parking lot at the southeast corner of Russell and Winder Streets.

For years it seemed that Greektown was the only place to go when visiting Detroit. Centered on Monroe Street, this enclave of Greek restaurants and bakeries was the place where after-theater diners could get a bite to eat or share a drink. The neighborhood was established well over a hundred years ago when Greek immigrants came to Detroit and set up homes around Lafayette and Monroe Streets. Greek businesses became commonplace on Monroe.

In the 1970s, Greektown became the focal point for efforts at revitalizing Detroit. The alley behind the buildings on the south side of Monroe was enclosed, creating a little multilevel mall called Trapper's Alley. The mall essentially failed, and in the 1990s, the Greektown Casino moved in. Within the last 30 years, the character of Greektown is less and less Greek, but several places still proudly stand true to their roots. **Pegasus Taverna** is the place for an authentic Greek meal, and **Astoria**

Pastry Shop is the place for dessert. Try their honey-sweetened baklava or maybe something less Greek, like cheesecake or the Black Forest torte.

In the southwest section of Detroit, another area has become known for its rich ethnic heritage. Mexicantown is just west off I-75 at Vernor Highway and Bagley Street. The neighborhood has several blocks of restaurants and taquerias offering authentic Latin American cuisine—everything from Columbian to Guatemalan to El Salvadoran. The real draw, however, are the Mexican restaurants.

Close to the highway there are three that pull a lot of traffic. Los Galane's, El Zocalo, and Xochimilco all share the corner of Bagley and 23rd Streets with the fourth corner the home of the La Michoacana Flour Tortilla Factory. There are more restaurants along Vernor. Worth a little bit of a drive is **Taquería Mi Pueblo,** which sits at the west end of Mexicantown, just past the Vernor-Dix fork. After a meal, be sure to stop at the **MexicanTown Bakery** for dessert.

There are several great hotels in Detroit—the Marriott, in Detroit's iconic Renaissance Center right downtown on the waterfront, and the new hotel/casino, the MGM Grand Detroit, are just two examples.

For more intimate accommodations, consider **The Inn on Ferry Street.** The inn is made up of four restored Victorian homes and two carriage houses comprising 40 rooms. It's fewer than 2 miles from the theater district and the baseball and football stadiums, and only a block from Wayne State University and the Detroit

Hostel Detroit is located in the city's Corktown neighborhood.

Institute of Arts. The rooms are finely appointed with Victorian touches—fully modern, but in keeping with the history of the neighborhood.

A bit closer to town is **The Inn at 97 Winder,** just two blocks from the Fox Theatre, Comerica Park, and Ford Field. Built in 1876, the 11,000-square-foot brick mansion home is truly an architectural delight. The 10 guest rooms on the second and third floors are luxuriously appointed, each a showpiece. Bathrooms are large and entirely modern, and each room has a comfortable sitting area.

For something at the other end of the spectrum, a hostel recently opened in North Corktown. **Hostel Detroit** opened its doors in the early spring of 2011 and has stayed open welcoming guests from around the world. If you want to get a feel for the "spirit of Detroit"—that combination of determination, entrepreneurialism, and creativity that is fueling much of the city's hopes—Hostel Detroit is your best bet.

Henry Ford, often called the father of modern industry, was born on a farm in what is now Dearborn, just west of Detroit. As the Ford Motor Company grew, Ford built the Ford River Rouge Complex in Dearborn. When completed in 1928, the Rouge Plant was the largest industrial complex in the world. And Ford's estate, Fair Lane, was just up the street from the plant. The history and trajectory of Dearborn has been, and continues to be, inextricably linked to Henry Ford and the automobile empire he created.

One of Ford's most lasting contributions to southeast Michigan is **The Henry Ford,** which is both the Henry Ford Museum and Greenfield Village in Dearborn. The museum began as Ford's personal collection of historic items. Today, exhibits pay tribute to the glories of human ingenuity and industry. Cars, planes, and trains are just the tip of the iceberg. The museum also houses vehicles that played some part in the course of American history, like the Rosa Parks bus and the Lincoln Continental in which President John F. Kennedy was shot.

Greenfield Village has exhibits of an entirely different nature—namely, buildings. Here you will find Henry Ford's childhood farm, Thomas Edison's Menlo Park laboratory, and the courthouse from Illinois where Abraham Lincoln once practiced law. In the summer, fields are farmed much like they would

This '56 Buick Century won the Curator's Choice award at Greenfield Village's Motor Muster, the first of the village's two annual summer car shows.

A brick farmhouse at Greenfield Village

have been in the 19th century. On weekends, teams play old-time baseball while fans watch from the shaded hillside. Two car shows—Motor Muster and the Old Car Festival—bookend the summer season. Hundreds of classic-car owners gather to swap stories and drive the village's brick streets.

While at The Henry Ford, check out the regular schedule of IMAX movies and special exhibits. Guests can also purchase tickets for the Ford Rouge Factory Tour.

Just across Michigan Avenue, across from the Fairlane Mall, is Henry Ford's palatial estate, **Fair Lane**. The property is cared for by the University of Michigan–Dearborn. Guests can take the self-guided tour of the grounds or sign up for a tour of the auto baron's mansion.

West of the Fair Lane estate, Ford Road takes you to Outer Drive. This picturesque boulevard was designed in the early 20th century as the perfect Sunday drive for city dwellers. It makes a grand horseshoe around Detroit. Over the years the route has evolved into a busy thoroughfare as the city has grown and burst its borders. Newcomers find it rather confusing, but it still connects historic neighborhoods and prime urban parks. Follow Outer Drive north through the Rouge River Park and past I-96, staying on Lahser Road when Outer Drive bends east. Just past Grand River you come to the next stop.

Plan ahead and you might get a chance to catch a movie at the **Redford Theatre.** This classic venue is owned and operated by the Motor City Theatre Organ Society. Built in 1928, a Barton Theatre organ was installed to accompany silent films. The fact that the organ survived intact where others had been dismantled or damaged attracted the Theatre Organ Society. They began restoring the organ with the theater owner's blessing in 1965. In 1977 they purchased the theater. Today the Redford Theatre offers folks a steady stream of classic films. Every show is preceded by a 30-minute "mini concert" on the old organ.

At 5 Mile and Beech Daly—2 miles west and 1 mile south—you will find another hidden gem. **Ackroyd's Scottish Bakery** has been in business for well over 60 years. Begun as a meat market in Detroit in 1948, the family soon discovered there was a demand for traditional Scottish meat pies. Soon they were making and selling shortbreads and tea cakes. Three generations of Ackroyds now run the bakery, and they are getting attention for having some of the most unique and tasty treats around.

Returning to 6 Mile, drive east nearly 9 miles to Northville Road and turn right. You will soon be in downtown Northville. This upscale burg is known by many because of the HGTV show *Cash & Cari.* It's hard to imagine a more suitable neighborhood for peddling high-end antiques. Deserving special attention is the **Mill Race Village,** owned by the Northville Historical Society. The property was given to the city by the Ford Motor Company and now features a number of historic buildings, including a blacksmith shop, church, rustic wooden bridge, and several attractive

Several historic homes have been moved to Northville's Mill Race Village.

homes. Check the village website for scheduled events, demonstrations, and concerts.

Continuing farther out into the suburbs, take Baseline Road/8 Mile east to Orchard Lake Road, then follow that north into Farmington Hills. Just before 14 Mile on the left is a large shopping center behind which you will find **Marvin's Marvelous Mechanical Museum**. The name says it all. A quick glance and you might dismiss Marvin's as a typical video game arcade, but it's not that at all. Terms like *penny arcade* and *carnival midway* come to mind. There are video games and classic pinball machines, but there is also a wonderful collection of arcade favorites—from a fortune-telling gypsy to an automaton that foretells the fate of the damned. And even though many of these attractions would be at home in a museum, they're here for anyone to play.

There are 13 Metroparks spread across five counties, creating a greenbelt of nearly 24,000 acres around metro Detroit. Add in the state recreation areas, various county parks, and innumerable city parks, and you will find that outdoor recreation is never far away in southeast Michigan. **Kensington Metropark** is one of the finest parks in the suburbs. From Farmington Hills it's an easy 17 miles away. Drive west on 14 Mile, which becomes Pontiac Trail. Turn north on Milford Road and drive 2.6 miles to the Huron River Parkway. Turn left and continue 1 mile to the park entrance on the right.

About 2.5 million people visit this metropark every year. The activities are seemingly endless. The park's lakes are used for swimming and boating (boat rental available), and there are campsites along the Huron River reserved for canoe campers. There's an 18-hole golf course and a disc golf course. For kids there's a nature center and farm learning center.

At Kensington Metropark, you can get quite close to the sandhill cranes. *Kim Forster*

The nature center is one of the best places around to see sandhill cranes. Several miles of nature trails are reserved for walkers—no jogging, no running, no pets—and one stretch of path is seemingly stocked with friendly birds that will eat out of your hand if you bring seed.

Return to Milford Road and drive north about 3 miles to **Milford**. The road makes a jog through town. Turn north on Main Street, and the road goes back to being called Milford Road.

A trailhead at the Holdridge Lakes Mountain Bike Area near Holly

Holly is 16 miles north of Milford on Milford Road. The town boasts nearly a dozen excellent antiques shops and the **Historic Holly Hotel.** The hotel was established around the turn of the 20th century to cater to guests arriving at the busy train station in town. Today there is no hotel per se, but a fine restaurant still serves guests in the dining room. Be sure to swing by **Holly's Main Street Antiques** for the biggest selection of antiques in town. In December, downtown Holly is transformed into a Dickensian village, complete with chestnuts roasting and wandering carolers clad in Victorian duds.

From downtown Holly, drive north on Saginaw about 1 mile to Grange Hall

Road. Heading east, take Grange Hall about 4.5 miles. Just after Dixie Highway, the road makes a sharp turn north. Ignore the turn and continue straight to **Holly State Recreation Area.** The park is bisected by McGinnis Road. The south side is for day use; the north has a campground. There are three lakes with a handful of beaches and picnic areas. The lakes are also popular with anglers. The north side has about 160 campsites on McGinnis Lake. The Holly Wilderness Trail is a nice 6.4-mile hike that winds through both sides of the park.

A short drive away, and also part of the recreation area, is the nearby Holdridge Lakes Mountain Bike Area. To get there, return back across I-75 on Grange Hall and turn north on Hess Road. You will see the parking area a little over 1 mile up on the left. Loops on the parking lot side of the road range from easy to moderate, and riders can easily customize a ride by combining different loops. Be sure to check out the map; these are all one-way trails, and you don't want to get stuck swimming against the current. The East Loop (aka Gruber's Grinder) is a tough, technical 15.5-mile trek that includes log jumps and rock climbs. I've known a few avid mountain bikers who have returned from Gruber's with quivering legs and aching knees.

Continue on the generally eastward bound Grange Hall Road. At Ortonville Road (MI 15) in Ortonville, turn right and drive south 3.5 miles to Seymour Lake Road; turn left. **Cook's Farm Dairy** is a few miles up the road. This working farm sells ice cream by the cone, bowl, or tub. Locals love to sit and watch the cows as they enjoy their favorite scoop. Beware: The small scoop is huge and too big for a little cone—get the waffle cone and be ready to experience something special.

Seymour Lake Road continues east, with a few jogs here and there, until it reaches Oxford. There the name changes to West Burdick Street for a few short blocks. In downtown Oxford, turn right and drive south on South Washington Street (MI 24). There are few nice restaurants in Oxford, and the Polly Ann Trail passes through town—you can see the pedestrian bridge over MI 24 just north of the center of town.

For a diversion, consider driving north on MI 24 to the town of **Metamora.** This is Michigan's horse country, with rolling green pastures hemmed in by whitewashed plank fences. The Metamora Hunt group, previously called the Grosse Pointe Hunt Club, moved here in 1928 and epitomizes the region's horse culture. During the season, with hounds ready, they ride the countryside in red coats and riding pants, looking for fox.

Downtown Metamora is 9 miles north of Oxford—1 mile east of MI 24 on East Dryden Road. Across the state, there are many towns with names that sound as if they are derived from the region's native peoples. Interestingly, the early Michigan explorer Henry Schoolcraft went about making up Native American–sounding

CLARKSTON

Settlement in Michigan did not happen as fast as in other territories. Surveyors sent by the government had reported that the entire region was swampy lowlands, impossible for farming or other industry. Some pioneers came anyway and soon discovered the surveyors' limited sight. The village of Clarkston was first settled in 1830 as a wave of adventurous souls followed the lead of one Maj. Oliver Williams, who had explored the lakes region beyond the settlement of Pontiac in 1818. A dam and a sawmill were built on the Clinton River, creating the village's signature Mill Pond.

Over the years, different owners put the mill to use as a sawmill, gristmill, plaster mill, and flour mill. The building was eventually torn down in 1917. In 1941, when Henry Ford was busy promoting his "Village Industries" program around southeast Michigan, the Ford Motor Company bought the old mill property and built a factory. The mill was intended to provide power to the factory but was never quite sufficient. The employees of the mill typically lived on small local farms. It was Henry Ford's philosophy that industry should not supplant agriculture, and he looked for workers who could keep "one foot in the soil."

Today, Clarkston is one of metro Detroit's bedroom communities. Its proximity to I-75 makes it very attractive to suburbanites, and its two-lane Main Street limits through-traffic. The downtown has seen a shift in the past 20 years. The old pharmacy is now a boutique grocery of sorts, and the once empty church on Main Street is now the widely acclaimed Clarkston Union. This restaurant is best known for its mac and cheese. Open for lunch and dinner; on Sunday they pull out the stops and serve a righteous breakfast.

The biggest thing to hit the village in recent years is the Union Woodshop. In some ways an extension of the Union, it was once the home of the Clarkston Café, which for years was one of north Oakland County's only five-star restaurants. In the past it was not uncommon for performers at Pine Knob Music Theatre (now the DTE Energy Music Theatre) to take in a meal here before or after their shows. The new joint is a favorite of Kid Rock and has been featured on the Food Network's *Diners, Drive-Ins, and Dives* with Guy Fieri.

For lodging, the Mill Pond Inn is a wonderful place to stay. Right on Main Street, a block from downtown, the inn has five rooms, all very affordable. Though the home is on Main Street, it's really quite quiet in the late evenings.

names for various settlements. Metamora was named after a popular play that was first performed in New York in 1829—*Metamora, or The Last of the Wampanoags.*

The Historic White Horse Inn has been a mainstay of the community since

1850—originally serving as a stagecoach stop and later as a traditional inn. Even after 150-plus years, the White Horse continues to get rave reviews. The menu is stocked with traditional American favorites, from steak and ribs to whitefish and their signature salads.

Diversions aside, return to MI 24 and drive south to Lake Orion (pronounced OR-ee-un). South and east of Lake Orion, the **Bald Mountain State Recreation Area** is plotted out in three separate areas. For swimming, Lower Trout Lake is in the central park. The entrance is south on MI 24 on the east side right after Waldon Road. The beach here is sandy, and families with younger children will appreciate the lake's wide shallows. Local mountain bikers revel in the 15 miles of bike trails.

One of the area's most impressive recreation features is the rails-to-trails success of the **Paint Creek Trail.** The trail follows the old Penn Central Railroad connecting Lake Orion and Rochester. The 8.5-mile path is surfaced in crushed limestone (except for a paved section near Rochester). With some riding on the roads, the trail connects with the Polly Ann Trail that continues north to Lapeer.

Two cider mills are conveniently located near the trail. The **Paint Creek Cider Mill** recently reopened its restaurant, serving pizza, wraps, and dogs year-round, as well as ice cream and doughnuts. Another mill, just 0.5 mile away, is the **Goodison Cider Mill.** In the fall they have great cider and doughnuts. While we're on the subject of cider mills, there's a historic mill on the other side of Rochester worth visiting (south and east of downtown at Dequindre and Avon). The **Yates Cider Mill** dates back to 1863, when the operation was first built as a gristmill alongside the Clinton-Kalamazoo Canal. The nearby Yates dam still provides the water that powers the mill.

Roughly following Paint Creek, Orion Road cuts southeast across the usual grid to Rochester Road and downtown Rochester. Back in the 1930s Red Knapp opened

Red Knapp's is a classic burger joint.

Red Knapp's Dairy Bar; the business was later sold and then repurchased by Red in the 1950s. It remains a classic '50s diner (the real thing, that is; it's not like Johnny Rockets in the mall). A hamburger here can take up a lot of room on the plate, but it keeps a low profile, so you can get your mouth around it. Egg salad sandwiches, chili dogs, and an old-fashioned sloppy joe—they all go down nice with one of Red Knapp's chocolate malted shakes.

There are a number of restaurants on Main Street in Rochester that regularly make the "Best of Metro Detroit" lists. A local favorite with families and folks looking for a cheaper option is **Lipuma's Coney Island.** Carrying on that great Coney dog tradition, Lipuma's serves up all sorts of dogs—from Chicago style to Texas style—but the real draw are the Coney dogs, served with chili and onions. Order a couple with a tray of fries and perhaps the soup of the day (a little-known specialty), and you're ready to sit back on their deck overlooking Paint Creek. Be sure to have cash on hand, because they don't take cards.

The Yates Cider Mill has been water powered ever since it was founded as a gristmill in 1863. *Kim Forster*

This stretch of Rochester Road, from town to MI 59, has every kind of restaurant you can imagine. Italian, Indian, Chinese, BBQ, steakhouses, classic Coney Islands—there's even an excellent Thai place on Auburn Road just west of Rochester Road. It is called **Sukhothai,** which means "dawn of happiness" in Pali. The uninitiated should try the pad thai or the pad bai kra prow with chicken. For dessert, the rotee—a Thai crêpe with chocolate—balances nicely with the spiciness of dinner. There are other Thai places around, but few do it this well with such an inviting atmosphere.

There's great Thai dining to be had in Rochester.

Rochester is the home of Oakland University. The property for the school was donated by Matilda Dodge Wilson (widow of auto pioneer John Dodge), and her mansion, **Meadow Brook Hall & Gardens,** still stands nearby, maintained by the university. Built in 1929 by Matilda

Dodge Wilson and her second husband, Alfred G. Wilson, a lumber broker, it is the fourth-largest mansion preserved as a museum in the United States. With 110 rooms, the Tudor revival mansion has 88,000 square feet of space. Tours are available daily; check the website for a schedule. Around Christmas, the home is decorated by various shops, and the public is welcome for the Holiday Walk.

IN THE AREA

ACCOMMODATIONS

Hostel Detroit, 2700 Vermont Street, Detroit. Call 313-451-0333. Website: hosteldetroit.com.

The Inn at 97 Winder, 97 Winder Street, Detroit. Call 313-832-4348 or 1-800-925-1538. Website: theinnat97 winder.com.

The Inn on Ferry Street, 84 Ferry Street, Detroit. Call 313-871-6000. Website: innonferrystreet.com.

Mill Pond Inn, 155 North Main Street, Clarkston. Call 248-620-6520. Just off the highway in Clarkston, this unpretentious B&B is central to north Oakland County. Website: millpondinn bb.com.

ATTRACTIONS AND RECREATION

Ackroyd's Scottish Bakery, 25566 5 Mile Road, Redford. Call 313-532-1181. Website: ackroydsbakery.com.

Bald Mountain State Recreation Area, 1330 East Greenshield Road, Lake Orion. Call 248-693-6767. Website: michigan.gov/baldmountain.

DeVries & Co., 2468 Market Street, Detroit. Call 313-568-7777. This historic cheese shop is open Tuesday through Sat. Website: devries1887.com.

Eastern Market, 2934 Russell Street, Detroit. Call 313-833-9300. Open year-round; closed Sun. Website: detroit easternmarket.com.

Goodison Cider Mill, 4295 Orion Road, Rochester. Call 248-652-8450. Open daily from September until Christmas, the mill has fresh pressed cider and warm cider doughnuts.

The Henry Ford, 20900 Oakwood Boulevard, Dearborn. Call 313-982-6001 or 1-800-835-5237. The Henry Ford has the Ford Museum, Greenfield Village, an IMAX theater, and tours of the Ford River Rouge Plant. Website: thehenryford.org.

The Henry Ford Estate: Fair Lane, 4901 Evergreen Road, Dearborn. Call 313-593-5590. Guided tours are offered year-round, with a limited schedule during the winter. Website: henryfordestate.org.

Holly's Main Street Antiques, 118 South Saginaw Street, Holly. Call 248-634-1800.

Holly State Recreation Area, 8100 Grange Hall Road, Holly. Call 248-634-8811. Website: michigan.gov/holly.

John K. King Books, 901 West Lafayette Boulevard, Detroit. Call 313-961-0622. Website: rarebooklink.com.

Kensington Metropark, 2240 West Buno Road, Milfod Call 248-685-1561 or 1-800-477-3178. Website: metro parks.com/parks/pk_kensington.php.

Marvin's Marvelous Mechanical Museum, 31005 Orchard Lake Road, Farmington Hills. Call 248-626-5020. Website: marvin3m.com.

Meadow Brook Hall & Gardens, 480 South Adams Road, Oakland Uni-

versity, Rochester. Call 248-364-6200.
Website: meadowbrookhall.org.

Mill Race Village, 215 Griswold
Street, Northville. Call 248-348-1845.
Website: millracenorthville.org.

**Model T Automotive Heritage
Complex,** 461 Piquette Avenue. Detroit. Call 313-872-8759. Website:
tplex.org.

Paint Creek Cider Mill, 4480 Orion
Road, Oakland Township. Call 248-
656-3400. Website: paintcreekcider
mill.net.

Paint Creek Trail, 4393 Collins Road,
Rochester. Call 248-651-9260. Website:
paintcreektrail.org.

Pewabic Pottery, 10125 East Jefferson Avenue, Detroit. Call 313-822-
0954. Website: pewabic.com.

Redford Theatre, 17360 Lahser Road,
Detroit. Call 313-537-2560. Website:
redfordtheatre.com.

Woodward Dream Cruise. Website:
woodwarddreamcruise.com.

Yates Cider Mill, 1990 East Avon
Road, Rochester. Call 248-651-8300.
Website: yatescidermill.com.

DINING

American Coney Island, 114 West
Lafayette Street, Detroit. Call 313-961-
7758. Website: americanconeyisland
.com.

Astoria Pastry Shop, 541 Monroe
Street, Detroit. Call 313-963-9603.
Website: astoriapastryshop.com.

Clarkston Union, 54 South Main
Street, Clarkston. Call 248-620-6100.
Website: clarkstonunion.com.

Cook's Farm Dairy, 2950 Seymore
Lake Road, Ortonville. Call 248-627-
3329.

Historic Holly Hotel, 110 Battle
Alley, Holly. Call 248-634-5208. Website: hollyhotel.com.

Historic White Horse Inn, 1 East
High Street, Metamora. Call 810-678-
2150. Website: historicwhitehorseinn
.com.

Lafayette Coney Island, 118 West
Lafayette Street, Detroit. Call 313-964-
8198.

Lipuma's Coney Island, 621 North
Main Street, Rochester. Call 248-652-
9862.

MexicanTown Bakery, 4300 West
Vernor Highway, Detroit. Call 313-
554-0001. Website: mexicantown.com
/bakery.

Pegasus Taverna, 558 Monroe Street,
Detroit. Call 313-964-6800. Website:
pegasustaverna.com.

Red Knapp's Dairy Bar, 304 Main
Street, Rochester. Call 248-651-4545.
Website: redknapps.net.

Sukhothai, 54 Auburn Road, Rochester Hills. Call 248-844-4800. Website:
sukhothai-thaicuisine.com.

Supino Pizzeria, 2457 Russell Street,
Detroit. Call 313-567-7879. Website:
supinopizzeria.com.

Taquería Mi Pueblo, 7278 Dix Street,
Detroit. Call 313-841-3315. Website:
mipueblorestaurant.com.

Union Woodshop, 18 South Main
Street, Clarkston. Call 248-625-5660.
Website: unionwoodshop.com.

OTHER CONTACTS

**Detroit Convention and Visitors
Bureau,** 211 West Fort Street, Suite
1000, Detroit. Call 1-800-DETROIT
(338-7648). Website: visitdetroit.com.

Turnip Rock makes kayaking on Lake Huron a bit of a treasure hunt.

2 Blue Water and a Green Thumb

PORT HURON, LEXINGTON, PORT AUSTIN, CASEVILLE, BAY CITY, AND FRANKENMUTH

Estimated length: 166 miles

Estimated time: 4 hours

Getting there: From Detroit, take I-94 north to exit 257, and then turn east on Fred W. Moore Highway 7 miles to St. Clair. The route follows MI 25 up to the tip of the Thumb and down into Bay City.

Highlights: Before this tour hits the Thumb's Blue Water region, where Lake Huron empties into the St. Clair River, we visit a county park with a fine historical village and farm museum: the Goodells County Park in Wales. Then the route heads to Port Huron for tours of the Huron Lightship Museum and the Fort Gratiot Lighthouse. Following the curve of the Thumb north, Lexington is the next stop on Lake Huron. Tourism being the main attraction, it's a nice place to browse shops or stop for a meal. You should also plan to stay at one of their excellent bed & breakfasts. Continuing north, visit the Sanilac County Historic Village & Museum and the historic Huron City Museums, the latter offering tours of the summer home of William Lyon Phelps. On the way to Port Austin, known for a few first-rate restaurants, stop and tour the Pointe aux Barques Lighthouse. If the weather permits, get out and enjoy the water and the beaches at Sleeper State Park or County Park Beach in Caseville. After touring Bay City's unparalleled Bay City Antique Center, the trip ends with a great family all-you-can-eat chicken dinner in Frankenmuth.

Look at a map of the United States, and you will find that the most readily recognizable feature is Michigan's Mitten. This has long been an advantage to Michiganders, who carry with them, at all times, a ready "map" of the state in their pocket. Ask locals, for example, where their summer cottage is, and they will pull out their left hand, palm down, and show you exactly where it is.

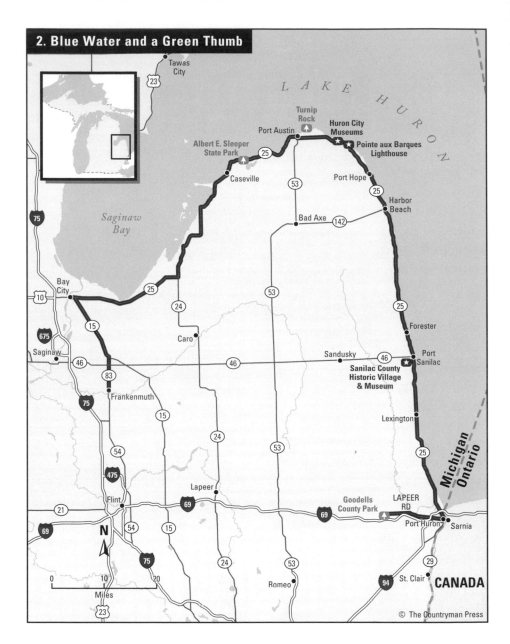

2. Blue Water and a Green Thumb

Native Americans and early European settlers, however, were at a distinct disadvantage in this regard. You can see on early maps, even those from the late 19th century, that Michigan was drawn more like an arrowhead with an inlet for Saginaw Bay than a mitten. It is no wonder then that the region, so obviously understood today to be the Thumb, was known by other names. A Dutch map from the 1600s names this region the Land of the Fox or the Skenchioe (from the Iroquois word for red fox). Later the French would dub this place Les Pays Plat (or "The Flat Country"), which is even more of a defining feature now that it's mostly farmland.

So thickly forested was the Thumb that when settlers came in the 1800s they found it easier to arrive by water and settle the shoreline. The abundance of mature pine attracted the lumbermen's ax, and by 1870 the area was heavily logged. In those days, loggers would leave behind the crowns of cut trees, a practice which would have tragic consequences. In 1871 and then in 1881, fires swept across the Thumb, fed by drought and fields piled with dead branches, dried pine needles, and flammable tree resin.

The first fire, known as the Port Huron Fire, was just one of several that burned on October 8, 1871. The fire took 200 lives and burned over 1 million acres across Michigan. The tragedy was largely overshadowed by two others that struck the nation the same day—the Chicago Fire in Illinois and the Peshtigo Fire in Wisconsin, the latter claiming 1,300 lives in one night.

The first blaze did not completely raze the Thumb, and lumbering continued until the Great Thumb Fire of 1881, which took 300 lives, left 14,000 people homeless, and destroyed thousands of buildings.

Every town in the Thumb was affected by these fires, which dramatically shifted the region's development. In a matter of days, forested areas were cleared and essentially open to agricultural development. Today, that agricultural tradition lives on in the Thumb's unrivaled production of navy beans and sugar beets. Sugar beets are processed at four facilities in the region by the Michigan Sugar Company, which is owned by some 1,200 farmers. They work together to produce the Pioneer Sugar brand of sugar.

Except for a detour here and there, most of the Thumb's tourism rests on the Lake Huron shoreline.

This route begins at one such detour. About 13 miles west of Port Huron sits a county park in the small town of Wales. **Goodells County Park** has some of the expected attractions—a splash pad and a playground, a butterfly garden, and facilities for horseback riding—and some unexpected: The barn that was once the centerpiece of this property is now the St. Clair County Farm Museum. The museum tells the county's agricultural history, with special attention to how farming was done between 1880 and 1945.

Adjacent to the farm, the county has moved in a number of historic buildings: the Columbus Bible Church (1860), the Mudge Log Cabin (1863), and the Lynn Township School (1885), to name a few. These are a part of the park's Historical Village and give visitors a chance to step back in time.

From the park, drive 12 miles east on Old State Highway 21 (aka Lapeer Road).

The Blue Water Bridge connects Port Huron, Michigan, with Sarnia, Ontario.

The road ends at Military Street at the Black River Bridge, where the river empties into the St. Clair River. This is the northern edge of Michigan's Blue Water region, which begins at Lake St. Clair to the south. The water that gives the area its name was also bestowed on the Blue Water Bridge that connects the Thumb with Canada. It's an appropriate designation. The water here is azure and bright cobalt blue, quite different from the steel blue waters found farther north.

Port Huron and Sarnia straddle the river, and they were once joined by ferry; the Blue Water Bridge was completed in 1938 and has become the fourth-busiest crossing between the United States and Canada. It's a pleasant walk along the river and under the bridge.

In 1925, the 32-foot sloop *Bernida* won the first of what would become an annual event, the Bayview Yacht Club's Port Huron to Mackinac Sailboat Race. Now, every year in July, revelers hit the streets of Port Huron to kick off the race in style (a more subdued "after party" on Mackinac Island bookends the race). According to recent estimates, the party draws more than one hundred thousand people to Port Huron to celebrate Boat Night. Looking past the beer-fueled revelry, the live bands on every street corner, and the ships on the river decked in wildly festive lights, Boat Night is about more than a race—it's a celebration of Port Huron's maritime history, a history that goes back to the first Europeans to explore the Great Lakes.

In early August of 1679, French explorer Robert de La Salle launched the first sailing ship on the Great Lakes, the *Griffin*. Setting sail from the eastern end of Lake Erie, he reached the Detroit River three days later. Heading north across Lake St.

Clair to the St. Clair River, the *Griffin* and her crew were hindered in their progress by weather. Strong winds from the north slowed them down, and near the present-day location of Port Huron, members of the crew were forced to go ashore with ropes to pull the ship through the river's rapids. The *Griffin* sailed north to Mackinac Island, and then Rock Island in Lake Michigan. La Salle sent the ship back east loaded with fur pelts. From Rock Island, the *Griffin* sailed into Michigan maritime history. The ship was never seen again—the first ship to sail the Great Lakes most certainly became the lakes' first shipwreck.

Several years later, France was looking to maintain its control over the Great Lakes fur trade. Daniel Greysolon Dulhut (often anglicized "Duluth") was instrumental in securing France's hold on Lake Superior and the trapping grounds of the upper Mississippi River. In 1686, he built a fort to keep English traders and trappers from traveling up the lake to the important trading centers of Sault Ste. Marie and Mackinac. The site he chose was at the northern end of the St. Clair River, at the base of Lake Huron. And so Fort St. Joseph, as it was named, was built on the site of modern-day Port Huron.

A lot of Port Huron's history, and that of the Blue Water region, can be learned at the **Port Huron Museum,** housed in the town's old library. A historic building in its own right, the library was funded by Andrew Carnegie and dedicated to the city in 1904. The museum oversees several other sites throughout Port Huron, including the **Huron Lightship Museum.** At one time, this ship was anchored in Saginaw Bay, warning other vessels of danger with a light on its mast and a foghorn. Today visitors can explore the ship from stem to stern, before heading north to tour another maritime site, the **Fort Gratiot Lighthouse.** This lighthouse, built in 1829, is Michigan's oldest. The original lighthouse towered 74 feet, and in the 1860s this was increased to its present height of 86 feet.

Between the lightship and the lighthouse, you can stop at a small museum that pays tribute to Port Huron's famous son, Thomas Alva Edison. The legendary inventor's family moved to Port Huron in 1854, when he was just a boy. He spent fewer than 10 years in Port Huron (from 7 to 16 years old), and he never returned except for one brief visit. The **Thomas Edison Depot Museum** can be found on Thomas Edison Parkway, in the shadow of the Blue Water Bridge. While stopping to learn more about the world Edison would have experienced as a boy in Port Huron, be sure to take a stroll along the river. There's a nice park here, and passing freighters seem close enough to touch.

For breakfast, lunch, or dinner, or just coffee, check out the **Raven Café** downtown. From the outside, this quirky coffeehouse looks like a British pub. Inside, it's plenty comfortable. Great coffee and sundry coffee-inspired drinks are complemented by soft couches and an excellent menu, which has an impressive selection of sandwiches, panini, and wraps.

For heartier fare, head north of town on MI 25 to **Palm's Krystal Bar and Restaurant.** (MI 25 goes by many names in Port Huron: Main Street turns into Military Street, which in turn becomes Huron Avenue and finally Pine Grove Avenue.) Palm's Krystal features Chicken in the Rough fried chicken. For those who don't know, Chicken in the Rough is a franchise that was started back during the Depression in Oklahoma. By 1950, there were 250 locations around the country selling their fried chicken dinners—often as a profitable supplement to an already established menu. (You didn't see a lot of restaurants named "Chicken in the Rough," just signs letting the public know that their chicken was served there.) That number has dwindled to less than a handful. Palm's Krystal stays busy in the evenings, passing boxed chicken dinners to hungry diners who have made the fried chicken here a local staple.

Continuing north on MI 25, Lexington is fewer than 20 miles from Port Huron. Established as a settlement in 1835, Lexington had a sawmill and several docks for schooners that came for the town's lumber. Soon there was a foundry, a couple of hotels, and an organ factory. By the time the town was incorporated in 1855, Lexington had become an important stop for ships on the Great Lakes.

Today the small lakeside town enjoys a brisk tourist industry. A short drive from metro Detroit, Lexington is popular with day-trippers who come for a little sun worshiping on the beach, shopping and dining on Huron Avenue, or possibly playing a round of golf at any number of nearby courses. A number of buildings survived from the town's heyday, and many folks come to stroll through the neighborhoods and take in Lexington's historic charm. Just west of the light on Huron Avenue, for example, sits the **Charles H. Moore Public Library.** Built as a law office in 1859, the property was given to the town and opened as a library in 1903. Over the years there has been some upgrading of the building, but it is worth a stop to see some of the architectural details, especially inside.

The road through downtown Lexington leads to Lake Huron.

Another way to appreciate Lexington's historic charm is a stay in one of its several bed & breakfasts. The **Inn the Garden B&B,** just west of town, is also on Huron Avenue. The builders of this brick home were inspired by Italianate country villas, and the current owners have a way with gardening that brings the yard to life with tastefully landscaped splashes of color. Inside the home, traditional decor is underscored by hardwood floors and high ceilings. Closer to downtown sits the **Captain's Quarter's Inn,** which has three rooms for guests as well as a two-room garden house. Just a block from that is the **Carroll House B&B.** This home was built in 1870 in classic Greek Revival style. There are three themed guest rooms, and breakfast is served in the beautifully remodeled kitchen or on the terrace. All of these lodgings are within walking distance (a few blocks at most) of downtown shops and restaurants, where you can find everything from T-shirts to home decor to fudge. For the latter, be sure to stop in at the **Oh! Fudge Shoppe.**

The Carroll House is just one of several excellent bed & breakfasts in Lexington.

The next stop is Port Sanilac, 11 miles north on MI 25. Approaching town from the south, the **Sanilac County Historic Village and Museum** is on the left. Even standing alone, it would be difficult to miss this yellow brick Victorian with its bright green shutters. But the mansion, built

Sanilac County Historic Village & Museum has several buildings to explore.

in 1872 for the town's doctor and his family, is simply the centerpiece of a 10-acre museum that features seven other historic buildings. Included in this number is the carriage barn, a general store (which over the years served as a feed store, barbershop, and place where you could take your hat to be blocked and cleaned), and a log cabin. During my last visit, there was a display of old working motors chugging along in the backyard.

When Port Sanilac's first settlers came to the area in 1844, they found a bark-covered shack that had been erected by a group of tanners from Detroit who had come a few years earlier to manufacture tanbark. The settlement was called

This small lighthouse in Port Sanilac is a private residence, but the Coast Guard still maintains the light.

Bark Shanty Point until 1857, when the town decided to name the town after Sanilac, a Wyandot chief. In 1886, the **Port Sanilac Lighthouse** was built. Located on Cherry Street, a block east of MI 25, the lighthouse sits on private property. The light is still active and is maintained by the U.S. Coast Guard.

At the north end of Port Sanilac you will find the finest dining on the Thumb. **The Van Camp House** opened in 2006, and in a few short years Chef Andy Fabian has built a reputation for creating a menu of exquisite dishes from local sourced ingredients. The menu changes weekly, and diners can expect nothing but the best service.

It is nearly 55 miles from Port Sanilac to Port Austin at the tip of the Thumb. Along the way, MI 25 passes through a mess of little towns like Forester, Harbor Beach, and Port Hope, to name a few.

As the highway turns and cuts west, two historic sites make the long drive more than worthwhile. At the tip of the Thumb is Pointe aux Barques, named "Point of Little Boats" in French by the trappers who met at this spot to trade. The first **Pointe aux Barques Lighthouse** was built on the point in 1848. Because of its height, the quality of its light, and the generally poor workmanship used in its construction, the original lighthouse was replaced in 1857 with the 89-foot light you see there today. In 1957, the Coast Guard automated the light, which is still in use today. The keeper's house is open to the public as a lighthouse museum. To get there, turn north on Lighthouse Road, which is 6 miles past Port Hope on MI 25.

The next stop is Huron City (also called the **Huron City Museums**). In the early 1900s, William Lyon Phelps made Huron City his summer home. Phelps, a professor at Yale University, was known nationally as a literary critic and speaker. Asked to preach at the local Methodist Episcopal church, Phelps was soon drawing crowds upward of a thousand. The church expanded its facilities twice. Huron City Museums has preserved Phelps's summer home, the House of Seven Gables (named after Hawthorne's masterpiece), built in 1886 by the family of Phelps's wife, Annabel. Many pieces of furniture and home decor are original, chosen by Annabel for her father.

Visitors can also visit the church where Phelps preached, the Community

House-Inn, and a log cabin built by Mitchell and Delia LeGassa in 1837. Considering this region was completely razed by numerous forest fires in the late 1800s (the House of Seven Gables was the third home built on the site), to see a log cabin preserved from the early 1800s is quite remarkable. To find this historic village, turn on Pioneer Street (about 8 miles east of Port Austin or 2.5 miles west of Lighthouse Road, on the north side of the road) — you can't miss it.

All of this is less than a 10-minute drive from Port Austin, the next town as you continue around the Thumb. This small town features a dozen excellent restaurants and several places to stay. It's also the location of the excellent **Port Austin Farmer's Market**. Few markets in the state compare to the 150 vendors that hawk their produce in this tiny town at the tip of the Thumb. If you are lucky, someone will be selling jars of country pickles — a perfect snack on a warm summer day. The market is open on Saturday mornings in the summer.

The Pointe aux Barques Lighthouse lights the way at the tip of Michigan's Thumb.

At the corner of Lake and State, you can't miss the classic brick building that was once the Winsor Snover Bank. Since 1984, the building has been home to Port Austin's classiest restaurant, **The Bank 1884** (the restaurant gets its name from the year the bank first opened). The blackened prime rib is excellent, as is the chicken Wellington, and kids are taken seriously with the thoughtfully considered children's menu.

A little outside of town sits **The Farm Restaurant,** specializing in what they call "Heartland" cuisine. The menu is prone to change, but the farmer's-style Swiss steak is pretty good, and they serve hearty fresh breads and soups.

To discover one of the state's most picturesque spots, travelers can rent kayaks at **Port Austin Kayak** and use them to paddle along Lake Huron to Turnip

The Port Austin Lighthouse is hard to see unless you take to the water.

Rock. It's about 3 miles from the put-in at the beach to this unique rock formation that attracts hundreds of visitors every year. Over the millennia waves ate away at the base of the cliffs along this stretch of shoreline. Turnip Rock, which was once part of the shore, stood firm against the onslaught and remains a teetering island of sorts. It is clear that the erosion would have eventually toppled this turnip, but efforts to shore up the base have put a halt to the ravages of time.

The land surrounding the rock is all private property, so the only way to view the rocks is to paddle out to them. Be aware of your limitations. It's a relatively easy paddle on calm days. When the waves pick up, however, it can be a struggle to skirt along parallel to the shore with waves hitting you broadside.

Another 18 miles on MI 25, now heading southwest, sits Caseville. The town is the self-proclaimed vacation capital of Huron County, and the moniker is most likely justified. In addition to a great summer festival, the two beaches in Caseville offer the best swimming on Lake Huron.

The **Albert East Sleeper State Park,** just a few miles east of town, straddles MI 25 (here called Port Austin Road). On the south side is a quiet wooded campground with a couple hundred campsites. On the north side visitors can set up towels and and an umbrella on 0.5 mile of sandy beach. Closer to town, the **Caseville County Park** has another great stretch of beach, and it also has a campground and marina. If your plans take you to Caseville in August, be sure to reserve lodging early—they fill to capacity for the Cheeseburger in Caseville Festival.

Cheeseburger in Caseville is Caseville's biggest annual event. Every year, in keeping with the Jimmy Buffet theme (remember his song "Cheeseburger in Paradise"?), the town is transformed into "Key North." For 10 days in early August, the town celebrates a summer of fun on the lake with music, games, and a big parade. The first festival was held in 1999, with five thousand people in attendance. Today even more guests take over Caseville for the event—an estimated seventy-five thousand cheeseburgers were sold at a recent festival!

There are a bunch of little mom-and-pop diners and cafés in town, many throwing their hat in the ring each year to win the coveted title of Best Cheeseburger in Caseville. **Lefty's Diner & Drive-In** is a great example. This classic '50s-style diner serves burgers and dogs, handmade onion rings, and shakes.

The highway continues through Caseville southwest to Bay City, where the Saginaw River empties into Saginaw Bay. The town was settled early, originally called Lower Saginaw to distinguish it from Saginaw, which is farther upriver. It quickly became a town of some repute, with lumber, milling, and shipbuilding driving the local economy. Since its formal incorporation in 1865, Bay City has seen its share of ups and downs (as have most American cities that once relied on manufacturing). Shipbuilding, which lasted until the Dafoe Shipbuilding Company folded in 1975, had a surprisingly good run.

Bay City's maritime legacy lives on in various ways. The town is home to two tall ships, both owned by **Bay Sail,** who offer the public a chance to experience these sailing vessels up close. There's a regular schedule of dinner sails, stargazer sails, and more aboard the *Appledore IV,* which is also used for overnight trips throughout the Great Lakes. The Tall Ships Challenge has made Bay City a port of call a number of times, and plans are under way to create a Maritime Heritage Center that will not only serve to preserve the town's lake-faring past but also will likely have space for classrooms, boat building and repair, and potentially a small shopping area.

Bay City has also become known as a great town for antiquing, and the best shops are in the town's Historic Riverfront District. The most extensive shop is the **Bay City Antiques Center,** the largest antique shop in Michigan. This block-long, three-story antiques shop has something for every collector—from Depression glass and French copper pots to 1950s Americana and 19th-century German furniture. They even carry architectural pieces like doors and windows, and a collection of antique hardware.

While you're in the neighborhood, swing by **St. Laurent Brothers** (right across the street from the Bay City Antiques Center), which has been selling nuts since 1904. Beginning with peanuts, the shop was soon roasting all sorts of nuts, from almonds to cashews to macadamia nuts. It didn't take long to add chocolate to the mix, and you have St. Laurent's as it is today, selling fresh roasted nuts and delicious candy confections. Rumor has it that Madonna stops by whenever she's in town. (The last reported sighting was in 2003 when she came with her now-former husband, Guy Ritchie.)

From Bay City, follow M 15 south to M 83 into Frankenmuth. Few towns in

This window display reveals just a peek at all Bay City Antiques Center offers.

Michigan have transformed themselves into an honest-to-goodness destination town as Frankenmuth has. Originally Frankenmuth was a quiet farming community settled by German immigrants seeking to share the love of Jesus with other Germans and the local Native American population in the mid-19th century. It is now a great place to eat chicken, buy Christmas decorations, and watch designers cut colorful candles.

The main attraction of this popular day-trip destination is the all-you-can-eat

fried chicken dinners at **Zehnder's of Frankenmuth** and the **Bavarian Inn**. Though both are owned by members of the ubiquitous Zehnder family, the former has been serving up the expected German-American fare for a bit longer. In 1929, William and Emilie Zehnder purchased the old New Exchange Hotel in downtown Frankenmuth. Across the street was the Fischer's Hotel. A little known fact: It was likely Herman and Lydia Fischer at the hotel who first introduced all-you-can-eat chicken dinners to Frankenmuth.

Zehnder's struggled for quite a few years through Prohibition and the Great Depression. It was only after World War II and the rise of the American family road trip that the restaurant took off. In 1950, Willie and Emilie's son, William Jr. (or "Tiny"), bought the Fischer's Hotel and along with his wife, Dorothy, set upon replicating his parents' success when they established the Bavarian Inn.

Today, both restaurants have their admirers. While the two family-style menus are very similar, both credit their respective family matrons for develop-

The Bavarian Inn, just across the street from Zehnder's

ing the recipes and overseeing the cooking that have made each so very popular.

Now, before you get to thinking that Frankenmuth is all about food, remember that this town was built by German immigrants. They were Lutherans, which is not a group of 19th-century Protestants prone to teetotalling. So it should come as no surprise that the oldest brewery in the state, the **Frankenmuth Brewery,** was founded right here in 1862. The company has changed hands and locations many times, but it has persevered, and beer aficionados come from all over the state to taste the suds and get the 20-minute brewery tour. And, of course, the brewpub serves a fine menu with obvious German-American leanings.

No trip to Frankenmuth would be complete without the shopping. Signs from all over—from Florida to Missouri—point visitors to **Bronner's CHRISTmas Wonderland.** Celebrating Christmas year-round, the store itself covers 7.5 acres. The founder, Wally Bronner, was a beloved local character who always insisted that "Christ" should be the focus of Christmas. That's why he had the name capitalized. He began Bronner's in 1945, and his fortunes were tied closely to the rise of the town itself.

A final stop, especially appropriate for families traveling with young kids, is **Grandpa Tiny's Farm.** Once the farm of William "Tiny" Zehnder, the same guy that founded the Bavarian Inn, today the property is used to teach folks about farming and farm animals. Like most immigrants, the German farmers that settled around Frankenmuth had their own way of doing things. For example, the old farmhouse has an authentic *backofen*—an outdoor oven for baking bread. The farm tour includes a horse-drawn wagon ride.

IN THE AREA

ACCOMMODATIONS

Captain's Quarter's Inn, 7277 Simons Street, Lexington. Call 810-359-2196. Website: cqilex.com.

Carroll House B&B, 7307 Simons Street, Lexington. Call 810-359-5702. Website: carrollhousebandb.com.

Inn the Garden B&B, 7156 Huron Avenue, Lexington. Call 810-359-8966. Website: inngarden.com.

ATTRACTIONS AND RECREATION

Albert East Sleeper State Park, 6573 State Park Road, Caseville. Call 989-856-4411. Website: michigan.gov /sleeper.

Bay City Antiques Center, 1020 North Water Street, Bay City. Call 989-893-0251. Website: bayantiquectr.com.

Bay Sail, 107 Fifth Street, Bay City. Call 989-895-5193. Website: baysailbay city.org.

Bronner's CHRISTmas Wonderland, 25 Christmas Lane, Frankenmuth. Call 989-652-9931. Website: bronners.com.

Caseville County Park, 6400 Main Street, Caseville. Call 989-856-2080. Website: huroncountyparks.com.

Charles H. Moore Public Library, 7239 Huron Avenue, Lexington. Call 810-359-8267. Website: lexington library.net/index.htm.

Cheeseburger in Caseville. Website: cheeseburgerincasevillefest.com. Also see Caseville Chamber of Commerce.

Fort Gratiot Lighthouse. Call 810-982-0891. Website: porthuronmuseum .org/Port_Huron_Museum/Fort_Gratiot _Light_Station.html.

Goodells County Park, on Lapeer Road, east of Goodells Road, Wales. Call 810-989-6960. Website: stclair county.org/offices/parks/goodells .aspx.

Grandpa Tiny's Farm, 7775 Weiss Street, Frankenmuth. Call 989-652-5437. Website: grandpatinysfarm.com.

Huron City Museums, 7995 Pioneer Drive, Port Austin. Call 989-428-4123. Website: huroncitymuseums.org.

Huron Lightship Museum. Call 810-982-0891. Website: porthuronmuseum .org/Port_Huron_Museum/Huron _Lightship.html.

Oh! Fudge Shoppe, 7296 Huron Avenue, Lexington. Call 810-359-5908.

Pointe aux Barques Lighthouse, 7320 Lighthouse Road, Lighthouse County Park, Port Hope. Website: pointeauxbarqueslighthouse.org.

Port Austin Farmer's Market, State and Lake Sts. Website: portaustin farmersmarket.com.

Port Austin Kayak. 119 East Spring Street Call 989-550-6651. Website: portaustinkayak.com.

Port Huron Museum, 1115 Sixth Street, Port Huron. Call 810-982-0891. Website: phmuseum.org.

Port Sanilac Lighthouse, end of Cherry Street, Port Sanilac. Website: michiganlights.com/portsanilaclh.htm.

St. Laurent Brothers, 1101 North Water Street, Bay City. Call 1-800-289-7688. Website: stlaurentbrothers.com.

Sanilac County Historic Village & Museum, 228 South Ridge Street, Port Sanilac. Call 810-622-9946. Website: sanilaccountymuseum.org.

Thomas Edison Depot Museum. Part of the Port Huron Museum (see above). Call 810-982-0891. Website: porthuronmuseum.org/Port_Huron _Museum/Thomas_Edison_Depot.html.

DINING

The Bank 1884, 8646 Lake Street, Port Austin. Call 989-738-5353. Website: thebank1884.com.

The Bavarian Inn, 713 South Main Street, Frankenmuth. Call 1-800-228-2742.

The Farm Restaurant, 699 Port Crescent Road, Port Austin. Call 989-874-5700. Website: thefarmrestaurant .com.

Frankenmuth Brewery, 425 South Main Street, Frankenmuth. Call 989-262-8300. Website: frankenmuth brewery.com.

Lefty's Diner & Drive-In, 6937 Main Street, Caseville. Call 989-856-8899.

Palm's Krystal Bar and Restaurant, 1535 Pine Grove Avenue, Port Huron. Call 810-985-9838. Website: palmskrystal.com.

Raven Café, 932 Military Street, Port Huron. Call 810-984-4330. Website: ravencafeph.com.

The Van Camp House, 135 North Ridge Street, Port Sanilac. Call 810-622-0558. Website: vancamphouse .com.

Zehnder's of Frankenmuth, 730 South Main Street, Frankenmuth. Call 989-652-0400. Website: zehnders.com.

OTHER CONTACTS

Blue Water Area Convention & Visitors Bureau, 520 Thomas Edison Parkway, Port Huron. Call 810-987-8687 or 1-800-852-4242. Website: bluewater.org.

Caseville Chamber of Commerce, 6632 Main Street, Caseville. Call 989-856-3818 or 1-800-606-1347. Website: casevillechamber.com.

Huron County Visitors Bureau, 250 East Huron Avenue, Bad Axe. Call 989-269-6431 or 1-800-35THUMB (84862). Website: huroncounty.com.

Port Austin Chamber of Commerce, 2 West Spring Street, Port Austin. Call 989-738-7600. Website: portaustinarea.com.

St. Clair Chamber of Commerce, 201 North Riverside Avenue. Call 810-329-2962. The chamber operates a Welcome and Information Center at this location. Website: stclairchamber .com.

Thumb Area Tourism Council, 157 North State Street, Caro. Website: thumbtourism.org.

The Mill Museum in Dundee not only features local history but hosts incredible traveling exhibits.

3 Forgotten Highways: The River Raisin and the Chicago and Territorial Roads

MONROE & DUNDEE, TECUMSEH, THE IRISH HILLS, ALLEN, COLDWATER, MARSHALL, CHELSEA, DEXTER, AND ANN ARBOR

Estimated length: 190 miles
Estimated time: About 4 hours

Getting there: This route starts near the shores of Lake Erie at the Sterling State Park in Monroe, about 40 miles south of Detroit. Take exit 15 on I-75 for North Dixie Highway. The park is less than 1 mile east of the interstate. From the park, the route follows MI 50 west from Monroe through a few small towns before it gets to US 12 in Cambridge Junction. Following US 12 east to Coldwater, the route turns north on I-69 toward Marshall, and then takes East Michigan Avenue and few other back roads east (paralleling I-94) to close the loop back in Ann Arbor.

Highlights: Your trip begins with a view of Lake Erie from the Sterling State Park. A paved path, which connects with a path into Monroe, offers a view of the area's diverse waterfowl. Following up the River Raisin, there's a stop at the River Raisin National Battlefield Park and several other historic sites in Monroe. In Dundee be sure to visit the Old Mill Museum. In Tecumseh, you can catch a short train ride between Tecumseh and Clinton. And while you're there, you might enjoy wine tasting at one of southeast Michigan's wineries, Pentamere Winery. After leaving Tecumseh, you pass through a portion of the Irish Hills. Along the way, be sure to stop for a tour of the 750-acre Hidden Lake Gardens. From the gardens, you will cut north to US 12, the Old Chicago Road. See remnants of the once-famous Irish Hills of Michigan, visit a shrine, and explore an important stagecoach stop, the Walter Tavern at the Cambridge Junction Historic State Park. If you enjoy auto racing, the

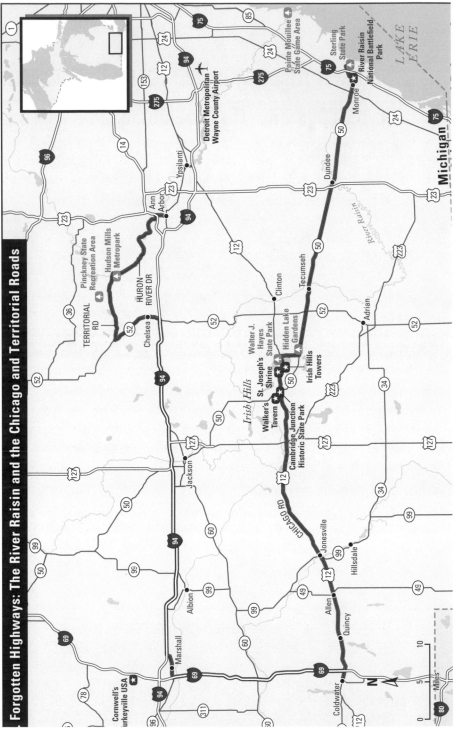

Forgotten Highways: The River Raisin and the Chicago and Territorial Roads

Michigan International Speedway is less than 1 mile away. The next town on the route, heading west now on US 12, is the little town of Allen, Michigan's Antique Capital. Though the town is small, you could spend a week browsing the antiques shops and malls along US 12. In Coldwater, stop for excellent Mexican at Los Tequilas and perhaps ride an authentic steam train. Heading north on I-69 brings you to the other road featured in this chapter, the Territorial Road. A walking tour of Marshall highlights the town's historic architecture, or you can experience it up close with an overnight stay at The National House Inn. This route winds down by heading east. Stop in Chelsea for a tour of the Chelsea Milling Company, the producers of the world-famous Jiffy Mix. Farther along, the Pinckney State Recreation Area is the perfect spot to get out your mountain bike or take a hike. Arriving in Ann Arbor, take your pick of a burger at the legendary Krazy Jim's Blimpy Burger or the perfect sandwich at Zingerman's Delicatessen—or choose from any of the town's three hundred restaurants.

Transportation is a theme that runs throughout this chapter. From well-paddled rivers to footpaths and early stagecoach routes to railroad lines and highways, the region has been defined by transportation. The earliest means of transportation in the region were its many waterways. Cutting west from Lake Erie, the primary cross-peninsula route was the Huron River, but the River Rouge and River Raisin also had their share of traffic. Part of our route follows the River Raisin from its mouth near Monroe.

When Michigan was still a territory, Congress approved the construction of the two roads that are also central to this trip. In 1825, Congress provided funds to build a road to connect Detroit and Fort Dearborn (on the Chicago River in what is now downtown Chicago). Road-building on the frontier in the early 19th century was not quite as sophisticated as it is today. In the case of the road to Fort Dearborn, crews followed a trail long used by the Sauk Native Americans. The path was widened to accommodate stagecoaches and carts, and where the earth was wet or boggy, logs were laid across the trail. The resulting "corduroy" road nearly jostled the teeth out of hundreds of subsequent travelers.

The Sauk Trail had been in use for centuries, and it was the principal route that linked the Mississippi River with Lake Erie. In all likelihood, Robert de La Salle followed the trail in 1680 as he sought a land route across the Lower Peninsula. A hundred and forty years later, during his survey of the territory in 1820, Henry Rowe Schoolcraft passed by the "river du Chemin" (meaning "river of the road") where it empties into Lake Michigan near present-day Michigan City, Indiana. He describes the nearby Native American trail that cut across the peninsula as "a plain horse path, which is considerably well travelled by traders, hunters, and others....

The paths at Sterling State Park are paved for better access to the nature areas.

The country is said to be handsomely diversified with prairies, woods, and streams, and furnishes every facility for waggon roads, settlements, water mills, &c."

It is this well-traveled horse path that was improved and widened and called the Chicago Road, or the Chicago-Detroit Post Road. Later it would be US 112. Today, as the road meanders east to west, it is called the Chicago Road or simply US 12.

Another settlement road to follow a native path was the Territorial Road, which connected Detroit with St. Joseph on Lake Michigan. Construction funds were approved by Congress in 1829, and surveying began a year later. It would play a key role in the growth of towns along the way, like Ann Arbor, Jackson, and Marshall. This road was eventually replaced by I-94, but the old highway still exists, often called Michigan Avenue, Old US 12, or the Red Arrow Highway (to explore the latter, see Chapter 5).

The interstate highway system dramatically reduced traffic on these roads, which were once significant conveyors of goods and commerce. Today, they are quiet two-lane highways passing through woods and farmland, with small towns scattered along the way. When the beaten path up and moved, these old highways became true back roads—notably convenient back roads—each with a history that is best told by visiting the towns they still serve.

When the first Europeans paddled the Great Lakes, the shores were buffered by an expanse of wetlands, the home to millions of birds—both local species and those passing through. Many migrating birds today still follow the ancient path down the St. Clair River and through the straits into Lake Erie. In the fall, birdwatchers stalk the coastline counting the raptors that pass on their way south. Restored wetlands farther north at places like the Pointe Mouillee State Game Area have helped some of these birds to return to the area in higher numbers. Another great place to see birds in the area, especially waterfowl, is the **Wm. C. Sterling State Park** in Monroe.

Just north of the River Raisin, the state park has several lagoons that attract thousands of birds. Even outside of migration season, you will see great blue herons, mallards, and double-crested cormorants. A wide paved path makes for an easy walk around these lagoons. The other side of the park has camping and a popular day-use beach on Lake Erie.

Dioramas illustrate scenes from the War of 1812 at the River Raisin Battlefield National Park.

The lagoon paths connect up with another biking/hiking path that leads up the River Raisin into Monroe, but unless you are up for a hike back to the car, you can drive to the next stop, the **River Raisin National Battlefield Park.** One of the newest historical parks in the national system, it is still a humble enterprise. The park commemorates a pivotal moment in the War of 1812.

In the winter of 1813, American troops marched into Frenchtown (present-day Monroe, Michigan) and repelled a contingent of British soldiers and their Native American allies. That previous summer the British had taken Fort Detroit when the commanding officer of the fort surrendered it without a shot. Taking Frenchtown was a step on the path toward expelling the British from the straits.

A few days after being forced out of Frenchtown, the British returned with more numbers and overwhelmed the Americans, who quickly surrendered. Anxious to make it back to Detroit before more American reinforcements came, the British's General Proctor turned north with his prisoners, leaving the wounded behind with a promise to return for them with stretchers. Once the British left, their Native American allies stripped wounded of their valuables, burned down the homes in which they were housed, and killed those who tried to escape.

Meanwhile, the prisoners who faltered on the march north with the British were dispatched with a tomahawk and left beside the road. One eyewitness reported "The road was for miles strewed with the mangled bodies." Few events of the War of 1812 served to incite the American people as did the Battle of the River Raisin. "Remember the Raisin!" became the American rallying cry.

At the corner of Elm and Monroe Streets in Monroe, General George Armstrong Custer sits atop his horse. This is not the tragic figure of the Battle of Little Big-

Custer sits ahorse, overlooking his childhood home of Monroe.

The Navarre-Anderson Trading Post is the oldest wooden structure still standing in Michigan.

horn. For this Custer, those events are still a decade away. Instead, with the River Raisin at his back, the youthful Custer looks toward the northeast, over the traffic and into a future that promises nothing but success. George Custer spent much of his boyhood in Monroe, and though he may be the most well-known piece of Monroe history, his story is just a taste of the whole historical pie.

The **Monroe County Historical Museums** include the county museum downtown as well as a number of historic sites. They do a good job of telling the story of French pioneers in this pre-Revolutionary settlement. West Elm Avenue, which parallels the River Raisin, becomes North Custer Road west of Telegraph Road. At the corner of North Custer and Raisinville Roads, you will find the Martha Barker Country Store Exhibit and the Navarre Anderson Trading Post Complex. The trading post is the oldest wooden home still standing in Michigan. It was built in 1789 by Utreau Navarre in what is now Monroe's Old Village Historic District. It was moved twice since it was built—once in 1894, and once in 1971. The complex attempts to recreate the original look and feel of the trading post, and there are plenty of activities and events to send the message home.

The Martha Barker Country Store has fewer years on it than the neighboring trading post. Built in the 1860s, this brick structure was originally a

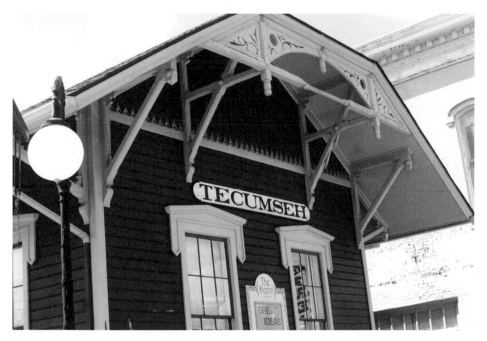

Catch the train for Clinton at the Old Tecumseh Depot.

schoolhouse. The building saw its last classes taught here in 1962. It's now a country store museum that has pulled together artifacts from general stores around the county.

Turning left on Raisinville Road, cross the river and turn right on South Custer Road (MI 50) and follow that into Dundee.

The River Raisin meanders a ways into the Lower Peninsula, traveling through four counties before it reaches its headwaters. Paddlers could paddle up the Raisin and their pick of routes to Lake Michigan, by way of the Grand, Kalamazoo, or St. Joseph Rivers. In an age before roads, this was a big deal. The river also allowed settlers to quickly establish commerce. Dundee, like most towns in the region, is built right alongside the river. The **Old Mill Museum** captures the town's history with three stories of exhibits. The mill itself is a bit of a time capsule and was once refurbished by Henry Ford as part of his rural industry initiatives.

Back in 1833, the newly formed Erie and Kalamazoo Railroad Company received the mandate to build a railway connecting the Kalamazoo River, via Adrian, to Lake Erie near present-day Toledo. The railroad was the very first west of the Allegheny Mountains. By 1853, a branch of that railroad was laid north through the towns of Tecumseh and Clinton, connecting the main line with Jackson (then Jacksonburg). After World War II, the profitability of rail transportation began to wane,

British Tea Gardens in Tecumseh

and slowly the once highly touted line was dismantled. In 1981, with little track remaining, three friends established the **Southern Michigan Railroad Society** and bought the track between Clinton and Tecumseh.

Throughout the year, the organization offers train rides between the two towns. In the summers, the train makes a couple runs each Saturday. In the fall there are fall color tours, and later in the year they have holiday tours. Though the route is relatively short, the trip has some history, and it's always fun to take a train ride.

While you're in Tecumseh, stop by the **Pentamere Winery.** Buying grapes grown around the Great Lakes, Pentamere (meaning "five seas") produces their wine right in town. The workings of the winery are out in the open, so guests coming to taste wine will get to witness the winemaking process as well. Tecumseh also has a surprising collection of shops catering to the epicurean's fancy. The **British Tea Garden and Rooftop Café** and the **Boulevard Market** both offer products not usually found in small-town Michigan.

For less elegant—though plenty satisfying—dining, consider stopping at **The Dog House** in Tecumseh. For a few years now, they've been dishing up excellent hot dogs to hungry diners. The "D to the T" takes the classic Detroit coney (with its chili and onions) and adds a Tecumseh twist by way of nacho cheese, shredded cheese, and Doritos. The truly brave will want to try the "Franken Dog," which is topped with every topping on the menu, from honey mustard and slaw to bacon and pineapple.

You will leave Tecumseh by driving west on MI 50. US 12 and MI 50 pass right through the heart of the Irish Hills, an area known as much for its rolling terrain as it is for the 52 spring-fed lakes that dot the map. (Rental cottages are available on more than half of those lakes. Check the Brooklyn–Irish Hills Chamber of Commerce website for a list.)

From Tecumseh it's 8 miles to **Hidden Lake Gardens,** a 755-acre botanical garden and arboretum managed by Michigan State University. The gardens began in 1926 as the pet project of retired businessman Harry Fee, who bought 200 acres of property surrounding Hidden Lake and began farming. The land was ideal for flowers and other nursery plants, so that's what he grew, creating picturesque bo-

Hidden Lake Gardens, west of Tecumseh, is maintained by Michigan State University. *Kim Forster*

tanical scenes. Later, he built a winding road with roadside parking areas for the public to drive through and enjoy the gardens.

In 1945, Fee donated the property to the university. Over the years the school has followed Fee's mandate that the gardens be maintained and developed for the benefit of the public. There is a small admission fee, and the entrance is found west of Nortley Highway.

Leaving the gardens, drive west a short distance on MI 50 to Pentecost Highway and turn north. In 2.5 miles, you will be at US 12—the Old Chicago Road. Turn west, and it is a little more than 0.5 mile to **Walter J. Hayes State Park.** This 654-acre park offers access to swimming, boating, and fishing on Wampler's Lake, as well as fishing and boating on Round Lake. The park's 185-site campground is filled to capacity nearly every weekend in the summer, and guests take advantage of the Irish Hills location and the proximity to the Michigan International Speedway.

Continuing west, less than 1 mile from the state park, you are sure to notice two hulking towers on your left. These are the fabled Irish Hills Towers, first opened in 1924. Now closed to the public, they were once a popular tourist attraction that featured a small collection of animals for children to feed, an arcade, and a restaurant. So popular were the towers, Greyhound opened a ticket office on the location, and in 1929, an estimated 50 buses brought passengers here every day.

The story of their construction, however, is more interesting than the towers themselves, which have fallen into disrepair. In 1924, the Michigan Observation Company asked Edward Kelly if they could purchase some of his property to build an observation tower. Kelly declined, so the company went to his neighbor, who was happy to sell a piece of his lot. The resulting tower was erected 6 feet from Kelly's property and obstructed the view from his house. Not one to take things lying down, Kelly built a tower of his own. Nearly identical to the first, Kelly's tower was a bit taller. The Michigan Observation Company soon raised the height of their tower to match Kelly's, and the threat of continued one-upmanship capped both towers at 60 feet.

For nearly half a century, the towers remained a successful tourist attraction. A subsequent owner bought both towers, and over the years, various people tried to return them to their former glory. In 2000, however, the lookouts were closed for good.

Another place to stop along US 12 is St. Joseph's Church and Shrine. This stone church was constructed by Irish settlers in the 1850s, and for the next 70 years, the church was remodeled and additions were made. In 1928, inspired by the grotto at Our Lady of Lourdes in France, **St. Joseph's Shrine** was added. Several years later, artisans created the 14 outdoor Stations of the Cross.

Built by Irish immigrants in the 1850s, St. Joseph's Church and Shrine is still an active church today.

When the church was first built, the Chicago Road was a busy route. Rest stops were few and far between, and westbound travelers must have looked upon the church with some relief, knowing that **Walker's Tavern** was only 3 miles away at Cambridge Junction. The tavern was built back in 1836, near the busy intersection of the Chicago Road (US 12) and La Plaisance Bay Road (MI 50). It was later purchased by Sylvester Walker in 1843 and appropriately renamed Walker's Tavern. Both roads were important thoroughfares, the latter connecting Jackson with Lake Erie, and the tavern

Walker's Tavern was an important stagecoach stop on the Chicago Road.
Kim Forster

was soon a thriving stagecoach stop. Hundreds of pioneer wagons would pass daily, and folks making the five-day journey between Detroit to Chicago would look forward to a stop at the tavern. Stagecoach drivers would change out horses, take on supplies, and see to necessary repairs, while their passengers could eat a meal or even take a room for the night.

Taverns and inns were necessary to early travelers—virtual islands of support in an empty wilderness—and the Walker Tavern soon became known for being a cut above the rest. Behind the inn Walker ran a small farm, his wife using the produce to fix hearty meals for weary travelers. Over the years, the inn played host to the likes of Daniel Webster and famed novelist James Fenimore Cooper.

In 1853, Walker built a three-story brick tavern across the street and made the original building his home. Today, the tavern sits on the Cambridge Junction Historic State Park, an 80-acre site that gives guests a chance to explore 19th-century life. Exhibits tell the story of Michigan's earliest settlers, life on the frontier, and what it was like to travel by stagecoach. The old Walker Tavern has been preserved, and a reconstructed New England barn houses a blacksmith's shop and other exhibits. Start your tour at the visitors center, which is located just north of US 12 on MI 50.

South on MI 50 from Cambridge Junction, you will find the **Dewey Lake Manor** bed & breakfast. As the name so aptly conveys, the inn is nestled on 18 acres on Dewey Lake. The hundred-year-old home has five guest rooms done up in Victorian decor. Guests are encouraged to take advantage of the location—grills and picnic tables are available for cookouts, and the inn has a paddleboat and canoe for you to enjoy on the lake.

From Cambridge Junction, continue west on US 12 to Allen. Leaving the hills behind, the countryside becomes flat again. The view on both sides of the road is dominated by farmland. As you pass through Jonesville, you might consider a detour south on MI 99 to visit Hillsdale, the home of Hillsdale College. In Jonesville, there is the **Munro House B&B.** Back in 1834, George Clinton Munro bought a wood frame house on this site. Six years later, a brick addition made the house the Greek Revival masterpiece it is today. The B&B has hosted many guests from around the world who have come to visit the college. This is a world-class inn worthy of its international reputation.

Allen, the Antique Capital of Michigan, is 29 miles west of Walker's Tavern. Antiques are this town's bread and butter, and there are several antiques stores downtown.

The best place to see a lot of dealers in a short time is west of town at any one of several antiques malls. Combined, these malls boast 100,000 square feet of retail space with one thousand different booths. One of these malls is a unique

The best Mexican restaurant around is Los Tequilas in Coldwater.

collection of 25 historic buildings called **Preston's Antique Gaslight Village.** Each building is its own antiques shop. (Take note: This "outdoor mall" is open Friday through Sunday.) Open daily is the **Allen Antique Barn,** which has three hundred booths on two floors and dealers who bring new stock every day.

Heading west on US 12, drive 10.5 miles to I-69. Some of the best Mexican food in the area can be found in Coldwater. The old train depot, just a block south of downtown, is now the home to **Los Tequilas.** The restaurant's dining room has excellent food and wide windows with a view of the tracks and the vintage cars of the **Little River Railroad.** The railroad is not just a left-over from the olden days. It makes regular runs to Quincy and Hillsdale powered by a steam locomotive. Be sure to check their website for a current schedule of trips. Coldwater is also the home of the **Chicago Pike Inn & Spa.** This Victorian home on East Chicago Street offers spa services as well as elegant candlelight meals.

The Chicago Pike Inn is right on Main Street in Coldwater. *Kim Forster*

Take the interstate 23.5 miles north and exit at West Michigan Avenue (exit 36). You are now on the old Territorial Road, 1 mile west of the historic town of Marshall. Today Marshall is best known for its historic architecture and small-town charm—a picture-perfect mid-American city.

In 1846, fewer than 10 years after Michigan had earned statehood, the state legislature began to discuss where to locate the state capital, which was temporarily in Detroit. The heated debate brought impassioned pleas from residents across the state, all touting their own hometown. Marshall was long considered a likely choice. In 1839, the **Governor's Mansion** was built, anticipating the arrival of state government. This historic home is currently owned by the Mary Marshall Chapter of the Daughters of the American Revolution, who gracefully open the mansion for tours in the summer.

Settled in 1830, the town was centrally located (a seemingly attractive quality for a future capital) and had already attracted a strong professional community of doctors, lawyers, and clergy. This was due much in part to the enterprising efforts of Sidney Ketchum, who bought land in Marshall in 1830 and then returned to his native New York to recruit settlers. By 1832, a schoolhouse was built and a teacher brought in from Ann Arbor to educate the town's handful of children.

An important stop along the Territorial Road, Marshall had an influence that extended throughout the territory. Two residents of the town, Isaac East Crary and John D. Pierce, created the state's public school system, which was written into the constitution in 1835. This system, which assured that education was uniformly available throughout the state, was adopted in some measure by every state that joined the union thereafter.

Alas, the legislators decided that choosing an already established town for the capital was too politically risky. Instead they moved the government to a sparsely populated township midway between Detroit and Grand Rapids. First called the Town of Michigan, it was later changed to Lansing.

Throughout the early and mid-1880s, settlers from back east continued to make their way to Marshall. They brought with them their New England sensibilities—a passion for education, hard work, and sound investment. Their influence can be seen in Marshall's many Greek Revival homes, a style popular in the mid-19th century. All told, 850 residences and businesses in Marshall have been included in its National Historic Landmark District.

The **Marshall Historical Society** owns three historic buildings that serve as museums—the Capitol Hill School, the Grand Army of the Republic Hall, and the Honolulu House. Right on Michigan Avenue as you pull into town is the Honolulu House. This home was built in 1860 by Judge Abner Pratt, who served as U.S. Consul in the Hawaiian Islands. His love of the Pacific is seen in the structure's blend of Victorian and Polynesian styles, and is said to resemble the mansion he lived in while he resided in Honolulu.

Two inns, both part of the National Historic Landmark District, are also listed on the prestigious Select Registry. The first is the historic **National House Inn.** Built in 1835, the inn is the oldest hotel in Michigan. It was, in its day, an important stagecoach stop on the Territorial Road, and for a time it served Marshall as a meeting place where town business was hashed out. As passenger railroad service became more and more popular after the Civil War, the number of people traveling long distances on Michigan roads diminished. This trend meant fewer lodgers, and in 1878 the once-bustling stagecoach stop was converted into a factory making

The National House Inn in Marshall is the state's oldest hotel.

windmills and wagons. A quarter-century later, the old inn was remodeled again and served as an apartment building.

In 1976, it was restored to its original purpose and reopened to the public. More than just a historic place to stay, the National House has a reputation for fine accommodations and service. Each of the inn's 16 guest rooms is individually decorated, most in a Victorian country style. A home-cooked breakfast is served each morning in the dining room. There are several comfortable parlors if you need a place to chat with friends or just relax, and there's even a little gift shop.

On the west side of town is the other historic bed & breakfast, the **Rose Hill Inn.** This Italian villa, built in 1860, is known as the Butler-Boyce House. The mansion was built by local businessman Edward Butler on property once owned by James Fenimore Cooper. It was purchased by William Boyce, the man who later brought scouting from England and founded the Boy Scouts of America. Boyce used the home and its accompanying 60 acres as a summer home. Today this proud structure sits on 3 acres—the grounds featuring fountains, a gazebo, a swimming pool, and a tennis court. The inn has six guest rooms tastefully decorated in Victorian style, all with private bath and cable TV, as well as amenities business travelers can appreciate, like wireless Internet and phones.

No visit to Marshall would be complete without a meal at **Schuler's Restaurant.** The restaurant traces its history back to 1909, when Albert Schuler opened a

A visit to Marshall is incomplete without stopping for the prime rib at Schuler's.

cigar store in Marshall, soon adding a lunch counter and bakery. Spurred on by his success, Schuler purchased the Royal Hotel and Restaurant in Marshall, which he renamed Schuler's. Business was good, but the restaurant did not receive national attention until Albert's son Winston took over. Seeing the long lines of guests arriving for dinner, often waiting for up to two hours for a table, Win decided there should be something for them to eat as soon as they were seated. Soon diners were raving about the Bar Scheeze (a cheese spread), bread, and meatballs—but especially about the Bar Scheeze. By 1968, Win Schuler's Bar Scheeze was available in grocery stores.

Over the years, the owners have continually updated the restaurant (the hotel was converted into corporate offices). The space is uniquely comfortable and elegant. The wood ceiling beams in the Centennial Room are tastefully inscribed with wise sayings, like that from Kit Carson, THE COWARDS NEVER STARTED AND THE WEAK DIED ON THE WAY, and Ralph Waldo Emerson, HE IS ONLY RICH WHO OWNS THE DAY. The menu is classic Midwest fare, including dishes like their popular prime rib dinner.

Heading east on I-94, on your way to Ann Arbor, stop in Chelsea to tour the

CORNWELL'S TURKEYVILLE USA

Begun as a small mom-and-pop eatery in 1968, Cornwell's Turkeyville USA has served up millions of delicious turkey dinners—and they're still just as mom-and-pop as they were back in the day. But now there is a bit more going on. About 5 miles north of Marshall, right off I-69, Turkeyville is a favorite stop with families, especially those looking to escape the frantic pace of the expressway and all the fast-food joints along the way. As you might have guessed, the menu at Turkeyville features turkey—everything from turkey sandwiches and tacos to full turkey dinners with all the fixings.

Located on a sprawling 400 acres, the Cornwell's farm is used year-round for special events. There are regular flea markets, art fairs, and antiques shows. On a hot summer day, be sure to try their ice cream, made right there and served at the old-fashioned ice cream parlor. And in the evening, stay for dinner and a show at the 185-seat dinner theater.

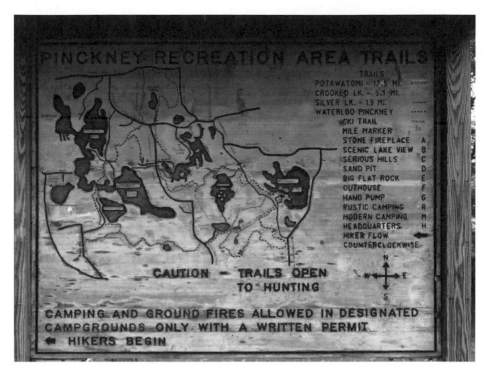

There are trails for hiking and biking at the Pinckney State Recreation Area.

Chelsea Milling Company (call ahead for reservations). The milling company is a family-owned business that produces 1.5 million boxes of Jiffy Mix every day. The mix goes back to 1930 when Mabel White Holmes came up with the original baking mix. They later added pie crust mix and corn bread mix. Today, without a lick of advertising, Jiffy Mix has 55 percent of the bake-mix market. For every 10 boxes of corn bread mix that leave the shelves across the United States, 9 are Jiffy brand.

Chelsea has a nice downtown, worthy of a stroll. For more rigorous activity, drive a little north to the **Pinckney State Recreation Area.** (You will need to check out a map for directions to this park.) Possibly the best spot for mountain biking in the state, the 11,000-acre park is known regionally for an abundance of great trails. The 17-mile Potawatomi Trail was developed years ago for backpackers wanting an overnight trip. It makes for a full day of trail riding.

Heading back toward Ann Arbor, start at the **Hudson Mills Metropark,** with their renowned disc golf course, and follow Huron River Drive through Dexter. This scenic route is particularly attractive in the fall. Along the way you will pass the **Delhi Metropark** and the **Bird Hills Nature Area.** After passing under MI 14, the road becomes Main Street, the main drag into downtown Ann Arbor.

The **University of Michigan** sits at the center of **Ann Arbor.** The university, whose existence benefited from a gift of 40 acres from the town fathers in 1837 (property they had hoped would attract the state capital), now employs more than thirty thousand employees. As people from around the world came here to take advantage of the school's research possibilities, people from around southeast Michigan began to recognize Ann Arbor as a regional cultural center.

Ann Arbor, a thriving community whose diversity is fed by fluctuating tides of incoming freshmen, grad students, researchers, and professors, is so much more than a quintessential university town. It is home to museums and art galleries, concert halls and clubs, and countless shops selling used and new books. The University of Michigan's **Hill Auditorium** hosts world-class musical guests, and in the folk-music community, the **Ark** has near-legendary status (up there with Club Passim in Boston). Borders bookstore began in Ann Arbor, and was home to the retail giant's corporate offices before its bankruptcy. And recently Google opened offices in town.

There are over three hundred restaurants in Ann Arbor, serving a truly international array of cuisine—from Ethiopian cuisine at the **Blue Nile** to Irish pub grub at **Conor O'Neill's.** Interestingly, one of the city's most widely touted eateries is a simple deli. It has been said that, for many years, you couldn't find a good delicatessen in Ann Arbor. Delis would quietly come and go, but none won the consistent patronage of Ann Arbor's persnickety diners. That all changed in 1982 when Ari Weinzeig and Paul Saginaw opened **Zingerman's Delicatessen** at the intersection of Detroit and Kingsley Streets. The building they chose was an old grocery (now on

People line up around the corner for a sandwich at Zingerman's Deli in Ann Arbor. *Kim Forster*

the National Register of Historic Places). Within a few years, the deli's reputation for great food began to spread beyond Ann Arbor. The company has expanded, adding **Zingerman's Bakehouse,** where they make artisan breads, pastries, and cakes, and **Zingerman's Roadhouse,** a restaurant that builds on their passion for quality ingredients.

At the deli, the sandwich menu is classic—the #2, Zingerman's Reuben, might be the best you'll ever eat. They also sell olive oils, barrel-aged balsamic vinegar, and fine cheeses from around the world. Another great way to enjoy Zingerman's is to take one of the classes that they offer through the bakery. Get a complete education on anything from making homemade pizza to doughnuts to wedding cakes.

If all of this sounds a little highfalutin for your tastes (and it really shouldn't), head over to **Krazy Jim's Blimpy Burger** for the town's best burgers. The restaurant used to be at the corner of Packer and South Division, but the property was recently bought to make way for some development. The owners promise to reopen, so check their website for the new location. This joint is a favorite with students, and like a lot of quirky dives known for great food, Blimpy Burger has its own culture. To fit in, you have to know the rules (as outlined on their website). There's an order to how you order, so newbies should be sure to pay attention to the people in line in front of them to see how it's done (if they haven't scanned the rules online first).

Since Ann Arbor has so many visitors—parents of students, business travelers, visiting professors—there are plenty of places to stay in town. Several bed & breakfasts are within walking distance of downtown Ann Arbor. The **Burnt Toast Inn,** for example, is three blocks west of Main Street. This typical American four-square has three rooms and a master suite; all have hardwood floors and are brightly decorated. The suite has its own private bath, and the entire home has wireless Internet.

A few blocks south, you will find the **First Street Garden Inn.** This B&B is a bit smaller but a touch more distinguished, offering two guest rooms with private bath. There are hardwood floors throughout, and the windows feature stained glass. This inn, too, has wireless Internet.

IN THE AREA

ACCOMMODATIONS

Burnt Toast Inn, 415 West William Street, Ann Arbor. Call 734-662-6685. Website: burnttoastinn.com.

Chicago Pike Inn & Spa, 215 East Chicago Street, Coldwater. Call 517-279-8744. Website: chicagopikeinn.com.

Dewey Lake Manor, 11811 Laird Road, Brooklyn. Call 517-467-7122. Website: deweylakemanor.com.

First Street Garden Inn, 549 South First Street, Ann Arbor. Call 734-741-9786. Website: firststreetgardeninn .com.

Munro House B&B, 202 Maumee

Street, Jonesville. Call 1-800-320-3792. Website: munrohouse.com.

National House Inn, 102 Parkview Street, Marshall. Call 269-781-7374. Website: nationalhouseinn.com.

Rose Hill Inn, 1110 Verona Road, Marshall. Call 269-789-1992. Website: rose-hill-inn.com.

ATTRACTIONS AND RECREATION

Allen Antique Barn, 9247 West Chicago Road, Allen. (Just west of Allen on US 12.) Call 517-869-2888. Website: allenantiquebarn.com.

The Ark, 316 South Main Street, Ann Arbor. Call 734-761-1451. Website: theark.org.

Boulevard Market, 102 East Chicago Boulevard, Tecumseh. Call 517-423-6000. Website: boulevardmarket.com.

British Tea Garden and Rooftop Café, 112 East Chicago Boulevard, Tecumseh. Call 517-423-7873. Website: thebritishpantry.com.

Chelsea Milling Company, 201 West North Street, Chelsea. Call 1-800-727-2460 or 734-475-1361. Website: jiffy mix.com.

Governor's Mansion Museum, 612 South Marshall Avenue, Marshall. Call 269-781-5260.

Hidden Lake Gardens, 6214 Monroe Road, Tipton. (South of US 12 on MI 50 west of Tecumseh.) Call 517-431-2060. Website: hiddenlakegardens.msu .edu.

Hudson Mills Metropark, 8801 North Territorial Road, Dexter. Call 734-426-8211.

Little River Railroad, 29 West Park Avenue, Coldwater. Call 260-316-0529 or 574-215-0751. Website: littleriver railroad.com.

Marshall Historical Society, 107 North Kalamazoo Avenue, Marshall. Call 269-781-8544. Their office is in the Honolulu House. Website: marshallhistoricalsociety.org.

Monroe County Historical Museums and Archives, 126 South Monroe Street, Monroe. Call 734-240-7780. Website: facebook.com/Monroe Museums.

Old Mill Museum, 242 Toledo Street, Dundee. Call 734-529-8596. Website: dundeeoldmill.com.

Pentamere Winery, 131 East Chicago Boulevard, Tecumseh. Call 517-423-9000. Website: pentamerewinery.com.

Pinckney State Recreation Area, 8555 Silver Hill Road, Pinckney. (From I-94, the park is northeast of Chelsea.) Call 734-426-4913. Website: michigan .gov/pinckney.

Preston's Antique Gaslight Village, 8651 West Chicago Road, Allen. (Just west of Allen on US 12.) Call 517-869-2928.

River Raisin National Battlefield Park, 1403 East Elm Avenue, Monroe. Call 734-243-7136. Website: nps.gov /rira.

St. Joseph's Shrine, 8743 US 12, Cambridge Township. Call 517-467-2183. Website: stjosephshrinebrooklyn .catholicweb.com.

Southern Michigan Railroad Society, 320 South Division Street, Clinton. Call 517-456-7677. Train rides begin at the depot in Clinton. They operate only on the weekends; check Website for seasonal schedule. Website: southernmichiganrailroad.org.

Walker Tavern Historic Site, 13220 MI 50, Onsted. Call 517-467-4401. Website: michigan.gov/walkertavern.

Walter J. Hayes State Park, 1220

Wamplers Lake Road, Onsted. Call 517-467-7401. Website: michigan.gov/hayes.

Wm. C. Sterling State Park, 2800 State Park Road, Monroe. Call 734-289-2715. Website: michigan.gov/sterling.

Zingerman's Bakehouse, 3711 Plaza Drive, Ann Arbor. Call 734-761-2095. Website: zingermansbakehouse.com.

DINING

Blue Nile, 221 East Washington Street, Ann Arbor. Call 734-998-4746. Website: bluenilemi.com.

Conor O'Neill's, 318 South Main Street, Ann Arbor. Call 734-665-2968. Website: conoroneills.com.

Cornwell's Turkeyville USA, 18935 15 1/2 Mile Road, Marshall. Call 269-781-4293 or 1-800-228-4315. Website: turkeyville.com.

The Dog House, 107 East Chicago Boulevard, Tecumseh. Call 517-301-4266. Website: thedoghouserestaurant.com.

Krazy Jim's Blimpy Burger, 551 South Division Street, Ann Arbor. Call 734-663-4590. Website: blimpyburger.com.

Los Tequilas, 32 Railroad Street, Coldwater. Call 517-278-0920.

Schuler's Restaurant & Pub, 115 South Eagle Street, Marshall. Call 269-781-0600 or 1-877-SCHULER (724-8537). Website: schulersrestaurant.com.

Zingerman's Delicatessen, 422 Detroit Street, Ann Arbor. Call 734-663-DELI (3354). Website: zingermansdeli.com.

Zingerman's Roadhouse, 2501 Jackson Avenue, Ann Arbor. Call 734-663-FOOD (3663). Website: zingermans roadhouse.com.

OTHER CONTACTS

Ann Arbor Area Convention and Visitors Bureau, 120 West Huron Street, Ann Arbor. Call 734-995-7281. Website: visitannarbor.org.

Brooklyn–Irish Hills Chamber of Commerce, 221 North Main Street, Brooklyn. Call 517-592-8907. Website: brooklynmi.com.

Marshall Area Chamber of Commerce, 424 East Michigan Avenue, Marshall. Call 269-781-5163 or 1-800-877-5163. Website: marshallmi.org.

The Ledges Trail follows the Grand River in Grand Ledge.

4 Through the Heart of Michigan: Following the Grand River

EATON RAPIDS, LANSING, GRAND LEDGE, LOWELL, GRAND RAPIDS, ROCKFORD, AND GRAND HAVEN

Estimated length: 150 miles

Estimated time: 2.5–4 hours, depending on whether you stick to back roads or take the expressway

Getting there: Eaton Rapids is south of Lansing, just 9 miles east off I-69 on East Clinton Trail (MI 50 at exit 60). Drive north to Grand River Avenue in East Lansing, then drive west of out Lansing on MI 43 (West Saginaw Street, which eventually becomes East Saginaw Street in Grand Ledge). From Grand Ledge, drive north and reconnect with the Grand River, heading west. South of Lowell, the road becomes Cascade Road. Drive north on Alden-Nash Avenue to Lowell, and then take MI 21 west to Grand Rapids. Continue following the river west on Luce Street, Linden Drive, and Leonard Street to Spring Lake and Grand Haven.

Highlights: The trip begins in the quiet town of Eaton Rapids on the Grand River. Consider a meal or lodging at The English Inn. In East Lansing, two used bookstores, the Curious Book Shop and Archives Book Shop, can provide hours of browsing. For entertainment, the wandering Ten Pound Fiddle coffeehouse has a regular schedule of folk performances, and the annual Great Lakes Folk Festival is worth a special visit. In Lansing's Old Town, the country's largest seller of stringed instruments, Elderly Instruments, is a musician's mecca. West of Lansing in Grand Ledge, the Ledges along the Grand River invite hikers and rock climbers. Just north of Lowell, Fallasburg Park features a covered bridge, and across the river is the ghost town of Fallasburg. In Grand Rapids, visit the Frederik Meijer Gardens & Sculpture Park and explore the city's architecture on Heritage Hill with tours of the Victorian Voigt

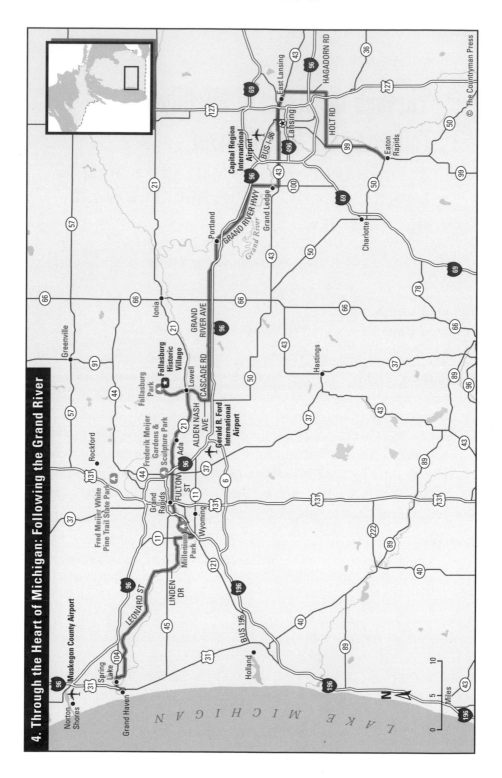

4. Through the Heart of Michigan: Following the Grand River

House and Frank Lloyd Wright's Meyer May House. Former president and Grand Rapids native Gerald Ford is remembered at the Gerald R. Ford Museum. West of town, the small John Ball Zoo is great for little kids. Once in Grand Haven, tour the boardwalk along the river, walk out to Grand Haven Pier and Lighthouse, or swim at the Grand Haven State Park or the City Beach.

The Grand River begins in spring-fed wetlands in southeast Michigan, and on its meandering path west to Lake Michigan it connects the larger towns of Jackson, Lansing, and Grand Rapids with quiet rural villages like Eaton Rapids, Grand Ledge, and Saranac. A relatively short portage separates the headwaters of the Grand River from the River Raisin, which flows east into Lake Erie. Other branches that feed the Grand are close to the rivers that flow into Lake Huron. It is no wonder Native Americans called the Grand *Owashtanong,* meaning "far away water." The Grand River is a water highway across the peninsula.

Grand River Avenue begins in the heart of Detroit and terminates in Grand Rapids. In the mid-1800s, the plank roads that connected Detroit and Lansing joined a road that followed the Grand River. Today, most of the route once called the Grand River Avenue exists. In metro Detroit it remains a busy thoroughfare, while farther west it follows a nearly direct path to Lansing, passing through small farming communities along the way. In Lansing, the road finally finds the river whose name it adopted, and the two run side by side until Grand Rapids (note that there's a jog near Lowell, and the road loses its name and ends before it reaches its historic terminus). West of Grand Rapids, there are still roads that run alongside the river, including Luce Street, Linden Drive, and Leonard Street. The latter continues to Spring Lake, just north of Grand Haven where the Grand River empties into the Great Lake.

This cross-state drive bypasses the highways, misses the truck stops and fast-food joints, and requires stops at the lights on the Main Streets of a dozen small towns. For the right person, it's a relaxing journey through mid-America—two lanes, speed zones, fields of corn and wheat, grain silos, once-grand Victorian homes, and empty downtown storefronts. This selfsame road will then take on a different personality as it passes through the heart of metro Detroit's suburbs or the student-filled streets of East Lansing.

Our route, however, keeps to the western portion of the old throughway—staying more true to the timeless river than the fickle demands of traffic patterns. Like most of the lower half of the Lower Peninsula, settlement began in the 1820s and 1830s. Timber was the going concern, and any settlement with a sawmill on the Grand would soon prosper. Eaton Rapids began just this way in 1835.

The English Inn in Eaton Rapids was the one-time home of Oldsmobile president Irving J. Reuter.

Just 17 miles south of Lansing, Eaton Rapids is on the Grand River. Houses in town date to the 19th century. In the 1920s, the president of Oldsmobile, Irving J. Reuter, built a Tudor revival home in Eaton Rapids named Medovue. Today it is a restaurant, pub, and bed & breakfast called **The English Inn.** The inn has six guest rooms in the main building and four more in two cottages, each exquisitely appointed, and antiques original to the house are found throughout. One room has a marble fireplace and others Jacuzzi bathtubs—the rooms balance historic and contemporary sensibilities.

The inn's dining room is open and well-lighted from banks of large windows. The menu includes classic prime rib, filet mignon, and a seafood dish or two. For a drink, drop by the wood-paneled, authentic English pub on the garden level.

From Eaton Rapids, take MI 99 for 9 miles north to Holt Road. Turn right and continue 8 miles to Hagadorn and turn left, continuing north on Hagadorn Road 6 miles to Grand River Avenue. Turning left on Grand River Avenue, the road is immediately in the heart of Michigan State University. The Red Cedar River flows through campus on its way to join up with the Grand River (inspiring the opening lines of the Spartans' fight song, "On the banks of the Red Cedar, there's a team that's known to all…").

East Lansing is primarily a college town, and Michigan State University dominates the downtown. The university was founded in 1855 as the Agricultural College of the State of Michigan. About 14,000 acres of state land was set aside for the school, and it was the country's first land-grant institution. Today the school has over forty-six thousand students, making it the nation's eighth-largest university.

Along Grand River, businesses catering to students thrive. There's the usual collection of bars and late-night dives, used-record stores, and textbook outlets. The **Curious Book Shop,** which has been around since 1969, has three stories of books, with everything from popular fiction to academic titles to rare collectibles. A little farther west, its sister store, the **Archives Book Shop,** has more rare titles. It's also next door to a nice coffee shop.

The **Wild Goose Inn** in East Lansing is a bed & breakfast with a lot of character. There are six rooms in two buildings, connected by a common deck. The smaller of the two is the Gosling. The innkeepers have gone to great lengths to offer guest rooms that are unique spaces: The Autumn Arbor has a custom-made bed with "branches" that support the canopy of leaves painted on the ceiling above, and the Great Lakes room has a white pine ceiling, fieldstone fireplace, and claw-foot Jacuzzi tub. The amenities throughout are top-notch.

Folk music has been a big part of the East Lansing entertainment scene for years. The **Ten Pound Fiddle,** for example, has become a folk-music mainstay. This roving coffeehouse brings top national folk acts, as well as local and regional performers, to East Lansing. Lou and Peter Berryman, and Michigan native Claudia Schmidt, are regulars. Once a month or so the coffeehouse holds a contra dance— newcomers welcome. Check their website for full concert and dance schedule.

Every year the city puts on the **Great Lakes Folk Festival,** featuring artists from around the world. The festival highlights folk music in the more global sense—mariachi, French-Canadian folk, zydeco, and the folk traditions of Europe and Africa—though there is always room for traditional American music as well. Recent festivals featured Czech-style polka and Piedmont-style blues. The festival runs the second weekend in August, Friday through Sunday.

A place to explore in nearby Lansing is Old Town. Right next to the Grand River, Old Town sprouted from the first settlement in Lansing Township, growing and prospering with the growth of Lansing. When the boom days were over, the neighborhood went into decline, but in recent years it has experienced a renaissance. Restaurants, bars and clubs, and many small businesses and shops call Old Town home. The **Golden Harvest,** for example, caters to a diverse clientele of busi-

Banjos line a wall at Elderly Instruments in Lansing's Old Town.

nesspeople, families, college students, and barflies. The menu is all breakfast, but they're open through lunchtime. Another place to eat in Old Town is **Pablo's Panaderia**—one of the best Mexican joints in Greater Lansing.

It's a nice place to spend an hour walking the streets. There are shops dedicated to bikes, skateboards, vintage apparel, and art. **Elderly Instruments** on Washington is the country's largest dealer of stringed instruments, and it has become one of the country's most respected sources for acoustic instruments, hard-to-find music books, and folk CDs. The shop was founded in 1972 by college friends Stan Werbin and Sharon McInturff. In 1984, they moved to their present location in the old Oddfellows' Hall. Elderly carries new and used instruments; they offer lessons on nearly every instrument you can pick, strum, or fret; and they have a full schedule of workshops, going to great lengths to preserve bluegrass music and promote local musicians.

Beginning in East Lansing, Grand River Avenue is also MI 43. Continuing west to Grand Ledge, stay on MI 43 as it becomes Oakland Avenue and then Saginaw Street. For a view of the Michigan State Capitol, head south five blocks on Capitol Avenue. The first state capital was Detroit, and when the territory was granted statehood, the new constitution required the capital to be established in a permanent location by 1847. The legislature was loath to pass this boon on to any of the contending cities and towns that sought this honor, so instead they chose the nearly uninhabited settlement in Lansing Township. Work began on a temporary capitol building in 1847, with the permanent structure you see today completed in 1879. Tours are available.

Continue 9 miles west on Saginaw Street to the town of Grand Ledge. Over the centuries, the Grand River cut a path through ancient sandstone and left ledges, rock outcroppings that rise 60 feet above the river. Folks today call these formations The Ledges. Native Americans who passed through this part of the state in the spring for the sap-rich maple trees called this area "Big Rocks."

In the late 19th century, Grand Ledge became a resort destination, and seven islands in the river sported a roller coaster and a small zoo. Second Island (now the town's Island Park) was the centerpiece of the Seven Islands Resort, with a high-class hotel and landscaped grounds. A dam was built downriver to maintain water levels for the paddleboats that carted tourists up and down the river. Attracted to the town's picturesque ledges, a group of spiritualists set up camp here in 1894. Their pavilion, a big red barn, still stands in **Fitzgerald Park.**

West of town and across from the old resort's Seventh Island, Fitzgerald Park has 3 miles of trails. The Ledges Trail follows the Grand River 1 mile back into town, ending at the bridge to Island Park. Rock climbers come from all over the state to climb the ledges in Oak Park, at the end of West Front Street (on the north side of the river).

Leave Grand Ledge, driving north on MI 100 to Grand River Avenue (about 3 miles north). Continue west on Grand River through Portland as the road name changes to Cascade Road. After driving 34 miles west, head north on MI 50 (Alden Nash Avenue). It's about 4 miles to Lowell.

The Flat River in Lowell is dammed just north of the confluence with the Grand River. Lowell is a small town with a respectable antiques shop, **Dovetail Antiques,** and a popular riverboat attraction, the Lowell Showboat. The boat, the *Robert East Lee,* was first conceived of in 1932, when town leaders were brainstorming ideas to bring business to Lowell during the Depression. Over the years, several ornate vessels have served as the showboat. The most recent was built after its predecessor was tossed upside down on the dock by a tornado-strength wind in 1978.

North of Lowell is **Fallasburg Park,** which straddles the Flat River. The Fallasburg Covered Bridge crosses the Flat at the south end of the park, and just east of the bridge is the historic village of Fallasburg. Back in 1837, the Fallas brothers brought their families here from upstate New York to make a new life, and the settlement became an important stop on the route from Ionia to Grand Rapids. Soon there was a sawmill and a gristmill. Later, a chair factory operated out of the upper floors of the sawmill—many see this as the beginning of Grand Rapids's prosperous furniture-manufacturing era.

Many of the buildings of historic Fallasburg have survived, and the Fallasburg Historical Society has been scooping them up as they become available. So far they have opened the schoolhouse, the Misner house, and the Fallas house as museum sites. There's also the Tower farm and the Waters house. Though you can drive

The Fallasburg Covered Bridge, north of Lowell, leads from the park to the ghost town of Fallasburg.

through the village anytime, at the Fallasburg School Museum, open on Sunday, you can talk to a volunteer about the village and get a map of the walking tour. Surrounded by government land, this historic district is isolated and retains much the rural charm it must have had nearly two hundred years ago. To get to the park, take Lincoln Lake Avenue north of Lowell to Fallasburg Park Drive. The bridge and the village are on Covered Bridge Road.

In Lowell, the **Flat River Grill** is a great place to stop for lunch or dinner. The restaurant has patio seating along the Flat River. A little finer than the usual stop, their wood-fired pizzas are excellent. Consider the sausage goat cheese or the fun BLT pizza. Sandwiches, steaks, and seafood are all on the menu.

Lowell's Main Street (MI 21) turns into Fulton Street west of town, and downtown Grand Rapids is 18 miles west on Fulton. About halfway, just before the Amway World Headquarters, the Thornapple River winds through the village of Ada and meets up with the Grand River. The **Ada Covered Bridge** connects the village with a town park. The original wood truss bridge was built in the 19th century. Efforts were made over the years to preserve the structure, but a fire destroyed the bridge, and the bridge in Ada today is reconstructed. It's open only to pedestrians.

Grand Rapids is the second-largest city in the state and the most prominent in west Michigan. Centered on the Grand River, the area was occupied over two thousand years ago when the Hopewell people made their homes in the Grand River Valley. In the earliest years of the 19th century, a fur trading post was established near the town of Ada, and in 1825 Louis Campau (the recognized founder of the town) built his log cabin near the river's rapids. In the mid-19th century, Grand Rapids began to earn its nickname, Furniture City. For some time the city was the world's leading producer of home furniture, and today companies like Steelcase help preserve that legacy; the city is still a world leader when it comes to the manufacture of office furniture. Grand Rapids is also home to Zondervan, Baker, and Eerdmans—all leading Christian book publishers.

North of Fulton on Beltline is one of Grand Rapids's finest attractions, the **Frederik Meijer Gardens & Sculpture Park**. From the English Perennial Garden to the Carnivorous Plant House to the Sculpture Park (over 30 acres), you could spend a whole day here. The 5-acre Children's Garden features 10 themed areas—the Rock Quarry, Wooded Wetlands, and the Tree House Village, to name a few—each telling a different story about the people, plants, and animals in the Great Lakes region. At the Michigan Farm Garden, where heirloom varieties of flowers and vegetables are grown, guests can visit a scale replica of the farmhouse from Lens (née Rader) Meijer's childhood. The family's hundred-year-old barn was moved to the site as well.

With the growth of the furniture industry, many of the city's well-to-do built homes in what is now called Heritage Hill. Many of these mansions, mostly Victorian in style, are too large for single-family use today. Heritage Hill is both a state and National Historic District, and to remain on the historic register, owners have to follow strict guidelines to make sure their homes retain historic character. While

The covered bridge in Ada is only open to pedestrians.

The Meyer May House in Grand Rapids was designed by Frank Lloyd Wright in 1908.

these homes are privately owned, the Heritage Hill Neighborhood Association sponsors a home tour every year in the fall.

Two houses, however, are open year-round, each revealing a very different side of turn-of-the-20th century architecture. The first is the more traditional Voigt House, maintained by the Grand Rapids Museum. One block north of Fulton on College Avenue, the three-story redbrick mansion was built in the grand Victorian style in 1896. The Voigt family had the first floor of the home decorated in 1907, and for over a hundred years now, that decor has not been altered. With its original rugs and tapestries and gas lamps, the home is a virtual time capsule.

For contrast, less than 1 mile away is Frank Lloyd Wright's Meyer May House. May was a successful clothier in Grand Rapids, and in 1908 he commissioned Wright to design a home; it was completed the following year. Considered one of the best preserved examples of Wright's Prairie style, the Meyer May House has been meticulously restored to Wright's original vision. The restoration was financed by Steelcase, and experts were consulted on every detail of the project. Inside are many of Wright's signature design features—wide banks of windows, cantilevered beams, lots of simple woodwork. The comparison to the Voigt House is astounding when you consider they were built within 14 years of each other.

For a more intimate experience of Heritage Hill, consider a stay at the **Peaches Bed & Breakfast,** less than a block south of Fulton on Gay Avenue. The inn is a Georgian country manor that was built in 1916 by the son of the founder of Old Kent Bank. There are five guest rooms, and breakfast is served each morning in the dining room. The house has much of its original charm, including unique atrium windows.

The next stop is the **Gerald R. Ford Museum,** honoring one of the city's favorite sons. The museum offers exhibits that illuminate history of a more national nature, telling the story of Ford's political career, with special attention given to the Nixon debacle. Raised in East Grand Rapids, Ford served 25 years in the House of Representatives for Michigan's fifth congressional district. He was chosen as Nixon's vice president after Spiro Agnew resigned, and in 1974 he became the fifth president of the United States not to have been elected.

The museum does a good job of putting Ford's presidency in the context of his own personal life story, his overall political career, and the cultural changes that shaped the 1970s. The Watergate exhibit looks at the constitutional crisis brought on by the burglarizing of the offices of Nixon's Democratic opponents and the following cover-up. And guests can view an exact replica of the Oval Office as it was during Ford's presidency. When Ford died in 2007, he was laid to rest on the museum grounds. (If you're looking for the Ford Presidential Library, it's in Ann Arbor.)

Just west of downtown in a quiet neighborhood is John Ball Park. Built into the hill on the north side of the 140-acre park is the surprisingly compact **John Ball Zoo.** The first record of the zoo is a mention in city records from 1891, seven years after pioneer/explorer John Ball donated 40 acres to Grand Rapids to be used as a park. It wasn't until the 1950s, after the John Ball Zoo Society was established, however, that it became an established institution. More than 1,200 animals call this zoo home—everything from chimpanzees and Komodo dragons to grizzly bears and lions. A short loop covers the entire zoo, making it great for little kids.

A grizzly wanders the pen at the John Ball Zoo in Grand Rapids.

The biggest event in Grand Rapids these days is **ArtPrize.** This unique art competition attracts artists from around the world. The cash awards are huge; anyone can enter their work; and the public gets to choose the winners.

Best of all, the contest means the city is flooded with art for 2 1/2 weeks. In 2012, this grand spectacle attracted 400,000 people to Grand Rapids.

Only one restaurant in Michigan has earned AAA's five-diamond rating, the 1913 Room in the **Amway Grand Plaza Hotel.** Built in 1913 in downtown Grand Rapids, the hotel was originally called The Pantlind. From the beginning, it was nothing short of opulent, its lobby featuring one of the world's largest gold-leaf ceilings. Within a few short years it was widely considered one of the finest hotels in the country. The Amway Corporation later purchased the property, adding the newer glass tower to the hotel. All told, the hotel has 682 rooms, a pool, and six restaurants. The 1913 Room on the lobby level keeps up the hotel's reputation for being one of the fanciest digs in the state.

For something a bit more casual than the 1913 Room, head east of town on 28th Street to the **Beltline Bar.** Originally built in the early 1950s, chili dogs and popcorn once topped the menu. Since 1966, however, the restaurant has served up a famous wet burrito. The primarily Mexican menu was rather unique when it first appeared, and this went a long way to establish the Beltline Bar's reputation. But it's more than just nostalgia that grows a simple watering hole into a full-fledged 250-seat restaurant.

For a side trip, consider a drive into Rockford. This town once drew its very life breath from the local shoe factory. Hush Puppy Shoes are still headquartered here, but in recent years, the town has reinvented itself as both a bedroom community of Grand Rapids and a fun weekend tourist town with great places to eat and shops to browse—from the colorful yellow and white façade of Aunt Candy's Toy Company to the sophisticated Urban Elements. Be sure to check out the shoes at **Rockford Footwear Depot.** This used to be a completely bare-bones factory outlet, with boxes of shoes piled on folding tables. Today it's a sprawling remodeled sales floor with fewer deals but better shoes than I remember from years back.

And if you missed lunch at the Beltline Bar, grab a hot dog at the **Corner Bar.** They started serving dogs here with their "special sauce" right after Prohibition (you needed to serve food if you were going to get a beer license). Inside, check out the Hot Dog Hall of Fame, celebrating over five thousand people who have eaten 12 of their chili dogs within four hours. (Eat 20 dogs, and they pick up the check.)

Returning to Grand Rapids, continue south and west on Front Avenue to Butterworth Street. Along the way, you pass Millennium Park, which has a large lake and beach area. Continue on Butterworth to Wilson Avenue (MI 11), turn north, drive for 3 miles, and turn left on Fennessy Drive. This road becomes Luce Street, Linden Drive, and Leonard Street as it follows the Grand River to Spring Lake. Watch for the left-hand turn that keeps you on Leonard Street after Crockery Creek.

THE WHITE PINE TRAIL

Stretching 92 miles from Cadillac in the north to Comstock Park in the south, the **Fred Meijer White Pine Trail State Park** is the longest state park in Michigan. (Incidentally, it also has the longest name of any state park.) The White Pine Trail was built on the grade of the old Penn Central Railroad, and it is relatively flat, with only gradual climbs. With the exception of two sections adding up to 20 miles of asphalt, the path is natural ballast and gravel.

Popular with hikers and cyclists, the trail sees a lot of snowmobilers and cross-country skiers in the winter. There are three trailheads—in Cadillac, Big Rapids, and Belmont. Though the park itself has no campsites, there are campgrounds nearby in the towns through which the trail passes.

If you hit I-96, you've gone too far. It's a very scenic drive in parts, but if you prefer to save time, drive west on I-96 to exit 9, and take MI 104 to US 31 south. Grand Haven is south of the bridge.

Madeline La Framboise was the daughter of a French fur trader and his Ottawa wife. She was born in 1780 in Fort St. Joseph but grew up in a Chippewa village near the mouth of the Grand River, near today's Grand Haven. In 1794 she married Joseph La Framboise, a French trader, and they went on to establish a number of trading posts throughout this part of the state—the most prominent in Ada. The city of Grand Haven traces its roots back to their establishment of the trading post Gabagouache (the Pottawatomie name for the region).

Today Grand Haven is the county seat for Ottawa County and boasts more than ten thousand residents. Not nearly as urban and industrial as Muskegon to the north, the town has a stunning waterfront. In the summer Grand Haven's beaches are packed with beachgoers. The **Grand Haven State Park,** with its 0.5 mile of Lake Michigan shoreline, sees over 1 million guests a year. The park has 174 campsites, simple slabs of asphalt surrounded by sand that make it clear that the beach is the real attraction here. The Grand Haven Pier along the north edge of the park is always rife with anglers and leads out to the Grand Haven Lighthouse. Just south of the state park is the Grand Haven City Beach, and Ottawa County has four other parks with beaches on Lake Michigan.

The 2.5-mile-long boardwalk begins alongside the Grand River at the City Marina, and it follows the river to the pier. Along the way, you pass the **Train Depot Museum.** Once the depot for the Grand Trunk Railroad, the museum houses displays that illustrate Ottawa County history, from fur trading and logging to railroads and the region's maritime legacy.

The boardwalk along the Grand River in Grand Haven leads up to the lighthouse on Lake Michigan. *Kim Forster*

Farther along the boardwalk, you might want to grab a bite at **Snug Harbor.** Open for lunch and dinner with a full bar, the restaurant sits right on the river and has patio seating when the weather is good. The dinner menu features steak, seafood, and pasta, and a nice selection of Mexican dishes. If you are a fan of the Reuben, be sure to try their turkey Reuben for lunch.

If you want to venture inland for some sight-seeing, catch the **Harbor Trolley,** which gives passengers a tour of Grand Haven with some historical narration en route. The trolley makes stops in Grand Haven, Spring Lake, and Ferrysburg. On summer nights, join the crowd that gathers around the city's musical fountain—the largest of its kind in the world—for a stunning display of water, lights, and sound.

Close to the beach, the **Bluewater Inn and Suites** is nothing fancy, but the hotel is certainly clean and affordable. For more sophisticated (and pricier) lodgings, check out the **Boyden House.** Built in 1874 and later owned by a lumber baron, the home features various woods throughout. There are eight guest rooms, each decorated in a contemporary style that complements the home's historical character. A gourmet breakfast is served each morning, and there is often a selection of items to please every palette.

IN THE AREA

ACCOMMODATIONS

Amway Grand Plaza Hotel, 187 Monroe Avenue NW, Grand Rapids. Call 1-800-253-3590. Website: amway grand.com.

Bluewater Inn and Suites, 1030 South Harbor Drive, Grand Haven. Call 616-846-7431. This affordable hotel is close to the beach. Website: bluewaterinngrandhaven.com.

Boyden House, 301 South Fifth Street, Grand Haven. Call 616-846-3538. Pricey, but the best in town. Also serves meals. Website: boydenhouse .com.

The English Inn, 677 South Michigan Rd., Eaton Rapids. Call 517-663-2500 or 1-800-858-0598. Ten guest rooms total, six in the main house. Weekends book early. Website: englishinn.com.

Peaches Bed & Breakfast, 29 Gay Avenue, Grand Rapids. Call 616-454-8000. Website: peaches-inn.com.

Wild Goose Inn, 512 Albert Street, East Lansing. Call 517-333-3334. Website: wildgooseinn.com.

ATTRACTIONS AND RECREATION

Archives Book Shop, 517 West Grand River Avenue, East Lansing. Call 517-332-8444.

ArtPrize, Grand Rapids. Website: art prize.org.

Curious Book Shop, 307 East Grand River Avenue, East Lansing. Call 517-332-0112. Website: curiousbooks.com.

Dovetail Antiques, 211 West Main Street, Lowell. Call 616-897-0898. Website: http://dovetailantiques.webs .com.

Elderly Instruments, 1100 North Washington Avenue, Lansing. Call

A tugboat working hard in Grand Haven *Kim Forster*

A sandy Lake Michigan beach

517-372-7880 or 1-888-473-5810. Website: elderly.com.

Fallasburg Historic Village, 13944 Covered Bridge Road, Lowell. Call 616-897-7161. Website: fallasburg.org.

Fallasburg Park, 1124 Fallasburg Road, Lowell. Call 616-336-PARK (7278). Website: accesskent.com (under the Parks & Leisure tab, click Parks, and then Parks Directory in the left column).

Fitzgerald Park, 133 Fitzgerald Park Drive, Grand Ledge. Call 517-627-7351. Website: eatoncountyparks.org.

Fred Meijer White Pine Trail State Park, 6093 MI 115, Cadillac. Call 231-775-7911. Website: michigandnr.com/parksandtrails.

Frederik Meijer Gardens & Sculpture Park, 1000 East Beltline Avenue NE, Grand Rapids. Call 1-888-957-1580. Website: meijergardens.org.

Gerald R. Ford Museum, 303 Pearl Street NW, Grand Rapids. Call 616-254-0400. Website: fordlibrarymuseum.gov.

Grand Haven State Park, 1001 Harbor Avenue, Grand Haven. Call 616-847-1309. Website: michigan.gov/grandhaven.

Great Lakes Folk Festival. Held annually in the summer in East Lansing. Website: greatlakesfolkfest.net.

Harbor Trolley, Grand Haven. Call 616-842-3200.

Heritage Hill Neighborhood Association, 126 College Avenue SE, Grand Rapids. Call 616-459-8950. Website: heritagehillweb.org.

John Ball Zoo, 1300 West Fulton Street, Grand Rapids. Call 616-336-4301. Website: johnballzoosociety.org.

Meyer May House, 450 Madison Avenue SE, Grand Rapids. Call 616-246-4821. Tours are available several days a week; call for current schedule.

Michigan State Capitol, Capitol

Square, Lansing. Call 517-373-2353. Reservations necessary for groups of 10 or more. Website: michigan.gov.

Rockford Footwear Depot, 235 North Main Street, Rockford. Call 616-866-9100. Website: facebook.com/ RockfordFootDepot.

Ten Pound Fiddle. Call 517-337-7744. Website: tenpoundfiddle.org.

Train Depot Museum, 1 North Harbor Drive, Grand Haven. Call 616-842-0700.

Voigt House, 115 College Avenue NE, Grand Rapids. Call 616-456-4600. Tours are available several days a week; check site for current schedule. Website: grmuseum.org/voigt_house.

DINING

Beltline Bar, 16 28th Street SE, Grand Rapids. Call 616-245-0494. Website: beltlinebar.com.

Corner Bar, 31 North Main Street, Rockford Call 616-866-4995. Website: rockfordcornerbar.com.

The English Inn, 677 South Michigan Rd., Eaton Rapids. Call 517-663-2500 or 1-800-858-0598. Open for lunch Monday through Friday; dinner daily. There is no dress code, but this is a fancy place. Website: englishinn.com.

Flat River Grill, 201 East Main Street, Lowell. Call 313-897-8523. Website: thegilmorecollection.com/flatriver.php.

Golden Harvest, 1625 Turner Street, Lansing. Call 517-485-3663. Open daily, serving breakfast through lunchtime. Website: facebook.com/pages/ Golden-Harvest/26493976313.

Pablo's Panaderia, 311 East Grand River Avenue, Lansing. Call 517-372-0887. Website: pablosoldtown.com.

Snug Harbor, 311 South Harbor Avenue, Grand Haven. Call 616-846-8400. Website: harborrestaurants.com/ SnugHarbor.

OTHER CONTACTS

Grand Haven Area Convention & Visitors Bureau, 1 South Harbor Drive, Grand Haven. Call 1-800-303-4092. Website: visitgrandhaven.com.

Grand Rapids Convention and Visitors Bureau, 171 Monroe Avenue NW, Suite 700, Grand Rapids. Call 616-459-8287 or 1-800-678-9859. Website: visitgrandrapids.org.

Greater Lansing Convention Center, 1223 Turner Street, Suite 200, Lansing. Call 1-888-252-6746. Website: lansing.org.

St. Julian in Paw Paw is Michigan's oldest winery.

5 The Grape Coast: Michigan's Wine Country

THREE RIVERS, KALAMAZOO, PAW PAW, COLOMA, HARBOR COUNTRY, ST. JOSEPH, SOUTH HAVEN, FENNVILLE, AND SAUGATUCK

Estimated length: 200 miles

Estimated time: 4–4.5 hours

Getting there: This route begins in Three Rivers, about 25 miles south of Kalamazoo. From there follow US 131 north to Kalamazoo. The Red Arrow Highway (Stadium Drive in town) heads west from there to stops in Paw Paw and Coloma. Jumping on I-94 head south to New Buffalo (exit 1) and drive 1 mile or so northwest to town. Leave New Buffalo heading northeast on East Buffalo Street, which becomes Red Arrow Highway and continues on to Union Pier and Benton Harbor. Through Benton Harbor and St. Joseph, northbound traffic stays on the main road, which becomes MI 63 (known here as Blue Star Highway). The Blue Star Highway continues north to South Haven and Saugatuck.

Highlights: This trip begins exploring southwest Michigan's rich history in Three Rivers, then north, passing through Kalamazoo on the way into the heart of Michigan's grape country. Winery tours and wine tasting begin at the state's oldest winery, St. Julian Winery, in Paw Paw. Heading west to Coloma, try chocolate truffles at The Chocolate Garden and pick seasonal fruit at Jollay Orchards. In Harbor Country, enjoy the many beaches along Lake Michigan. There's the beach in New Buffalo, of course, but don't miss out on the incredible dunes at Warren Dunes State Park. For a break from the water, consider a short hike through Warren Woods or explore the natural diversity of Grand Mere State Park. Heading north to South Haven, there's more fun to be had on the city beach, or visit the Michigan Maritime Museum and schedule a short trip on their sloop, Friends Good Will. Finally, continue north to

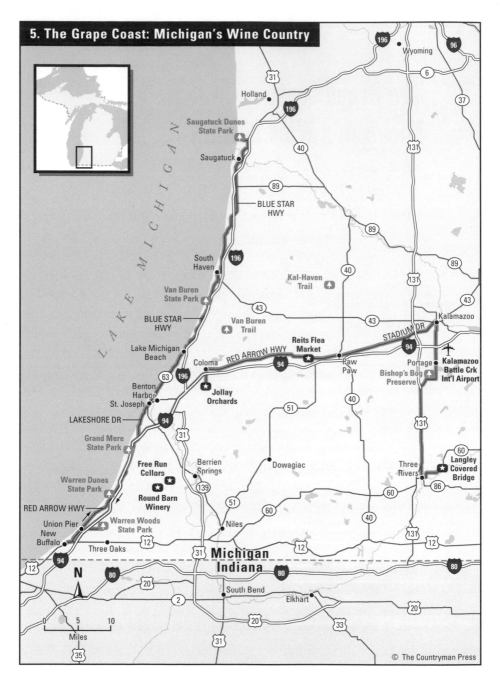

Saugatuck. En route, stop and tour the SS *Keewatin* Ship Museum. In Saugatuck, take the Chain Ferry across the Kalamazoo River and climb the steep steps to the top of Mount Baldhead. Down the other side you can relax on Oval Beach. Later, take a dune ride at Saugatuck Dunes State Park with the folks at Saugatuck Dune Rides.

L aced with rivers all leading west to Lake Michigan, the southwest corner of Michigan has a fascinating history. The Pottawatomie and Miami called this corner of the peninsula home. In the early 1800s, settlers came to farm the region's rich soils. They built mills alongside the St. Joseph and Kalamazoo Rivers, and soon the railroad was collecting crops and commerce for other parts of the country.

In Three Rivers, men would build barges to carry their harvest out to Lake Michigan where it could be shipped to Chicago. Since it was a lot easier to float a full barge downriver than pole the empty barge back against the current, they dismantled their boats and sold the wood, making a profit on both the raft and its cargo.

In the late 1870s, George Sheffield, a mechanic for the Three Rivers Pump Factory, grew tired of walking the 7 miles or so to and from work. Since his property butted up against the tracks for the Michigan Central Railroad, he usually walked the rails. Considering how he might make the trek easier, he created a three-wheeled hand-powered vehicle that would ride the tracks. The railroad eventually got wind of his invention and ordered a few for its track inspectors. A patent, some investors, and a few years later, the Sheffield Car Company was born. For several decades, the company drove the Three Rivers economy—employing up to 1,500 people. You can see one of George's velocipedes in the lobby of City Hall.

About the time Sheffield was tinkering away at his invention, Arthur Silliman was building a small factory on the banks of the St. Joseph River. The three-story brick structure was never used as a factory. The Silliman family moved in on the main level, and Arthur set up a blacksmith shop on the basement level. Today, the **Sue Silliman House & Blacksmith Shop** is maintained by the local chapter of the Daughters of the American Revolution. Tours are catch-as-catch-can. Typically in the summer there's someone there on Fridays. Otherwise give them a call and someone will be happy to let you look around. There's a neat collection of local artifacts on the third floor.

East of town, the **Langley Covered Bridge** stretches 282 feet over the St. Joseph River, making it the longest covered bridge in the state. To get there, you take MI 60 east to Schweitzer Road. About 2.5 miles on, you come to Covered Bridge Road, and the bridge is on your left.

Returning to US 131, head north toward Portage and Kalamazoo. About 12 miles north of Three Rivers, the highway eases westward, and there's an exit ramp of sorts for Shaver Road. At 1.6 miles, turn right on West Osterhout Avenue; 1 mile east is Schrier Park. Anyone interested in the natural history of southeast Michigan will appreciate the several interconnected parks here in Portage. Beginning at Schrier Park, visitors can take the Bishops Bog Trail to the **Bishop's Bog Preserve.** At 152 acres, this is the largest relict bog in southern Michigan. On the city website,

The Silliman House in Three Rivers had a blacksmith shop on the lower level.
Kim Forster

there's an excellent guide for appreciating the unique ecology of the bog. A hike from Schrier Park to the trail's end is about 1.75 miles—so count on a 3.5-mile out-and-back if you want to hike the whole thing.

Heading north on Westnedge takes you right into the heart of Kalamazoo, the home of Western Michigan University and Kalamazoo College. Right downtown, the **Kalamazoo House Bed & Breakfast** is one of the finest B&Bs around. While it's a fine place to crash for the night, you might wish you booked more nights and made it the centerpiece of a romantic weekend.

From Westnedge, turn left on West Michigan Avenue, which becomes Stadium Drive and eventually turns into the Red Arrow Highway, the main path for the next leg of the trip.

The Lake Michigan Shore Appellation is Michigan's oldest American Viticultural Area, and commercial vineyards in this region of the state date back to 1867. Lake Michigan helps temper the local climate—the vast body of water holds the summer's warmth and prolongs the growing season by a couple months. The sandy terrain, formed by retreating glaciers, is sloping, which allows for air drainage, reducing the risk of frost.

This grape-growing region (with nearly 12,000 acres of vineyards) accounts for more than half of the wine grapes grown in the state of Michigan. Of the state's vineyards, 90 percent are found in this area—most producing Concord and Niagara for juice and jelly. Visitors, however, come to explore the region's wineries and wines. Overall, a mere 11 percent of the state's vineyards are growing wine grapes, and half of these vineyards are in southwest Michigan. The rest are found in northwest Michigan, on the Leelanau and Old Mission Peninsulas (see Chapter 6 for a related trip).

Paw Paw is the unofficial wine capital of Michigan. This is due in no small part to the state's oldest winery. **St. Julian Winery's** humble beginnings can be traced back to Windsor, Ontario, where in 1921 a young Italian immigrant named Mariano Meconi founded Border City Wine Cellars. He moved the winery to Detroit in 1934 (Prohibition had just been repealed the year before), and two years later he moved it to its present location in Paw Paw. The final move brought the winery into the heart of the Lake Michigan grape-growing region. Over the years, the company's name was changed several times. St. Julian was the patron saint of Meconi's home village in Italy, and that name was finally settled on in 1941.

Coming south from Red Arrow Highway on Kalamazoo Street, St. Julian is hard to miss. The winery sits on the west side of the road; its exposed aggregate façade looms just several feet from the street. The winery has a tasting room and gives regular tours of the facility, including a look into how they make their fruit brandies. Though wine is their specialty, the winery produces more nonalcoholic sparkling juices than fermented products.

Next to St. Julian, nestled cozily alongside the Paw Paw River, is **Warner Vineyards Winery,** the state's second-oldest winery. While aesthetically more pleasing than many other wineries in the area, this one is a bit easier to maintain since their wine is made elsewhere. An old train car sits on the meticulously landscaped lawn, and you cross a covered bridge to reach their tasting room and restaurant. The tasting room, called the **Warner Wine Haus,** was once the local waterworks. The Warner family bought the property in 1967 and restored it to its current condition. With the river gently curving around the front and the tall shade trees, it's very picturesque.

A little downstream, where the dam creates Maple Lake, you will find the perfect place to eat on the water, **La Cantina Restaurant.** This classic Italian eatery has been serving Paw Paw for generations. A deck out back overlooks the lake. The portions are huge, and the pizza is a local favorite.

Every year in September, regional wineries get together in Paw Paw to celebrate the annual **Paw Paw Wine and Harvest Festival.** It's the town's biggest event and always draws a crowd.

Returning north on Kalamazoo Street, turn left on West Michigan Avenue (at the light in the center of town). Continuing west, Michigan Avenue becomes Red

The picturesque Warner Vineyards Winery offers wine tasting and a nice restaurant.

Arrow Highway, once known as the Territorial Road, which was built between Detroit and St. Joseph in the 1830s. About 5 miles west of town is **Reits Flea Market.** On weekends in the summer, 450 dealers display everything from antiques and collectibles to tacky velvet oil paintings and bandannas featuring wizards and dragons.

Farther west, you will pass through the quiet towns of Lawrence, Hartford, and Watervliet before you get to Coloma. While this region is firmly established as part of the fruit belt, Coloma is home to **The Chocolate Garden,** which specializes in the art of the chocolate truffle. South of town on Friday Road, this small chocolate shop is nestled between acres of fruit trees. Featured on the Food Network, the truffles have a unique texture and taste that consistently win over visitors—even those who have no particular passion for chocolate.

The Chocolate Garden's truffles alone are worth a trip to Coloma.

Drive another 1 mile farther south

MORE WINERIES

If you'd like to visit more wineries while you are in the area, stop at **Round Barn Winery** in Baroda and **Free Run Cellars** in Berrien Springs. While they are only 7 or 8 miles from the expressway, getting there can be a little tricky. (Check their respective websites for directions.) Conveniently, both have tasting rooms in Union Pier just off I-94, exit 6. For a price, the Round Barn offers tours for groups of 20 or more with reservations, but not in the summer or fall months.

---

on Friday Road to **Jollay Orchards,** a Centennial farm that has been in the Jollay family for over 150 years. Throughout the summer, people come out to pick their own fresh fruits and berries, like raspberries, peaches, and apples. In the fall, the orchard gives you a chance to see cider being made while you chomp down the traditional Michigan cinnamon-and-sugar cider doughnut. For kids there is a hayride, pumpkin patch, and corn maze during the annual harvest festival.

As you continue west, Red Arrow Highway gets a bit lost through Benton Harbor and St. Joseph. It makes good sense to get on I-94 here in Coloma and bypass the rigmarole of those twin cities, driving straight to New Buffalo (exit 1) and Union Pier (exit 6) on Lake Michigan.

The seven towns south of Benton Harbor along the lakeshore, and Three Oaks (7 miles inland), make up the region known as Michigan's Harbor Country. In the 1800s, this stretch of Lake Michigan prospered from the logging boom. Sawmills, ships, and docks and piers dominated the coastline. Most of the timber was shipped to Chicago to feed its incredible growth, and later the wood was needed to rebuild the city after the Great Chicago Fire of 1871.

When the lumber industry began its decline, the railroads that serviced this part of the state switched gears and began to promote tourism. Just a mere 70 miles from Chicago, this stretch of Lake Michigan has been welcoming vacationers from the Windy City since the late 19th century. The list of Chicago-based personalities, both famous and infamous, who had summer homes in these lakefront towns is impressive. As such, the towns of Harbor Country are well suited for tourists. There are plenty of restaurants, ice cream shops, galleries, and hotels and inns. For longer stays, resorts are popular, as are cabin rentals. New Buffalo, for example, is the perfect spot to waste away an afternoon, walking through town or along the small harbor where condos overlook boat slips.

Outside of the obvious harbor towns, the well-established community of homes along the lake might prove frustrating for newcomers longing for a view of the

New Buffalo Lighthouse

water. Driving along the Red Arrow Highway, you are at times 0.5 mile from the shore—a very wooded 0.5 mile. But access to Lake Michigan and its beaches is not hard to come by, and locals boast they have the warmest water for swimming on the Great Lakes. New Buffalo Beach Park, a short walk from downtown New Buffalo, is a great location. A wide ribbon of sand stretches north from the Galien River Channel, and there's a concession stand and restrooms conveniently located near the parking lot.

Another way to get your feet wet in the Great Lake, and to get in touch with the region's natural beauty, is to visit one of two state parks. The first, **Warren Dunes State Park**, is about 7.5 miles north of Union Pier. Nearly 2,000 acres were purchased in the 1880s by a businessman from nearby Three Oaks, East K. Warren. At the time, his neighbors thought he was a fool. The property was considered so worthless that many owners saw no point in paying property tax and let their lots revert to state ownership. In 1930, Warren's property was set aside as a state park.

Warren saw in the dunes something of value that people today can also appreciate. Each year 1 million visitors clamber up the dunes for a view from the top (Tower Hill rises over 250 feet above Lake Michigan), or spread a towel on the park's 3 miles of beach, or simply hike the trails (there are 6 miles of paths here). For campers, there are over two hundred sites, both modern and semimodern. In recent years, the emerald ash borer beetle has done quite a number on the park's campground (as it has across the state). Over four thousand ash trees have been removed, which has dramatically changed the feel of the campground.

Just off Red Arrow Highway 8 miles farther north is **Grand Mere State Park.** This park is a naturalist's wonderland. Listed as a National Natural Landmark, one of 12 statewide, the unique qualities of the terrain have preserved several stages of ecological development—from the sandy beaches and dunes near the lake to climax forest—in one relatively small area (a mere 985 acres). As such, the park presents an abundance of ecological diversity.

The big dune at Warren Dunes tempts many to climb, but not all.

Most visitors come for the 1 mile of sandy beach or a hike around one of the three interdunal lakes. The park allows dogs, and this is a big draw. The beach is not close to parking, however, and visitors should be aware that at the end of the 0.5-mile hike a steep and somewhat strenuous-to-climb dune springs up as the final hurdle before reaching the water. To get there, head north to West John Beers Road, backtrack under I-94 (near exit 22), and take a left onto Thornton Drive. The park entrance is just 0.5 mile south on the right.

When you're ready for a bite to eat, try **Red Arrow Roadhouse** in Union Pier. This place is a classic roadhouse, though perhaps a little more family-friendly than others of its ilk. With its knotty-pine interior and old hardwood floors, you'd expect that they would have great hamburgers and fries. Even the char-grilled steak and Lake Superior whitefish on the menu are no surprise. What you might not expect is mahimahi fish tacos or whole wheat fusilli, or appetizers like blue cheese potato chips and Buffalo fantail shrimp.

March 1 is a big day for diners in New Buffalo: It's the day **Redamak's** opens after its annual winter sabbatical. Known for serving great burgers (perhaps the best in the state), this tavern and legendary burger joint keeps it down-to-earth. The restaurant was the passion of the Redamak family, who started it in the 1940s

---

THE WARREN WOODS

Most visitors get this close to Lake Michigan and find it hard to see anything else. Just a few miles inland, Warren Woods State Park is worth a visit. This 311-acre park is home to the state's last known beech-maple forest, which is what scientists call a climax forest (meaning it is the last in a series of ecological stages that are typical for eastern woodlands). The forest takes up about 200 acres of the park. The trees here are old—many over 450 years old. The smooth-barked silver beeches are tall, creating a 100-foot canopy above that blocks out most of the sunlight. The sugar maples are shorter, picking out sunlight where they can. A 3.5-mile trail leads back into the woods, following and crossing the Galien River.

The park was the result of a local businessman's incredible foresight. East K. Warren purchased this property in 1878 with the purpose of preserving it for posterity, and in keeping with the park's mission to remain undeveloped; the facilities are sparse (including pit toilets and a rustic picnic area). Visitors come to view the beautiful changing of the leaves in the fall, and throughout the year, the park is popular with bird-watchers.

Warren Woods, administered by the Warren Dunes State Park, is a little over 2.5 miles east of I-94 on Elm Valley Road (at exit 6; west of the interstate, the road is called Union Pier Road).

and sold it to the Maroney family from Chicago in 1975. Just as it has been for decades, the beef is cut and ground on-site. Each patty weighs 5.3 ounces when it hits the skillet. The burgers are then dressed (with Velveeta when you ask for a cheeseburger), wrapped in wax paper, and tossed in a basket with your sides. The dining room is big enough to accommodate a lot of diners, so don't be afraid if you see a line. And be sure to bring your cash; they don't take checks or plastic.

Folks say that Redamak's in New Buffalo serves the best burgers in Michigan.

A region as popular with tourists as Harbor Country is sure to have great lodging, but a couple of places really stand out. Halfway between Red Arrow Highway and the expressway on Union Pier Road, the **Garden Grove Bed & Breakfast** in Union Pier is certainly one of the most romantic places to stay. The inn has four rooms in the main house, and in 2004, owners Paula and Jerry Welsh added the Deluxe Carriage House, which offers another two rooms and a large suite. Most of the rooms have a Jacuzzi tub big enough for two. The property is nearly 1 full acre, and rooms overlook the lovingly tended gardens. The entire house seems to open up to the outdoors, admitting the lush landscaping. Breakfast is served each morning, and guests enjoy dishes like the popular blueberry pancakes and apple-stuffed sausage.

Also in Union Pier, a bit closer to the lake, is the **Inn at Union Pier.** Built in the 1920s, it was originally billed as Karonsky's Hotel. The original resort offered 39 rooms, all quite tiny. Dramatically remodeled, the inn now has 16 guest rooms distributed among the Great House, the Pier House, and the Four Seasons Cottage. The inn is decorated with distinctive Danish and Swedish antiques, and most rooms feature a traditional Swedish *kakelugn* (a highly decorative wood-burning stove), each of which has an interesting history. Outside there's a hot tub and sauna, both of which are available year-round. In the summer, the beach is only a block away.

Finally, there is a small boutique hotel in New Buffalo, **The Harbor Grand,** that offers guests another kind of experience. Built in 1994 overlooking the harbor downtown, the hotel has 55 guest rooms and offers little touches not normally found at the bigger chain hotels—like an extensive DVD library, beach cruiser bikes, and

BERRIEN SPRINGS

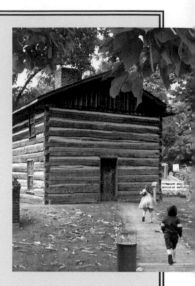

Originally platted in 1831, Berrien Springs is best known for its large community of Seventh Day Adventists. The Adventist school Andrews University is located here, and you will find fewer establishments open for business on Saturdays.

The town was the seat of Berrien County government from 1837 to 1894. The towering Greek Revival courthouse in the old town center was built in 1839. After the county seat was moved to St. Joseph, the courthouse limped along for several decades, until it was eventually vacated. In the 1960s, there was a push to preserve the courthouse and its neighboring structures, and thus was born The History Center at Courthouse Square.

The property's claim to fame is that it is the oldest surviving county government complex in the Midwest. In addition to the courthouse itself, visitors can wander through the 1830 Murdock Log House (moved from just 1 mile down the road), the old sheriff's residence and the adjoining footprint of the county's unique round jail, and a blacksmith's shop. There's a museum and museum store on-site as well.

From I-94, the exit for Scottdale Road (exit 28) will get you there. (Niles Road, exit 27, cuts the corner a little bit if you are coming from the south.) Just follow MI 139 into downtown Berrien Springs and turn left on East Ferry Street. The courthouse complex is a block down on the left.

delivery of Ben & Jerry's ice cream to your room 24 hours a day. The rooms are fashionably comfortable, and many have fireplaces, water views, and flat-screen TVs. This is a great spot if you want more modern amenities on your vacation.

Passing through St. Joe's on the route north, don't miss a chance to stop at Silver Beach. There's a great playground right on the beach, an intense splash pad, a picturesque lighthouse, and a classic carousel. Not to be missed is the famous Silver Beach Pizza. Waits here are incredibly long, so either plan on coming at an off time or bring an engaging dinner partner, one whose stimulating conversation can make an hour pass in an instant. If neither of these is an option, you can always order carryout at the window.

The next stop is South Haven, a little over 45 miles north. To get there on the back roads, drive north on Red Arrow Highway. In Benton Harbor, the road changes names—it becomes Lakeshore Drive and soon joins with MI 63. Follow the signs for MI 63 north until you get to the town of Lake Michigan Beach, where MI 63 makes a sharp turn to the east on Hagar Shore Road. The road you were on, however, continues north, now called the Blue Star Highway. Stay on that for 12.5 miles. As the highway veers east, it crosses MI 140. Take a left and continue north 1.5 miles to downtown South Haven, which centers on Phoenix Avenue.

The story of South Haven begins humbly enough. A man by the name of Jay R. Monroe secured a land patent for 65 acres along Lake Michigan in 1833, and he and his wife moved into a log cabin he had built on the property. He hoped to found a village there where the Black River emptied into the lake; however, no more settlers came until the 1850s. In the intervening years, Monroe and his wife moved to Lawrence, Michigan, and raised a family. Their son, Charles J. Monroe, returned to the family property and served as the town's bank president (now Clementine's restaurant).

Early on, the Black River helped transport lumber down to ships waiting in South Haven's harbor. Today the harbor is more popular with leisure ships, and the economy centers on tourism and fruit production. In particular, South Haven is known for blueberries. Each year, since the town's centennial celebration in 1969, the town has put on the **National Blueberry Festival.** Festival highlights include live bands, a 5K run, and a blueberry pie social. Inland, there are several U-pick blueberry farms, and right in town is the aptly named **Blueberry Store,** located on Phoenix Street. They carry all sorts of blueberry products, including jelly and jam, salsa, dessert toppings, and BBQ sauce—not to mention blueberry coffee, dried blueberries, and blueberry concentrate. All of their food items are made with fruit from local berry farms.

The take-out window at Silver Beach Pizza *Kim Forster*

With a huge playground, kids love Silver Beach even when it's too cold for swimming.

With a spacious harbor, classic pier lighthouse, and sandy beach, South Haven is yet another spot where you can appreciate Lake Michigan up close. The Black River runs through town, and Phoenix Street becomes Water Street as you walk west toward Riverfront Park and the lake.

The **Michigan Maritime Museum** is a block north of town, just past where the Dyckman Avenue drawbridge crosses the Black River. The museum offers several ways to experience South Haven's maritime history. Exhibits at the museum itself include a fishing tug and several U.S. Coast Guard rescue boats, and the museum even has its own reproduction sloop, the *Friends Good Will*, modeled on a ship of the same name that sailed the Great Lakes in the early days of the 19th century. The museum tells the story of this vessel, which began as a merchant craft, was later seized by the British, and then was won back by the Americans during the War of 1812. The British eventually had the last word, burning the ship as it lay on the beach near Buffalo, New York. Throughout the summer, the ship takes passengers out for 90-minute cruises.

To see the harbor from land, the Harbor Walk is a self-guided tour of the harbor, complete with signposts that tell about the town's lifesaving station, fruit industry, and shipbuilding. Beginning on the north side of the Black River, the walk takes you around the harbor and out toward the lake on the south side of the river. You'll pass a block from the center of town, so the historic stroll can segue nicely into a lunch break or some time spent browsing South Haven's shops.

Book lovers will want to stop at **Black River Books**, a block south of Phoenix on Kalamazoo Street. Book collecting began as a hobby for Dick and Pam Haferman. Soon they were selling volumes online, and in 2007 their hobby became a full-time business. With over thirty thousand used books, the store is spacious and allows for easy browsing, and the titles are all carefully organized. Two Labradoodles greet customers with a welcoming wag of their tails. The comfortable atmosphere is inviting, and bibliophiles can spend half a day browsing the extensive collection without realizing where the time has gone.

Ask anyone, and they will tell you there are two great places in town for dinner. The first is **Clementine's,** right downtown in the old Citizen's Bank building (built in 1897). The restaurant retains much of the old bank's historic charm—from the impressive wood trim to the hammered tin ceiling. The menu is full of hearty variety, with steaks, seafood, pasta, and burritos. Entrées with names like the Gunslinger, Carlita's Way, or the Drunken Sailors may seem a little hammy, but it fits the atmosphere. They offer good food and a nice place to eat it.

The other, the **Thirsty Perch Watering Hole & Grille,** is the place for fish. They serve a bottomless bucket of beer-batter-fried perch that comes with fries and coleslaw. Take note of the tabletops in the dining room: The restaurant used to be a bowling alley, and the tabletops are what's left of the old wooden lanes.

Just north of Silver Beach is the stunning St. Joseph Pier Lighthouse.

For breakfast, stop by the **Golden Brown Bakery.** They have been in the business of baked goods since 1938, and in the mornings they have a great selection of fresh baked doughnuts, Danishes, and other treats.

Overnight accommodations in the area include the **Yelton Manor Bed & Breakfast,** essentially two Victorian homes located on a beautifully landscaped property near the heart of South Haven. This large bed & breakfast would technically qualify as an inn in some books: The main house (or the Manor House) has nine rooms and two suites, and the adjacent Manor Guest House has three rooms and three suites. But regardless of the size, owners Elaine Herbert and Rob Kripaitis have created a B&B where everyone feels welcome and at home. Every morning, breakfast is served in the dining room, often featuring dishes that more easily accommodate 20-plus guests, such as breakfast casseroles and frittatas. The guest house has all the amenities of the main house, but without the social dynamic (there's no office or kitchen, and a continental breakfast is served in the guest rooms, picnic style).

The next stop is one of Lake Michigan's most popular tourist towns, Saugatuck. Drive north on the Blue Star Highway; it's just 18 miles up the road. Along the way, moored on Kalamazoo Lake in Douglas, the highway passes the **Keewatin Maritime Museum,** which is actually a Great Lakes steamship, the SS *Keewatin*. Built in Scotland and delivered to the Great Lakes in 1907, the *Keewatin* picked up rail passengers from the Georgian Bay and brought them to railroads heading into western Canada from Thunder Bay in the far corner of Lake Superior. Beautifully

Don't forget the concessions at South Haven Beach.

The SS *Keewatin*, at one time a luxury steamship, is now a maritime museum.

appointed, the ship is a masterpiece of craftsmanship. Tours include a viewing of crew quarters, first-class staterooms, lounges, and drawing rooms.

Tourism has taken such root in Saugatuck that the once quaint downtown can seem more like a mall at Christmastime than a quiet waterfront village. To avoid the crowds and the traffic, a weekday visit is preferable. However, it can sometimes be fun to dive into the hustle and bustle of the busy streets and join the milling throng of people who are out enjoying a warm summer weekend.

Saugatuck sits on Kalamazoo Lake about 2 miles from where the Kalamazoo River empties into Lake Michigan, and the deep river and adjoining lake make a perfect harbor for pleasure craft. Water Street follows a section of the river along the west edge of town, and at the intersection of Water and Mary is Saugatuck's famed Chain Ferry. For a small fee, this pedestrian ferry will take you across the river, where you will find the path and staircase up to the top of Mount Baldhead. This majestic dune rises 262 feet, and from the top you can see Lake Michigan, Kalamazoo Lake, all of Saugatuck, and neighboring Douglas. Tucked up against the bottom of Mount Baldhead, on the other side, is Oval Beach, which *Condé Nast Traveler* magazine ranked among their 25 finest summer shorelines in the world.

More dunes are north of town at **Saugatuck Dunes State Park.** The park has a nice 2-mile stretch of beach and 13 miles of hiking trails. For a more adventurous

Pedestrians cross the Kalamazoo River in Saugatuck via the Chain Ferry.

visit, stop by **Saugatuck Dune Rides.** Since 1954 they've been showing guests just how much fun you can have on a giant pile of sand.

With dozens of places to eat in Saugatuck, you really have your pick. A nice place to grab a bite for lunch is **Pumpernickel's Eatery,** which offers a mess of great sandwiches. For breakfast, be sure to try their Saugatuck Cinnamon Roll.

For a nice meal down by the water, try the **Mermaid Bar & Grill.** Located on Water Street, the restaurant has a large outdoor eating area with a view of the docks, great for watching the boats pass by. The Mermaid has a great seafood menu, as well as sandwiches, steaks, chicken, and burgers. Something for everyone, to use the cliché.

A nice B&B right on the water is the **Bayside Inn**—originally built in 1927 as a boathouse. In fact, two of the inn's suites were once a boat garage. Over the years the property took a beating, much of it submerged under high water. But innkeepers Kathy and Frank Wilson saw promise. In 1990 they bought the old building and began fixing it up. Today it's one of Saugatuck's nicest spots to stay. Right on Water Street, the inn overlooks the river, with Mount Baldhead for a backdrop. There are six rooms and four roomy suites, all close to downtown and just a few steps down from the Chain Ferry. Guests love the French toast casserole served for breakfast.

A little farther from the water but with a charm all its own is the **Beechwood Manor Inn & Cottage**. Built in 1874 in the Greek Revival style, the inn's three guest rooms each have a private bath—two with a claw-foot tub. Adjacent to the inn is a cottage with three rooms and one bath that is available for larger parties—the 1,100-square-foot cottage has a full kitchen, living room, deck with patio furniture and a BBQ, and even a washer and dryer. Breakfast, however, is not included with a stay at the cottage. The inn is located on a quiet neighborhood street within a short walk of downtown.

IN THE AREA

ACCOMMODATIONS

Bayside Inn, 618 Water Street, Saugatuck. Call 269-857-4321. Website: baysideinn.net.

Beechwood Manor Inn & Cottage, 736 Pleasant Street, Saugatuck. Call 269-857-1587 or 1-877-857-1587. Website: beechwoodmanorinn.com.

Garden Grove Bed and Breakfast, 9549 Union Pier Rd., Union Pier. Call 269-469-6346 or 1-800-613-2872. Website: gardengrove.net.

The Harbor Grand, 111 West Water Street, New Buffalo. Call 269-469-7700 or 1-888-605-6800. Website: harbor grand.com.

Inn at Union Pier, 9708 Berrien Street, Union Pier. Call 269-469-4700. Website: innatunionpier.com.

Kalamazoo House B&B, 447 West South Street, Kalamazoo. Call 269-382-0880. Website: thekalamazoo house.com.

Yelton Manor Bed & Breakfast, 140 North Shore Drive, South Haven. Call 269-637-5220. Website: yeltonmanor .com.

RAILS TO TRAILS

The rails-to-trails movement has taken off across Michigan, and in the southwest part of the state there are two trails that have really put old railroad beds to good use. The first is the Van Buren Trail, which runs 14 miles from Van Buren Trail State Park in Hartford to Van Buren State Park on Lake Michigan. The trail is ungroomed—mainly dirt and gravel.

The second is the much longer Kal-Haven Trail, which runs 34 miles from Kalamazoo to South Haven. The railroad ties that once marked the route have been replaced with crushed limestone. To reach the trailhead in Kalamazoo, take US 131 to MI 43. Drive west to North 10th Street, and turn north. The trailhead is just past H Avenue.

Both trails are open for hiking and biking, and in the winter, cross-country skiing and snowmobiling. For both trails, trail passes are necessary; places where they can be purchased are listed on the Kal-Haven Trail website, kalhaventrail.org.

ATTRACTIONS AND RECREATION

Bishop's Bog Preserve, 9920 South Westnedge Avenue, Portage. Website: portagemi.gov/Departments/Parks Recreation/ParksAmenitiesListing/ BishopsBogPreserve.aspx.

Black River Books, 330 Kalamazoo Street, South Haven. Call 269-637-7374. Website: blackriverbooks.net.

The Blueberry Store, 525 Phoenix Street, South Haven. Call 269-637-6322. Website: theblueberrystore.com.

The Chocolate Garden, 2691 Friday Road, Coloma. Call 269-468-YUMM (9866). Website: thechocolategarden .com.

Free Run Cellars, 10062 Burgoyne Road, Berrien Springs. Call 269-471-1737. Website: freeruncellars.com.

Grand Mere State Park, Thornton Drive, Stevensville. Call 269-426-4013. Website: michigan.gov/grandmere.

The History Center at Courthouse Square, 313 North Cass Street, Berrien Springs. Call 269-471-1202. Website: berrienhistory.org.

Jollay Orchards, 1850 Friday Road, Coloma. Call 269-468-3075. The harvest festival runs every weekend from Sept. through Oct. Website: jollay orchards.com.

Keewatin Maritime Museum. Call 269-857-2464. The SS *Keewatin* sits in Lake Kalamazoo, right along the Blue Star Highway. Open every day all summer, Memorial Day to Labor Day. Website: keewatinmaritimemuseum .com.

Langley Covered Bridge, at the intersection of Schweitzer Road and Covered Bridge Road, Centreville.

Michigan Maritime Museum, 260 Dyckman Avenue, South Haven. Call 269-637-8078 or 1-800-747-3810. Website: michiganmaritimemuseum.org.

National Blueberry Festival, South Haven. Website: blueberryfestival.com.

Paw Paw Wine and Harvest Festival. Call 269-655-1111. Website: wine andharvestfestival.com.

Reits Flea Market, 45146 Red Arrow Highway, Paw Paw. Call 269-657-3428. Open weekends and holidays from Apr. through Sept.

Round Barn Winery, 10983 Hills Road, Baroda. Call 1-800-716-9463. Website: roundbarnwinery.com.

St. Julian Winery, 716 South Kalamazoo Street, Paw Paw. Call 269-657-5568. Michigan's oldest winery has a tasting room and winery tours. Website: stjulian.com.

Saugatuck Dune Rides, 6495 Washington Road, Saugatuck. Call 269-857-2253. Website: saugatuckdunerides .com.

Saugatuck Dunes State Park, Saugatuck. Call 269-637-2788. Website: michigan.gov/saugatuckdunes.

Sue Silliman House & Blacksmith Shop, 116 South Main Street, Three Rivers. Call 269-273-5391. Website: michigandar.com/silliman_house.htm.

Van Buren State Park, 23960 Ruggles Road, South Haven. Call 269-637-2788. Two hundred campsites, 1 mile of sandy Lake Michigan beach, and some dunes make this a great place to camp. Website: michigan.gov/van buren.

Van Buren Trail State Park, Hartford. Located a few blocks north of Hartford on Prospect Street, west of Center Street. Call 269-674-8011. Website: michigan.gov/vanburen.

Warner Vineyards Winery, 706 South Kalamazoo Street, Paw Paw.

Call 1-800-756-5357. Website: warner wines.com.

Warren Dunes State Park, 12032 Red Arrow Highway, Sawyer. Call 269-426-4013. Website: michigan.gov/warrendunes.

Warren Woods State Park, Sawyer. Call 269-426-4013. Website: michigan.gov/warrenwoods.

DINING

Clementine's, 500 Phoenix Street, South Haven. Call 269-637-4755. Website: ohmydarling.com.

Golden Brown Bakery, 421 Phoenix Street, South Haven. Call 269-637-3418. Website: goldenbrownbakery.com.

La Cantina Restaurant, 139 West Michigan Avenue, Paw Paw. Call 269-657-7033. Website: lacantinapawpaw.com.

Mermaid Bar & Grill, 340 Water Street, Saugatuck. Call 269-857-8208. Website: mermaidofsaugatuck.com.

Pumpernickel's Eatery, 202 Butler Street, Saugatuck. Call 269-857-1196. Website: pumpernickelssaugatuck.com.

Red Arrow Roadhouse, 15710 Red Arrow Highway, Union Pier. Call 269-469-3939. Website: redarrowroadhouse.com.

Redamak's, 616 East Buffalo Street, New Buffalo. Call 269-469-4522. Website: redamaks.com.

Silver Beach Pizza, 410 Vine Street, St. Joseph. Call 269-983-4743. Website: silverbeachpizza.com.

Thirsty Perch Watering Hole & Grille, 272 Broadway Street, South Haven. Call 269-639-8000. Website: thirstyperch.com.

OTHER CONTACTS

Greater South Haven Chamber of Commerce, 606 Phillips Street, South Haven. Call 269-637-5171. Website: southhavenmi.com.

Harbor Country Chamber of Commerce, 530 South Whittaker Street, Suite F, New Buffalo. Call 269-469-5409. The chamber has an office and visitors center in the old train depot as you pull into town from the south on La Porte Road. Open weekdays in the summer and for a couple of hours on Saturday; closed Sunday. Website: harborcountry.org.

Lake Michigan Shore Wine Trail. Website: miwinetrail.com.

Saugatuck and Douglas Visitors and Conventions Bureau. Call 269-857-1701. Website: saugatuck.com.

A trail over the dune off Pierce Stocking Scenic Drive

6 The Cherry Coast

SILVER LAKE, LUDINGTON, SLEEPING BEAR DUNES, THE LEELANAU PENINSULA, AND OLD MISSION POINT

Estimated length: 200 miles
Estimated time: 4.5 hours

Getting there: This trip begins near Mears, Michigan, at the Silver Lake State Park. From points south, drive north on US 31 to the exit for Shelby. Turn west onto West Shelby Road and continue 6.5 miles to County Road B15 (CR B15, also called South Scenic Drive and South 16th Avenue). CR B15 continues north past the Silver Lake Dunes, all the way to Pentwater. From Pentwater, get back on US 31 and take that to the South Pere Marquette Highway. From Ludington, take US 31 to Manistee, where you switch to Lake Shore Road (MI 110). This road becomes MI 22 in Onekama. The route gets very scenic between here and Frankfort. Stay on MI 22, skirting the Sleeping Bear Dunes National Lakeshore to Empire. From Empire, drive north 2 miles to MI 109; turn left. Stay on MI 109 until Glen Arbor. There you rejoin MI 22, which follows the outline of the Leelanau Peninsula, passing through Leland, Northport, Suttons Bay, and then Traverse City. In Traverse City, turn north on MI 37 to explore Old Mission Point.

Highlights: This route begins with Mac Wood's Dune Rides and the Little Sable Point Lighthouse at Silver Lake State Park. A scenic drive north ends in Ludington, which has a handful of excellent B&Bs and restaurants, and miles of Lake Michigan beaches. There's paddling and fishing on Hamlin Lake at Ludington State Park, and Ludington is also the home of the Lake Michigan Carferry, the SS *Badger*. Tour the SS *City of Milwaukee* in Manistee for some history on Lake Michigan ferries. More than a day can be spent exploring the Sleeping Bear Dunes National Lakeshore (including North and South Manitou Islands). At the very least, take the Pierce Stocking Scenic Drive, stop for the Dune Climb, and visit the restored logging village

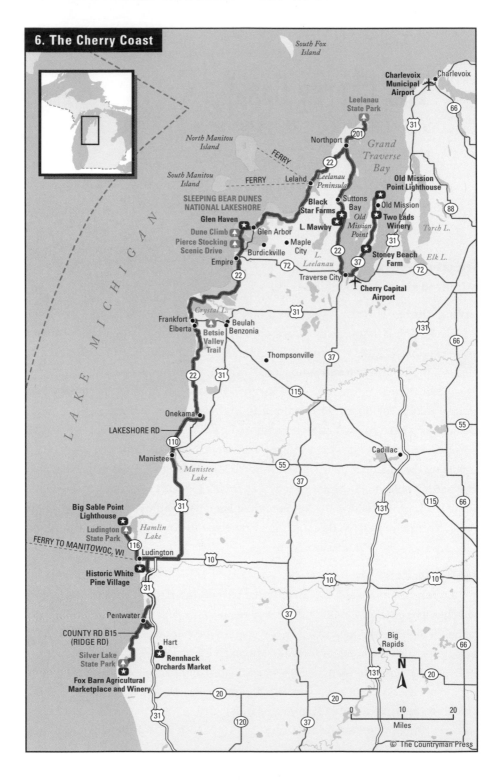

6. The Cherry Coast

of Glen Haven. In Leland, visit the historic old fishing shanties of Fishtown. Then head to the tip of the peninsula to Northport, for shopping and a tour of the nearby lighthouse. To the south in Suttons Bay, there are several Leelanau Peninsula wineries to see before you continue south to Traverse City and visit Old Mission Point: tour wineries, stop at the Old Mission General Store, and check out the Old Mission Lighthouse.

From Ludington to the Leelanau Peninsula, the Lake Michigan shoreline is edged by miles upon miles of sandy beaches and dunes. Inland, the terrain is progressively more hilly toward the north. Farmers take advantage of the sandy soil, the glacial sloping of the land, and the longer growing season near the water to grow everything from apples, cherries, and grapes to asparagus and pumpkins. Country roads are lined with gray alder or poplar—planted close, these trees act as hedgerows that protect growing fruit from bruising winds. Farther north, on the Leelanau and Old Mission Peninsulas, vineyards produce about half of the state's wine grapes, supporting a host of wineries and a robust local wine culture.

Still, the northwest corner of the Lower Peninsula is cherry country. Michigan farmers produce 75 percent of the tart cherries grown in the United States—and they make a sizable contribution to the sweet cherry market as well. In nearby Traverse City, the **National Cherry Festival** is celebrated every year in early July, drawing more than a half million people. Many come to compete at cherry-pit spitting and pie eating; most come for good food, drink, and music by Grand Traverse Bay.

Buying cherry pies and touring the wineries aside, visitors come to this region for Lake Michigan, the green rolling hills, small lakeside towns, and the dunes. The big ones, of course, are at Sleeping Bear Dunes, but for an all-out recreational experience of these piles of sand towering over the Great Lake, start at Silver Lake near Mears.

ORCHARDS AND FARM MARKETS

This part of the country has small orchard and farm markets tucked away on many back roads. South of Silver Lake, the Fox Barn recently changed its name to the **Fox Barn Agricultural Marketplace and Winery**. The market has everything in its season—asparagus, cherries (sweet and tart), peaches, apples, and pumpkins. You can pick produce fresh from the farm or buy it at the market, which also sells jellies and jams, and even wines. Closer to US 31 in Hart, **Rennhack Orchards Market** is another choice stop.

The dunes on the far side of Silver Lake separate the smaller lake from Lake Michigan.

The **Silver Lake State Park** nearly surrounds Silver Lake and the sand dunes that separate the lake from Lake Michigan. There are 2,000 acres of sand dunes open for exploration, and Silver Lake has set aside 450 acres for off-road vehicles. Rent dune buggies at **Silver Lake Buggies** in Mears, or leave the driving to professionals at **Mac Wood's Dune Rides.** When Mac Wood first began driving people around the dunes in 1930, passengers were taken out in customized Ford Model As and Studebakers. They could seat four to six at a time. Today, with his grandchildren at the helm of the business, guests ride in customized Fords and a few old Internationals that can seat up to 20 passengers. The 7-mile dune outing lasts about 40 minutes and takes you from the top of the highest dune right down to Lake Michigan.

At the southwest corner of the state park is the Little Sable Point Lighthouse. The light began burning in 1874, three years after the schooner *Pride* was grounded on Little Sable Point. The lighthouse today looks much like it did during the 19th century. (In fact, it looks a lot like the Big Sable Lighthouse used to before the latter was wrapped in reinforcing iron bands.) In 1900, it was painted white for greater visibility during the day. But in 1955, when the light was automated, the paint was sandblasted off, and the keeper's house and other buildings were torn down to save on maintenance costs. A state park vehicle permit is required to get into the parking lot, and a small donation buys a climb up the tower.

Silver Lake is bounded on the east by private land (with the exception of the state park campground). Along the lake are dozens of cottages and summer homes, and across the street are bumper boats and miniature golf, jeep rentals, pizza places, and souvenir stores. For campers who like to be right in the middle of things, the state campground is walking distance from all the touristy fun.

Leaving the Silver Lake area, drive north on CR B15. The road ends at West Monroe Road (the business spur of US 31). East or west, the road returns to US 31. To the west it passes through Pentwater along the way. Take US 31 north to Pere Marquette Highway, the exit for Ludington.

South of Pere Marquette Lake, 25 buildings have been gathered on 23 acres to create a museum that preserves the history of Mason County. The **Historic White Pine Village** first opened in 1976 on the site of the original Mason County seat. The Mason County Courthouse stands very close to where it was originally built in 1849, but other buildings were moved here, like the 1850s Trappers Cabin and the Pere Marquette Town Hall. And some, like the Phoenix Hose Company #1 firehouse, are fine reproductions of historic structures. Throughout the year, teachers bring their fourth-grade classes to spend a day in the Marchido School, a one-room school-house, to learn what school was like in the 19th century.

French explorer Père Jacques Marquette died near present-day Ludington in 1675. His body was later returned to the mission he founded in St. Ignace, but his name remained behind. The river, the lake, and even the first settlement there were called Pere Marquette. The village was founded by Burr Caswell when he built the first frame house in 1849 (later to become the aforementioned courthouse). For a while, the Caswells were the only settlers for miles, but over the next several de-cades, that number grew steadily.

The river, the natural harbor, thousands of acres of lumber, and James Lud-ington's sawmill eventually added up to the boomtown that took his name. James Ludington never lived there, but he did own a big store, platted out the city, and

The Phoenix Hose Company No. One firehouse is one of several buildings on display at the Historic White Pine Village in Ludington.

The Skyline Trail at Ludington State Park follows the crest of an ancient dune.

founded the first local newspaper. The railroad came near the turn of the 20th century, and ships ferried railroad cars across Lake Michigan to Milwaukee, Kewaunee, and Manitowoc, Wisconsin.

At the end of Ludington's sunny main drag, one of the last ferries built still makes the run today. The SS *Badger* has been plying the waters of Lake Michigan since 1953. After the railroad traffic died out, the *Badger* saw some years of inactivity, but in 1992, the **Lake Michigan Carferry** restarted the service with a focus on cars and their drivers. The ship now makes the run between Ludington and Manitowoc, and it is a registered historic site in two states. Once outfitted to carry railroad freight cars, the ship's fine passenger accommodations—including movie room, restaurant, and more—have made it a favorite with travelers. It's a seven-hour drive (through Chicago, no less) from Ludington to Manitowoc, but the ferry makes it in four.

Downtown, the carferry and the

The beach south of Ludington State Park stretches for miles.

BIG SABLE POINT LIGHTHOUSE

The sister light of the Little Sable Lighthouse near Silver Lake, the Big Sable Point Lighthouse at Grand Pointe au Sable sits in the northern portion of Ludington State Park, at the northern end of Lighthouse Trail. Visitors leave their cars in the Beach Café parking lot and follow the shore north 1.5 miles. For the purist, this seems right, as lighthouses were most often far from roads and civilization, and their only connection to the world was the ships that brought supplies. This light was originally built of yellow brick in 1867. By the 1890s, however, the brick was beginning to crumble. Iron bands were wrapped around the light's exterior, and concrete was poured between the iron and brick. To make the lighthouse more visible during the day, the black-and-white-striped pattern seen today was added.

The tower is open for tours (for a small donation), and guests enamored of the lighthouse can consider the Volunteer Keeper Program, which offers participants the chance to live and work at the lighthouse for two weeks at a time. Some orientation and training are necessary, but what better way is there to truly experience a lighthouse?

beach are the center of attention, but to the north is **Ludington State Park,** straddling the stretch of land between Lake Michigan and Hamlin Lake. The park seems to have two identities. On one hand, there's a stunning stretch of sand where beachgoers spend the day sunning or swimming in Lake Michigan. They rent tubes and inflatable rafts from the park concession stand and float lazily down the Big Sable River, which connects the two lakes. Near the beach, there's dining at the classic stone beach house, which is now the Beach Café, and 1.5 miles up the beach is a lighthouse (see the Big Sable Point Lighthouse sidebar).

On the other hand, campers can come and pitch their tents in one of the park's 344 wooded sites. Though thoroughly modern, the campground is completely immersed in the surrounding nature. Visitors can also visit the Great Lakes Visitors Center, which has a small museum explaining the region's history and ecology, as well as hike the 1-mile-long Skyline Trail, near the visitors center parking lot, which climbs a tall sand dune south of the river. There's also the Canoe Trail, which winds along Hamlin Lake. (Canoes, paddleboats, kayaks, and rowboats are available for rent from the concession stand on Hamlin Lake.)

Downtown Ludington has a number of beautifully maintained historic homes along East Ludington Avenue. Fortunately, several are now bed & breakfasts. The **Cartier Mansion Bed & Breakfast** is a neoclassical mansion, originally built in 1905. Inside is extensive woodwork, each room featuring a different species, from

Sleeping Bear's scenic overlooks offer stunning views.

white oak to black walnut. The inn has six guest rooms, each with bath and shower. The King Suite is particularly comfortable with its own sitting room, balcony, and enormous bathroom with both a tub and period shower. Breakfast is served in the grand dining room.

Just a few doors down is the **Ludington House Bed & Breakfast.** A classic Victorian home built in 1878 by local lumber magnate Antoine Cartier, the inn has eight guest rooms, each with its own bath; several feature a whirlpool tub. Also on East Ludington, just a few blocks farther east, is the **Inn at Ludington.** Built in 1890, this Victorian home has seven guest rooms, each with private bath. Two rooms have original fireplaces.

There is no shortage of places to eat in Ludington. Families love the **House of Flavors Restaurant,** a short walk from Ludington Beach. Playing up the '50s theme, the House of Flavors serves classic diner food like meat loaf and hot turkey sandwiches. The ice cream is made locally (just behind the restaurant, actually), and waffle cones are made on the spot when you order. For more upscale dining, **P. M. Steamers** is a block south of the main drag on Loomis. Serving dinner daily, Steamers features steak and plenty of seafood. And for pancakes, French toast, and omelets, the **Old Hamlin Restaurant** has been voted best spot for breakfast for a number of years.

Leaving Ludington, return to US 31 north (about 5 miles east of where the highway ended at US 10). North of downtown Manistee, the **SS** *City of Milwaukee* is docked on the right, in Manistee Lake. Now a maritime museum, the ship served the railroad companies from 1930 to 1981. The steamship's deck could carry an entire 32-car freight train. From April through September, guests can explore the car deck, engine rooms, and wheelhouse on the guided one-hour tour.

North of the carferry museum 0.5 mile, turn left on Lake Shore Drive (MI 110). In Onekama, MI 110 becomes MI 22, which will continue over progressively more hilly terrain to Frankfort.

The small towns of Frankfort and Elberta sit on either side of Betsie Lake. The Betsie Valley Trail connects these towns with Benzonia and Beulah to the east. A classic rail-to-trail project, it was built on the grade of the old Ann Arbor Railroad. Beginning at Lake Michigan, the trail follows the Betsie River to the eastern end of 10,000-acre Crystal Lake. In Beulah the trail turns southeast, terminating in Thompsonville. End to end, the trail is 22 miles long. The first 6 miles are paved; the remainder are aggregate. The trail is popular with runners, in-line skaters, and cyclists. In the winter, the section from Beulah to Thompsonville is open to, and popular with, snowmobilers.

The **Sleeping Bear Dunes National Lakeshore** begins just north of Crystal Lake. This 72,000-acre national park stretches 35 miles along the shore of Lake Michigan. Many visitors will begin and end their visit in the portion of the park just north of Empire (22 miles north of Frankfort on MI 22), but there is much, much more to explore. Begin at the **Sleeping Bear Dunes Visitors Center** in Empire. Close to the intersection of MI 22 and Front Street, it's hard to miss. This is the place to purchase the required vehicle pass; get a schedule of the day's ranger-led activities; and ask any questions you might have about historic sites, the park's ecology, the nature of dunes, and (of course) hiking, camping, and swimming.

First-time visitors will want to take the scenic drive, tackle the dune climb, and possibly visit historic Glen Haven. Leaving the visitors center, turn right on MI 22, drive 2 miles to the South Dune Highway (MI 109), and turn left. In the 1960s, before this was designated a national park, Pierce Stocking got it in his mind to build a road to the top of the dunes. The entrance to his road is 3 miles north on the South Dune Highway. Having worked as a lumberman,

It's 450 steep feet down to the lake, and yet people still think it will be an easy climb down and back up.

The sandy trails of Sleeping Bear Dunes

The Dune Climb at Sleeping Bear Dunes National Lakeshore

he was uniquely qualified for the task of creating the 7.5-mile stretch of road that now bears his name, the Pierce Stocking Scenic Drive. At the ranger station at the entrance to the drive, there's a handy flyer. Be sure to check out the views of the dunes at the stops marked #3, #9, and #10. The Lake Michigan Overlook (#9) is particularly awesome—ambitious guests often step off the 450-foot drop to Lake Michigan. Just be aware, it's an arduous climb back up.

Just 2 miles from the scenic drive is the Dune Climb, a 150-foot wall of sand that offers views of Glen Lake from the top. A little farther north is the historic town of Glen Haven. The village cannery now houses a collection of historic Great Lakes boats, and the general store carries a surprisingly sophisticated collection of goods. The Life Saving Service Station just down the beach is a maritime museum that highlights the service of the surfmen and the equipment they used to save lives when ships floundered in the busy Manitou Passage.

There are several excellent places to stay in the area if you are not up for camping. East of Empire on MI 72 is the **Sleeping Bear Bed & Breakfast.** Nestled along a maple-lined country drive, this 19th-century home has been lovingly restored and offers great access to the dunes and the central Leelanau Peninsula area.

Glen Arbor sits on the edge of

Sleeping Bear Dunes, a small cottage community whose tree-lined side streets dead-end on Lake Michigan. The main street through town, Western Avenue, is lined with a few choice shops, restaurants, and two great inns. The **Sylvan Inn,** built in 1885, offered hot meals and rooms to lumbermen and sailors. In the old part of the inn, the guest rooms each have a wash basin, and guests share the three modern baths. An addition in 1987 added six rooms, each larger and with private bath. In the center of town, there's the **Glen Arbor Bed & Breakfast.** At one time a boardinghouse for loggers, the building was used by all sorts of businesses over the years. The inn has four rooms (two share a bath), two suites, and two guest cottages. For food, **Boone Docks** in Glen Arbor is a festive place. The large restaurant and bar has live music nightly, and the large outdoor patio is a great place to unwind.

In Glen Haven there's a blacksmith shop.

The Glen Haven General Store is worth a stop.

With so many small towns scattered across the Leelanau Peninsula, it's no surprise that little gems of restaurants and inns can be found almost anywhere. Beyond Empire and Glen Arbor, guests rave about the Italian food at **Trattoria Funistrada** in Burdickville. And **La Bécasse** in Maple City serves traditional French country cuisine.

One of the most remote camping experiences in the Sleeping Bear Dunes is offshore on North and South Manitou Islands. The passage between the mainland and the islands was a major shipping lane, and ships would stop to pick up supplies and fuel. Today North Manitou, the larger, 15,000-acre island, is true backcountry, with no park services and open camping. South Manitou, on the other hand, has three campgrounds and a ranger station. There is a lighthouse to explore, as well as the old town cemetery and schoolhouse. Walking the shore of the island, you can see the shipwrecked freighter *Francisco Morazan* above the waves. With so many ships

A view of Leland's Fishtown from the dam *Catherine Forster*

making their way through the narrow Manitou Passage, it's no surprise that other shipwrecks wait just below the surface.

To get to either island, **Manitou Island Transit** operates a ferry that takes passengers to both daily. Be aware that even South Manitou, the most visited, has very little in the way of amenities, so bring food, water, and weather-appropriate clothing. The ferry company also has a shoreline tour of the Sleeping Bear Dunes.

While you're in Leland, be sure to stop at the **Stone House Bread Café** on Main Street. This is the place for artisan breads, soup, sandwiches, and a great cup of coffee. Once the road crosses the bridge, turn west on River Street to visit Fishtown. In 1971, this old strip of fishing shanties along the Leland River was wasting away. The fishing industry was no longer the economic powerhouse it had once been, and tourism was becoming more and more a part of Leland. Local fisherman Bill Carlson, who grew up in Leland, saw an opportunity to prop up the town's commercial fishing industry and preserve its culture. He began buying up property along the river, and rather than razing the shanties, he restored them.

Today, the cedar-shake shanties along the dock house shops like the **Reflections Art Gallery,** which carries art and goods with a nautical theme, and **Manitou Outfitters,** selling a mess of sportswear. There's also a bead store, a sandwich shop, and a place to buy hats. Also along the Leland River is **The Cove,** which is open for lunch and dinner. Whitefish, perch, and walleyes top the menu. There's steak and chicken for those not partial to seafood, but have no doubt, this is a fish joint.

Farther upriver, **The Riverside Inn** waits right on the water. Built in 1902 and remodeled over the years, the inn has two rooms and two suites. The accommodations either offer a view of the Leland River or the shady River Street. They all have a private bath. Downstairs, the inn has a dining room and lobby bar. They serve dinner nightly in the summer, and the menu is not at all shabby, featuring lobster, whitefish, and Alaskan halibut.

Driving around the peninsula, US 22 breaks south in Northport. This quiet community is far from the annual run of tourists that flood the streets of Leland and Suttons Bay, though that may be changing. The town has a small harbor on Grand

Traverse Bay, and a number of little shops and places to eat. Be sure to stop at **Barb's Bakery** for their excellent cinnamon rolls, or browse the Petoskey stones at **Nature Gems Rock Shop.** On Waukazoo Street, a used-book shop and fine-art gallery share space—**Dog Ears Books** and the **Painted Horse Gallery.**

Another 8 miles farther north, in Leelanau State Park, is the **Grand Traverse Lighthouse**, one of the more important in northern Lake Michigan. It served foremost to alert ships to the very presence of the Leelanau Peninsula, marking the entrance to Grand Traverse Bay and the Manitou Passage as well as the Straits of Mackinac. The original light only lasted several years. The current light, in the rooftop tower of a two-family home, has been there since 1858. Open daily in the summer, the lighthouse museum has a nice gift and camp store.

South of Northport 12 miles is Suttons Bay. Ships pass by this way on their way to Traverse City, and the deep harbor made it a natural spot for steamships to stop and pick up cordwood for their engines. The first wooding station was set up by Harry Sutton in 1854. By 1880, the community boasted 250 residents. A sawmill, two hotels, and a handful of stores were soon a regular stop for the railroad servicing the peninsula.

Today downtown Suttons Bay is a tourist town in the summer. Great

Do not miss a cinnamon twist at Barb's in Northport.

The bark-covered Nature Gems Rock Shop in Northport specializes in Petoskey stones.

The Grand Traverse Lighthouse, Leelanau State Park

Suttons Bay Marina

restaurants and numerous shops line the streets. Stop at **North Country Grill & Pub** for burgers or steak. This newer addition to the Suttons Bay dining scene has an outdoor grill and bar with patio seating. After dinner, walk down St. Joseph Avenue. Stop in at the **Michigan Artists Gallery** for contemporary pieces by regional artists. Or if it's early enough, check out the pastries and other breakfast and lunch items at **Martha's Leelanau Table**—they have an espresso bar.

The **Korner Kottage Bed & Breakfast**, a 1920s bungalow right in town, is one of the nicest B&Bs in Michigan. The innkeepers go all out to make their guests feel at home. Original art decorates the walls, and the three rooms, each with a private bath, are bright and warmly decorated, featuring 700-thread-count sheets (ironed

The vineyard lines the drive to Black Star Farms.

no less), profoundly relaxing mattresses, and great coffee with breakfast in the morning.

The surrounding countryside is home to numerous cherry orchards and vineyards, as well as several outstanding wineries. **Black Star Farms**, south of Suttons Bay, just off MI 22 on Revold Road, has a tasting room, farmer's market, and a bed & breakfast as part of their vineyard estate. The eight-room inn is nestled between hills of grape vines. A little farther on toward Traverse City, you can tour **L. Mawby**, a winery specializing in sparkling wines. Their tasting room is open year-round. The winery is on Elm Valley Road, between Fort and Hilltop Roads, one road west of MI 22.

The highway continues south to Traverse City. The largest city in northern Michigan, its greater metro area has over 130,000 residents. US 31 is lined with hotels and motels, restau-

Many folks make the trip north in the colder months simply for a stay at Great Wolf Lodge.

rants and ice cream shops, putt-putt golf and bumper boats, and it is the home of Michigan's only **Great Wolf Lodge.** Downtown has **Horizon Books,** which has remained a family-owned business since 1961. Their store rivals Barnes & Noble and its ilk for selection.

As you enter Traverse City, turn north on MI 37 to explore Old Mission Point, a slight promontory that bisects Grand Traverse Bay. It got its name from the mission that was established here in 1839. Henry Schoolcraft visited the point that same year and helped establish a school for Native Americans. Located near the northern end of the peninsula is a replica of the log mission church. Leaving Traverse City behind, very quickly you find yourself surrounded by open countryside, vineyards, orchards, and, of course, views of Grand Traverse Bay.

First stop on the peninsula tour is **Stoney Beach Farm,** featuring a farm stand and a summer full of opportunities to pick your own fruits and vegetables. The farm has been around since the mid-1800s. The barn, though it looks rather new,

Out on Old Mission Point, the Old Mission General Store has been taking care of customers for over 160 years.

The reproduction Old Mission on Old Mission Point

has been around since the 1850s—or at least the oldest part of the barn has.

For lunch or dinner, stop by the **Peninsula Grill** or the **Bad Dog Deli.** The latter closes in the late afternoon, but the Peninsula is open much later. Though favorites with locals, both are pretty low-key, and crowds are minimal. Expect great sandwiches at the deli and a slightly more sophisticated menu next door.

All along the drive you will pass wineries—there are at least a half dozen on the peninsula. If you turn off Center Road (MI 37) onto Mission Road, you will pass **Two Lads Winery** before you get to Old Mission. They have a tasting room, and if they're not too busy with customers, they will gladly show you around the winery and explain how they have incorporated gravity-flow techniques into their winemaking.

The center of Old Mission village is the **Old Mission General Store.** A classic of its kind, the store has been taking care of folks on the peninsula for over 160 years. Nearby you can tour the replica of the original **Old Mission,** a log structure built in 1840 as a church and school for the local Chippewa Native Americans (see Chapter 7 for the story of the mission's beginnings in Elk Rapids across the bay). The first frame house built on the point, the **Dougherty House,** is also close by. It was built in 1842 by Peter Dougherty, the Protestant missionary serving on the peninsula. Later owners added the small Victorian porch you see today.

At the far northern tip of the peninsula sits the **Old Mission Point Light-**

house, part of the Peninsula Township park. Built in 1870, the light is aptly described as a schoolhouse-style lighthouse. Also at the park is the **Hessler Log Home,** built in 1858.

For accommodations on the peninsula, drive back along the west side. On Tucker Point, overlooking Bowers Harbor on the west side of the peninsula, the **Neahtawanta Inn** was built in the late 1800s as a private summer cottage. Early on the home was transformed into a hotel, and over the years several additions to the original property have been made. The inn has four

At the tip of Old Mission Point is the Old Mission Lighthouse.

rooms and a suite, with views of either the lake or the surrounding woods. Quiet and somewhat secluded, the B&B captures the essence of an unpretentious "up north" vacation. The innkeepers are passionate about environmental responsibility: Their gardens are maintained without chemicals, breakfast is often a vegan affair, and yoga is taught in their beautiful yoga studio.

IN THE AREA

ACCOMMODATIONS

Cartier Mansion Bed & Breakfast, 409 East Ludington Avenue, Ludington. Call 231-843-0101 or 1-877-843-0101. Website: cartiermansion.com.

Glen Arbor Bed & Breakfast, 6548 Western Avenue, Glen Arbor. Call 231-334-6789. Website: glenarborbnb.com.

Great Wolf Lodge, 3575 North US 31 South, Traverse City. Call 1-866-478-9653. Website: greatwolf.com.

The Inn at Black Star Farms, 10844 East Revold Road, Suttons Bay. Call 231-944-1251. Website: blackstarfarms.com.

Inn at Ludington, 701 East Ludington Avenue, Ludington. Call 231-845-

7055 or 1-800-845-9170. Website: inn-ludington.com.

Korner Kottage Bed and Breakfast, 503 North St. Joseph Avenue, Suttons Bay. Call 231-271-2711 or 1-888-552-2632. Website: kornerkottage.com.

Ludington House Bed & Breakfast, 501 East Ludington Avenue, Ludington. Call 231-845-7769 or 1-800-827-7869. Website: ludingtonhouse.com.

Neahtawanta Inn, 1308 Neahtawanta Road, Traverse City. Call 1-800-220-1415. Website: neahtawantainn.com.

The Riverside Inn, 302 River Street, Leland. Call 231-256-9971 or 1-888-257-0102. Website: theriverside-inn.com.

Sleeping Bear Bed & Breakfast, 11977 South Gilbert Road, Empire.

Call 231-326-5375. Website: sleeping bearbb.com.

Sylvan Inn, 6680 Western Avenue, Glen Arbor. Call 231-334-4333. Website: sylvaninn.com.

ATTRACTIONS AND RECREATION

Big Sable Point Lighthouse. Call 231-845-7343. Website: splka.org.

Black Star Farms, 10844 East Revold Road, Suttons Bay. Call the tasting room at 231-944-1271 or the inn at 231-944-1251. Website: blackstarfarms.com.

Dog Ears Books, 106 Waukazoo Street, Northport. Call 231-386-7209. Website: dogearsbooks.net.

Fox Barn Agricultural Marketplace and Winery, 500 South 18th Avenue, Shelby. Call 231-861-8050. Website: thefoxbarn.com.

Grand Traverse Lighthouse, 15500 North Lighthouse Point Road, Northport. Call 231-386-7195. The lighthouse is inside Leelanau State Park. Website: grandtraverselighthouse.com.

Historic White Pine Village, 1687 South Lakeshore Drive, Ludington. Call 231-843-4808. Website: historic whitepinevillage.org.

Horizon Books, 234 East Front Street, Traverse City. Call 231-946-7290 or 1-800-587-2147. Website: horizon books.com.

L. Mawby, 4519 South Elm Valley Road, Suttons Bay. Call 231-271-3522. Website: lmawby.com.

Lake Michigan Carferry, 701 Maritime Drive, Ludington. Call 1-800-841-4243. Website: ssbadger.com.

Ludington State Park, 8800 West MI 116, Ludington. Call 231-843-2423. Website: michigan.gov/ludington.

Mac Wood's Dune Rides, 629 North 18th Street, Mears. Call 231-873-2817. Website: macwoodsdunerides.com.

Manitou Island Transit. Call 231-256-9061. Website: leelanau.com/manitou. The ferry leaves from the end of River Street.

Michigan Artists Gallery, 309 North St. Joseph Avenue, Suttons Bay. Call 231-271-4922. Website: michigan artistsgallery.com.

National Cherry Festival. Website: cherryfestival.org.

Nature Gems Rock Shop, 101 North Mill Street, Northport. Call 231-386-7826.

Old Mission General Store, 18250 Mission Road, Traverse City. Call 231-223-4310. Website: oldmissiongeneral store.com.

Painted Horse Gallery, 106 Waukazoo Street, Northport. Call 231-386-5828.

Rennhack Orchards Market, 3731 West Polk Road, Hart. Call 231-873-7529. Website: rennhackorchards market.com.

Silver Lake Buggies, 8288 West Hazel Road, Mears. Call 231-873-8833. Website: silverlakebuggys.com.

Silver Lake State Park, 9679 West State Park Road, Mears. Call 231-873-3083. Website: michigan.gov/silver lake.

Sleeping Bear Dunes National Lakeshore Headquarters & Visitors Center, 9922 Front Street, Empire. Call 231-326-5134. Website: nps.gov/slbe.

SS *City of Milwaukee*, 99 Arthur Street, Manistee. Call 231-723-3587. Website: carferry.com.

Stoney Beach Farm, 10295 Center Road, Traverse City. Call 231-922-

8191. On Old Mission Point, 6 miles up the peninsula, is a farm stand and U-pick produce. Website: stoneybeach farm.com.

Two Lads Winery, 16985 Smokey Hollow Road, Traverse City. Call 231-223-7722. Website: 2lwinery.com.

DINING

Bad Dog Deli, 14091 Center Road, Traverse City. Call 231-223-9364. Website: tcgrills.com/bad-dog-deli.

Barb's Bakery, 112 North Mill Street, Northport. Call 231-386-5851.

Boone Docks, 5858 South Manitou Boulevard, Glen Arbor. Call 231-334-6444. Website: boonedocksglenarbor .com.

The Cove, 111 River Street, Leland. Call 231-256-9834. Website: thecove leland.com.

House of Flavors Restaurant, 402 West Ludington Avenue, Ludington. Call 231-845-5785. Website: houseof flavors.com.

La Bécasse, 9001 South Dunn's Farm Road, Maple City. Call 231-334-3944. Website: restaurantlabecasse.com.

Martha's Leelanau Table, 413 North St. Joseph Avenue, Suttons Bay. Call 231-271-2344. Website: marthas leelanautable.com.

North Country Grill & Pub, 420 North St. Joseph Avenue, Suttons Bay. Call 231-271-5000. Website: boones northcountrygrillandpub.com.

Old Hamlin Restaurant, 122 West Ludington Avenue, Ludington. Call 231-843-4251. Known for great breakfasts. Website: oldhamlin.com.

Peninsula Grill, 14091 Center Road, Traverse City. Call 231-223-7200. Website: tcgrills.com/peninsula-grill.

P.M. Steamers, 502 West Loomis Street, Ludington. Call 231-843-9555. Serves dinner nightly; specializes in seafood. Website: pmsteamers.com.

The Riverside Inn, 302 River Street, Leland. Call 231-256-9971 or 1-888-257-0102. Website: theriverside-inn .com.

Stone House Bread Café, 407 South Main Street, Leland. Call 231-256-2577. Website: stonehousebread.com/ cafe.

Trattoria Funistrada, 4566 West MacFarlane Road, Burdickville. Call 231-334-3900. Website: trattoria -funistrada.com.

OTHER CONTACTS

Leelanau Peninsula Chamber of Commerce, 112 East Philip Street, Lake Leelanau. Call 231-994-2202. Website: leelanauchamber.com.

Leelanau Peninsula Wine Trail. Website: lpwines.com.

Ludington Area Convention and Visitors Bureau, 5300 West US 10, Ludington. Call 1-877-420-6618. Website: pureludington.com.

Silver Lake Sand Dunes Area Chamber of Commerce, 2388 North Comfort Drive, Hart. Call 231-873-2247 or 1-800-870-9786. Website: think dunes.com.

Wineries of Old Mission Peninsula. Website: wineriesofoldmission .com.

Grand Traverse Bay

7 The Great Northwest

ELK RAPIDS, THE CHAIN OF LAKES, CHARLEVOIX, BEAVER ISLAND, PETOSKEY, AND BAY VIEW

Estimated length: 125 miles

Estimated time: 3 hours (another 4 on the ferry if you visit Beaver Island)

Getting there: From Detroit and points south via I-75, get off in Grayling (exit 254) and head west on MI 72. At MI 605 (Elk Lake Road), turn north to Elk Rapids. Coming from Chicago, take I-94 to I-196 north, on to US 131. Continue north to the town of Fife Lake, turning left on MI 605 (Fife Lake Road). Continue north to Elk Rapids. From Elk Rapids, follow the east shore of Torch Lake on MI 593. MI 88 cuts over to Central Lake and Bellaire. US 31 continues north to Charlevoix and east to Petoskey and Bay View.

Highlights: The town of Elk Rapids is a great place to stop, check out an art gallery (be sure to stop at the Twisted Fish Gallery), and grab a bite. There's scenic driving around Torch Lake and paddling along Antrim County's Chain of Lakes. North on US 31, stop for pie at Royal Farms and then cherry doughnuts, fresh produce, and country gifts at Friske's Farm Market. And be sure to stop at the Bier Gallery, housed in a restored schoolhouse, before you meander into Charlevoix, which has art galleries, boutique shopping, a fudge shop, and a beautiful marina on Round Lake. This is also where you would catch the ferry to Beaver Island. Farther east in Petoskey, stroll the Gaslight Village or visit the Crooked Tree Arts Center. Finish your tour by traveling through the Tunnel of Trees to Cross Village and a meal at the Legs Inn.

There are no breathtaking dunes along the shores of Grand Traverse Bay. Following the coastline north and to the east into Petoskey, you will not find any Pictured Rocks. The countryside is not teeming with waterfalls, and the small towns along

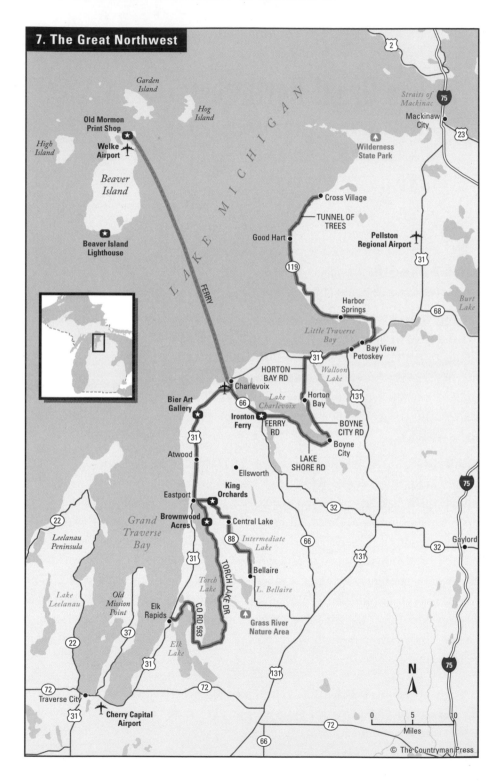

7. The Great Northwest

Garden Island

Hog Island

Straits of Mackinac

Mackinaw City

Old Mormon Print Shop

Welke Airport

High Island

Beaver Island

Wilderness State Park

Cross Village

TUNNEL OF TREES

Pellston Regional Airport

Good Hart

LAKE MICHIGAN

Beaver Island Lighthouse

119

Harbor Springs

Burt Lake

68

Little Traverse Bay

FERRY

Bay View
Petoskey

31

Walloon Lake

HORTON BAY RD

Charlevoix

Bier Art Gallery

66

Lake Charlevoix

Horton Bay

131

Ironton Ferry

FERRY RD

BOYNE CITY RD

Boyne City

31

Atwood

LAKE SHORE RD

Ellsworth

75

King Orchards

Eastport

32

22

Brownwood Acres

Central Lake

Grand Traverse Bay

88

Intermediate Lake

66

Gaylord

Leelanau Peninsula

131

32

Bellaire

L. Bellaire

31

Lake Leelanau

Old Mission Point

Torch Lake

TORCH LAKE DR

CO RD 593

Grass River Nature Area

22

Elk Rapids

37

Elk Lake

31

72

72

Traverse City

31

Cherry Capital Airport

N

131

72

75

0   5   10
Miles

66

© The Countryman Press

2

75

23

the way sport far fewer fudge shops than you will find in Traverse City and Mackinaw City. Nevertheless, thousands of people will happily attest that this northwest section of Michigan's Lower Peninsula is the most beautiful vacation spot in the state.

Rolling green hills give way to numerous inland lakes—Lake Charlevoix, Torch Lake, and Elk Lake, just to name a few of the biggies. Rivers wind lazily, connecting these lakes with the big lake, Lake Michigan. From Grand Traverse Bay to Little Traverse Bay, the Lake Michigan shoreline alternates from stones to sandy beaches. Close to the shore, there are woods thick with northern white cedar and airy stands of paper birch. And as you travel inland, deeper into Antrim and Charlevoix Counties, the rich agricultural heritage of the region is seen in lush farm fields and sprawling orchards.

In the early part of the 20th century, Ernest Hemingway summered here at his family's house on Walloon Lake. It was here that the aspiring author tramped through the countryside, fishing and hunting as he went. Many of Hemingway's Nick Adams stories recall this time, a time when life was hard and the people just a bit harder still. Life here was more rustic then, and lumbermen and Native Americans still mingled in town. Up and down the coast, a sawmill and a dock were the economic center for numerous plucky lumber towns—towns that did not survive long when the lumber was gone. Many, like the town of Antrim, which features so prominently in Nancy Stone's children's novel, *Whistle up the Bay,* are only remembered by a few posts in the water that mark the town's one-time dock and a graveyard along the Old Dixie Highway.

Lumber played a big role in the development of this part of the state, and as the supply of timber played out, the railroads and shipping lines that connected the region with points south suffered greatly. The railroad companies went to work drumming up new business, encouraging city dwellers from Chicago to become tourists. Several of the area's historic resorts were the result of the railroad looking for ways to make northern Michigan attractive to potential train passengers. Railroads pushed the image of northern Michigan as a sportsman's paradise and Edenic retreat for the whole family, and people came, by train and later by car. Tourism has been a staple of the economy ever since.

It might seem that towns that do not sit on Lake Michigan would have a tough job selling themselves as tourist destinations, but a dozen substantial inland lakes and, as in the case of Boyne City, a few hills big enough to ski down have been attracting travelers for years. Even so, for many years it seemed Petoskey was the only town in the region (outside Traverse City to the south) large enough to support a substantial year-round population. For several decades now, however, a year-round tourism industry has been firmly established—due much in part to the grow-

Part of the Chain of Lakes, Intermediate Lake is accessible from the town of Central Lake.

ing number of people using their summer homes in the winter to take advantage of the heavy north Michigan snows for snowmobiling, cross-country skiing, and snowshoeing.

Towns like Bellaire and Central Lake have capitalized on their natural small-town charms. Quaint bed & breakfasts make for a homey home base after a day exploring the nearby Chain of Lakes. In fact, paddlers have found they can make a weeklong exploration of this inland waterway—stopping along en route at excellent restaurants, and spending their nights in the pure comfort of local inns and B&Bs.

One town that rather successfully resisted the influx of tourism was Elk Rapids. In recent years, however, the town has been undergoing a transformation. Given Elk Rapids's proximity to Traverse City, its ideal water-sports location between the bay and Elk Lake, and its active harbor, it's a surprise the town wasn't taken over by tourists years ago. So far, the development has been restrained, but several excellent restaurants have established themselves, and more and more people are discovering that Elk Rapids is a great little town.

Many of the qualities that make this a great place to visit are what attracted Native American people here years ago. In the 1830s, Protestant missionaries settled in with a group of Native Americans that were camping on the site; however, the camp soon moved to present-day Mission Point across the bay. It took several more years before the area was truly settled, and Elk Rapids gets its name from its earliest permanent settler, Abram Wadsworth. As the story goes, Wadsworth came across a river that emptied into Grand Traverse Bay while on a surveying trip in 1847. In the river's rapids he discovered a set of elk antlers, and thus the Elk River and Elk Lake were named. In 1848, he returned and settled along the river, building a cabin and a sawmill, giving birth to the town of Elk Rapids.

One of the town's treasures is the library. At one time, this wooded piece of property was a sand dune, but town father and successful businessman Edwin Noble transformed the land by covering it with clay and soil. Over 60 different kinds of trees were planted, and in 1865 the Island House was built. It is connected to River Street by a wooden bridge, which you can find just west of downtown. In 1949, the building was donated to the village. Ever since it has been home to the Elk Rapids District Library. It's worth a visit just to browse books at the perennial book sale or take in the shady lawn overlooking the Edward C. Grace Memorial Harbor. There's even a reading porch with rockers for those who take their reading and relaxing seriously.

For a pleasant experience of the harbor, stroll by the docks and check out the boats. The boardwalk continues between the Upper and Lower Harbors of the Elk River and eventually makes its way under US 31. A great place to eat right on the water with views of the Elk River and Elk Lake, the **Riverwalk Grill** is just the place if this water wonderland has you craving fresh whitefish, perch, and walleyes. They also have great steaks and ribs. When the weather is good, be sure to ask for a table on the deck so you can take in the scenery. One other restaurant in town deserves mention: **Pearl's New Orleans Kitchen,** serving Cajun and Creole cuisine, is a short 0.5 mile drive east of the light at US 31.

Art lovers will not want to pass up the **Twisted Fish Gallery.** Art galleries are a big part of the "up north" experience for many travelers, and while most of

King Orchards is a great place to taste the region's produce.

the touristy towns have a nice selection, there are also a number of artists and gallery owners who have claimed property outside of the usual artsy venues. South of Elk Rapids, where US 31 meets Bayshore Drive, the Twisted Fish combines a wonderfully varied selection of art pieces with beautiful flowers. The grounds are spotted with outdoor sculptures, and it has become sort of a gateway gallery for those located farther north along US 31.

If there's a need to abbreviate your itinerary, getting from Elk Rapids to Charlevoix and Petoskey is an easy shot north along US 31. More scenically inclined travelers, however, take advantage of MI 593, which hugs the curve of Elk Lake and then turns to follow the eastern shoreline of Torch Lake. Whereas US 31 pulls away from the shoreline and offers little lake scenery, MI 593 dives headlong into the thick hilly forest that defines Torch Lake's eastern shore. More often than not, the lake can be glimpsed just beyond the many cabins and cottages. Torch Lake is spring-fed, and the water is a sparkling cobalt blue. Unfortunately, the water stays so cold—even after a long, hot summer—that cobalt blue is also the color swimmers turn after taking a dip in the water.

One of Torch Lake's oldest attractions is **Brownwood Acres.** Located on the east side of the lake on MI 593, Brownwood began in 1957 when Mary Louise Morse had the old Eastport Inn moved across Torch Lake. The plan was to move the building across when the lake was frozen, but the building fell through the ice. When you stop by the Brownwood Country Store, be sure to check out the pictures that tell the story of the move and how the building was eventually retrieved from the water. Once a thriving venture, Brownwood has diminished some in recent years, but it's still worth a visit for their Famous Kream Mustard and Famous Cherry Butter. Generations of visitors have made their requisite annual visit to stock up on a year's supply of their favorite fruit butters and mustards. (I've always been partial to the apple butter myself.) With a new production facility in Williamsburg, Brownwood Farms now offers a huge variety of items—from cherry BBQ sauce, which is great on ribs, to new varieties of mustard—which are available at their store in Eastport on US 31 and grocery stores throughout the state.

Not far from Brownwood Acres, on MI 88, stop at **King Orchards** to pick a bushel of apples or gather up some of their other produce. In their season they have cherries, sweet corn, strawberries, peaches, and pears.

At the north end of Torch Lake, MI 88 cuts east and south to the little villages of Central Lake and Bellaire. These two towns sit on the Chain of Lakes—a 75-mile stretch of connected water that begins with Six Mile Lake southeast of Ellsworth, and then winds its way through five smaller lakes before emptying into Intermediate Lake south of Central Lake. And the first six lakes are just the upper half of the chain. The waterway continues from Intermediate Lake to Lake Bellaire, Clam Lake, Torch Lake, and Lake Skegemog on its way to Elk Lake and, finally, Grand Traverse Bay.

For those who love to paddle, you will not find a more accessible and worthwhile stretch of water for an extended trip in the northern Lower Peninsula, and because there are towns positioned along the entire route, you can travel with or without the luxuries of civilization. Anglers appreciate the route's many hidden waters—small lakes and streams far from most of the region's recreational boaters and Jet Skiers.

The Lower Chain begins south of the town of Central Lake. These lakes are larger and more accessible than the Upper Chain, and one way to get out on the water and explore is to rent a pontoon boat for the day in Bellaire. The **Riverside Marina** in Bellaire is, as the name suggests, located on the river that connects Intermediate Lake and Lake Bellaire. They rent pontoon boats and have maps of the local water routes. Heading downstream, boaters eventually pass through the **Grass River Nature Area**. The river passes through 1,325 protected acres, and quiet attentiveness will pay off with sightings of herons, sandhill cranes, loons, and eagles. For landlubbers, the nature area can be explored on foot thanks to 3 miles of very accessible trails—boardwalks have even been built where the earth is too wet for hiking.

Bed & breakfasts abound east of Torch Lake, from Bellaire up into Ellsworth. The **Applesauce Inn** is south of Bellaire, right on MI 88. This classic four-square was built in 1900 and used to sit on a 160-acre farm. The house stayed in the same family for nearly one hundred years. In 2002, David and Wendy Keene bought the home and converted it into this bed & breakfast. Since opening the inn in the spring of 2003, they've played host to hundreds of guests. Each of the three available rooms

Mōka in Bellaire has outdoor dining, which can be very nice in the summer.

has their signature "snugglebed," a queen-sized mattress with an inordinate amount of layered comfort — mattresses topped with a 4-inch featherbed and wool-pile mattress pad. Breakfast might include Applesauce Inn Pancakes or other treats featuring Traverse City cherries. July is their busiest month, so summer travelers should reserve rooms early.

Bellaire is also home to several great restaurants. **Mōka** on Bridge Street has a menu of gourmet sandwiches, pizzas, and salads, and there's a great patio for eating *en plein air*. Since we're on the subject of food, a little farther to the north, 9 miles north of Central Lake in Ellsworth, is **The Rowe Inn**, a place you won't want to miss. This French country inn stands out from the usual local family dining and the tourist-trap eateries. It is certainly one of the finest restaurants in Michigan. It was here that the chef of the now-gone Tapawingo cut his teeth. The ever-changing menu takes full advantage of local produce, but maintains a particular French flair.

For more paper-plate dining, however, you will want to stick with **Classic Pizza** on Main Street in Central Lake. The pizza is good, and the sandwiches are even better. Best of all, the bill won't bust the travel budget.

In Ellsworth, **The House on the Hill Bed & Breakfast** is a converted farmhouse that offers four guest rooms in the main house and three in the carriage house. The rooms are spacious, and all include a private bath. The home is tastefully decorated with a cozy yet contemporary touch. The gourmet breakfast served every morning features homemade muffins and flavored butters.

To get back to US 31, head north on Main Street (MI 88) from Central Lake, following the road west as it winds toward Eastport and US 31. Just before Eastport, as the road crests the final hill, good weather will reveal the blue water of Grand Traverse Bay and possibly the Leelanau Peninsula resting on the distant horizon.

Once you're back on US 31, head north toward Charlevoix. This portion of the journey can be breathtaking on a warm summer day after a recent rain. It is simply beautiful country. The road is sided with rolling wooded hills and lush green farmland. Often travelers will catch a glimpse of Grand Traverse Bay to the west. About halfway between Eastport and Charlevoix, the speed limit drops to 45 mph through the little hamlet of Atwood, which does not have much more than a gas station and a John Deere dealership. Just north of town, across from the miniature drive-up prayer chapel, is **Friske's Farm Market.** The market has some of the best cherry doughnuts on the planet, so if at all possible, make this a morning stop.

For years, the Elzinga family operated a small market on this site, which sat next to their orchards. In 2000, the Friske (pronounced FRISK-ee) family purchased the market, along with part of the Elzinga farm, and went to town expanding the place. Today, the farm market is open year-round with seasonal offerings of apples, cherries, asparagus, rhubarb, and more. There's a special cold storage room to keep produce fresh. The market's Orchard Café serves soup and sandwiches, and guests can get lost in the market's several gift shops. Throughout the year, Friske's holds various events. In October, for example, they have Fall Fun Saturdays for the kids.

Just south of Friske's on US 31, **Royal Farms** is the place to go for cherry pie. Sure, they sell cherries by the pint and a load of other products—cherry pie filling, syrups and preserves, dried fruit—but take a cherry pie to warm up later. For a hand-held treat, go with the cookies instead.

Farther along US 31, a bright red schoolhouse sits on the east side of the road. This is the **Bier Art Gallery.** Back in 1972, two artists, Ray and Tami Bier, decided to buy and renovate the old Hilton schoolhouse. (At the time, another couple, both artists, were their partners in the venture.) The school was built in 1878 and was used for classes until 1950. Located a short drive from Charlevoix, on the main north-south highway, the schoolhouse was the perfect spot for an art gallery. The Biers themselves work mainly in clay—Tami sculpting in clay and Ray making stoneware pottery. Like with most enterprises, the first couple of years were the hardest, but travelers who once raced north and south along the highway, eyes on the scenery, soon began to stop, and as word of mouth spread, more people stopped. Today, many people make an annual pilgrimage to this unique shop. When they started, the Biers displayed only their own work and that of their two partners, but today they display the work of nearly 60 artists. Even their son, Tyler, is contributing to the family business with his popular line of imaginative piggy banks.

Located between Lake Michigan and Round Lake, the town of Charlevoix (pronounced SHAR-la-voy) has become a popular stop for leisure boaters and day-tripping tourists. In the busy summer season, the crowds browsing Charlevoix's galleries and gift shops can be overwhelming, as can be the perennial traffic jam. The main road, US 31, goes right through downtown and narrows to two lanes, creating an amazingly effective bottleneck—a bottleneck that is made even more difficult by the drawbridge in town that is raised every half hour. The only alterna-

One of Earl Young's fairy cottages in Charlevoix

tive is a lengthy 30-mile detour around Lake Charlevoix, which includes a ride on the Ironton Ferry.

The people that make their way here every summer are not fools—the town has much to offer: There's an American Spoon, the Koosky Gallery, and a Murdick's Fudge Shop. It's also a great town for boat-watching, as all sorts of craft tie up at the docks on Round Lake—everything from glamorous yachts to leisure fishing boats to sailboats with polished hardwoods and gleaming hardware. In town, one gallery stands out for its unique offerings of art and furniture: the **North Seas Gallery,** located downtown in the old Charlevoix County Bank building. This is not your typical tourist-town art gallery. They display an amazing collection of 19th- and early-20th-century European art. Browsing is like walking through a museum, and the bank has proven to be an excellent location to hold not only their paintings but also a collection of museum-quality furniture.

There are several excellent beaches near Charlevoix, the best possibly being the Charlevoix City Beach. And if you have time, be sure to drive through the neighborhoods north of downtown (along Lake Michigan). Beginning in the 1920s and up into the 1950s, Charlevoix real estate broker and architect Earl Young built some 30 stone houses in town. These summer homes are reminiscent of English country cottages, but their organic design—whimsically curving walls and flowing cedar-shake rooflines—have earned them names like the Mushroom Houses or the Earl Young

Fairy Cottages. Young was an imaginative self-taught architect; often working without plans, he would simply walk out the design on-site, explaining to the builder what he wanted.

Over the years, he kept an eye out for boulders that he would later use in his projects. One such stone can be found in the **Weathervane Restaurant.** The restaurant, located on the north side of Pine River, overlooks the boat traffic in and out of the marina and has great views of both Round Lake and Lake Michigan. Originally a gristmill stood on this site. Young bought the mill on August 1, 1954, and began building the Weathervane the same day. Much of the mill was torn down, but the original foundations and the timbers of the first level remain. The fireplace inside displays Young's prized boulder—shaped like a map of northern Michigan—which sits as the keystone for the mantle. The stone weighs 9 tons, and because of an error in measuring, some of the rafters had to be removed to make room for its installation. The Charlevoix Chamber of Commerce has a map of all of Earl Young's homes, which makes for a great walking tour (and a great excuse to get away from the bustling crowds on Bridge Street).

A favorite bookshop in Charlevoix is **Round Lake Books.** Now located at the north end of town, it seems only a few years ago the bookstore was tucked behind the Bridge Street shops. Since its coming out, Round Lake Books has become a regular bustling commercial enterprise.

Petoskey is northeast of Charlevoix on US 31, but, again, the adventurous will want to go around Lake Charlevoix. West of town, turn south on MI 66. In a little fewer than 5 miles, turn left on Ferry Road for the Ironton Ferry. This historic ferry, established in 1879, holds four cars at a time—the fare is currently up to $3.25. Ferry

The Ironton Ferry is the shortest way around Lake Charlevoix.

BEAVER ISLAND

There are few back roads or byways as remote as Beaver Island, located 36 miles from the mainland by ferry, and with only 450 year-round residents. A trip to the island is like stepping back in time—a time before all of Lake Michigan's coastal communities had become boomtowns, a time when people didn't come back from vacation needing a vacation. About 13 miles from north to south,

and 6 miles at its widest, the island is richly wooded and spotted with lakes, ponds, streams, and bogs. With only one small town in the north, the island is mostly sparsely populated, a perfect spot to get away from it all.

On the southern tip of Beaver Island stands the Beaver Island Lighthouse. First lit in 1851, it was one of Michigan's first lighthouses. The original tower toppled early on, and the one you see today was erected in 1858. A rise in lake traffic in the mid-1800s made it necessary to direct ships through Beaver and North Fox Islands, and around the dangerous waters of the Beaver Archipelago. Ships passed up the east side of the island and down the west, and a sandy harbor at the north end was a place to stop and ride out a storm if necessary.

It is said that the island was called Turtle Island by the Ottawa, who took advantage of the many fish in these waters. Though they claim to have never set up camp here themselves, the oral tradition recalls that when their ancestors first came to this area they saw other people living in fishing settlements along the island's shores. The French named it Île du Castor (or "Island of Beaver"), which was directly translated into the English as Beaver Island.

The most fascinating chapter in the island's history begins in 1844 with the death of Joseph Smith in far-off Illinois. The death of Mormonism's founder was quite a blow to his followers. For a time, there was a struggle to fill the void his death left. Most followed Brigham Young, but a young man, James Jesse Strang, established his own church, claiming it was the true successor to that begun by Joseph Smith. Early on he had some success, leading twelve thousand adherents. In 1848, he moved the church headquarters to Beaver Island. Taking the mantle of leadership to heart, he declared himself king in 1850.

For six years, Beaver Island was home to the only monarchy in U.S. history. Though Strang only claimed sovereignty over his followers, the island was mostly inhabited by Strangites, and there was a patent blurring of the line between church and state. A productive lot, the Mormons founded the town of St. James on the island's north harbor. In 1856, Strang was shot by two disgruntled followers, and the Mormons were soon driven from Beaver Island by a mob from Mackinaw City. The only Strangite building left today is the Old Mormon Print Shop, now the home of the Beaver Island Historical Society and Museum.

Irish fishermen soon arrived in droves—many from Ireland's County Donegal—giving the island much of its cultural character. (It's no wonder the island is billed today as America's Emerald Isle.)

There are two ways to get to the island—by boat or plane. The Beaver Island Boat Company operates a ferry from Charlevoix. In the high season, there are boats leaving Charlevoix and St. James twice daily. The ferry trip is two hours long. Day trips are possible, and catching the early ferry in the morning leaves you about six hours to play on the island. Two companies serve Beaver Island by air: Island Airways and Fresh Air Aviation take passengers on the 15-minute flight to Beaver Island.

A plane is a great way to get back and forth from Beaver Island. *Kim Forster*

Day-trippers might want to explore the island by car. Geo Trackers are available for four-hour or all-day rental at the Beaver Island Marina. The roads are generally level and make for a decent bike ride—bikes and mopeds can be rented at Lakesports & Paradise Bay Gifts. They also rent canoes and kayaks if you want to explore by water.

For food, the Dalwhinnie Bakery and Deli is exceptional for breakfast, lunch, and dinner. Upscale dining with a fantastic view of Lake Michigan is yours at The Restaurant at Beaver Island Lodge.

The Beaver Islander ferry has been making the trip to the island from Charlevoix since 1962.

The Horton Bay General Store remains much as it was in the days when Ernest Hemingway was a customer.

Road continues on to Boyne City (changing its name to Lakeshore Road and Front Street along the way). In Boyne City, turn north along Charlevoix–Boyne City Road, which passes through Horton Bay, the town made famous for its association with Ernest Hemingway. The general store in town is much as it was nearly a hundred years ago in Hemingway's time, and a wall full of memorabilia pays tribute to the celebrated writer. In Horton Bay, you can continue along that lake or head north on Horton Bay Road. Both terminate at US 31, still west of Petoskey.

The Crooked Tree Arts Center in Petoskey has a gallery that features local artists.

Several communities huddle along the shores of Little Traverse Bay, including Petoskey and Bay View on the southern edge and Harbor Springs on the north. The story of Petoskey is similar to most in the region. Missionaries first came to what was then the Ottawa village of Bear River in 1855. Within 25 years, the town was renamed Petoskey (after a local Ottawa chief, Petosega).

Lumber and tourism fed the town's economy—railways and steam ships bringing eager travelers to experience the luxurious resorts of the north.

Petoskey has a great arts community, as witnessed by the **Crooked Tree Arts· Center,** located in the repurposed Petoskey United Methodist Church. This Victorian edifice was initially erected in 1877, and the arts center purchased the building in 1979 as a cultural center. Be sure to check out their galleries and the sales gallery. There are also numerous galleries and eateries in Petoskey's Gaslight Village. Also in Gaslight Village is **McLean & Eakin Booksellers,** which has a surprising inventory for such a compact location. The bookstore has two levels and takes advantage of every inch of space, and the staff seems to really know their stuff.

In 1875, the Methodist Church established a camp meeting that would eventually become the community of Bay View. Adjacent to Petoskey, the Bay View Association is a National Historic Landmark. The community has nearly 450 Victorian cottages—well worth a drive or walk through the neighborhood. The bulk of the cottages sit south of US 31 (Woodland Avenue) as the road passes east of Petoskey. Still maintained by the Methodist Church, the Bay View Association has maps of town and a summer program that highlights the many activities, festivals, and cultural events happening in Bay View.

As this is a thriving resort area, you will find many opportunities for lodging.

Stafford's Perry Hotel in Petoskey still maintains its Victorian charm.

THE TUNNEL OF TREES

North of Harbor Springs, the lakeshore is markedly different than what is found south along Lake Michigan. Gentle approaches and the often sandy beaches suddenly give way to high wooded bluffs. MI 119 begins in Bay View, north of Petoskey, and continues west through Harbor Springs. As it follows the graceful curve of the lake northward, the road begins to wind and twist with the landscape.

Between Good Hart and Cross Village, the road that follows this shoreline is one of the most scenic drives in the state. The town of Good Hart marks the entrance to Michigan's legendary Tunnel of Trees. The Good Hart General Store serves this tiny community as the post office, grocery, bakery, and deli. The store is known for baking an excellent pot pie. Next door is Primitive Images. Housed in a 19th-century log cabin, dismantled and moved here from Quebec, the shop sells unique furniture and accessories. In the back is the Good Hart & Soul Tea Room.

The Tunnel of Trees *Catherine Forster*

For the next 7 miles to Cross Village, the branches of the trees along the road create an arboreal arch. The narrow road is so twisty in parts that cars slow to a snail's pace. Now and then the trees part to stunning views of

Stafford's Perry Hotel in downtown Petoskey was built at the turn of the 20th century. It is the last remaining resort from the town's heyday, when Petoskey hosted 20 such hotels. The Victorian decor has been updated over the years, but guests can certainly sense the hotel's 19th-century sensibility. There are 79 guest rooms, and those with a private balcony overlook Little Traverse Bay.

The Terrace Inn, down the road in Bay View, was built in 1911. The hotel features bed & breakfast–style accommodations, but with a full restaurant and 38 rooms, it is definitely an inn. The hotel is surrounded by the Victorian cottages of Bay View. From Fairview Avenue, rows of trees line the sidewalk to a tall staircase leading to the hotel. The dining room is open to the public Thursday through Saturday for dinner—reservations are required.

Lake Michigan. The trip is beautiful in the summer, but in the fall the changing colors will leave you breathless.

While in Cross Village, be sure to check out the Legs Inn. Built in the 1920s, this incredible fieldstone inn has one of the best scenic views around, sitting on a high bluff overlooking Lake Michigan. The roof is creatively decorated with inverted stove legs, hence the name. Legs serves a variety of international and Polish dishes, and they have cottages available for rental during the season.

This little corner of the state has virtually been forgotten by the masses who stop just short in Petoskey or bypass the region altogether on their way to Mackinac Island. One of the state's most attractive parks, Wilderness State Park, is located a little farther north on Lake Michigan. In addition to campsites, the park has six cabins on the lake that can be rented on a nightly basis.

IN THE AREA

ACCOMMODATIONS

Applesauce Inn, 7296 South MI 88, Bellaire. Call 231-533-6448 or 1-888-533-6448. Pet friendly. A parking area with room for snowmobile trailers. Website: applesauceinn.com.

The House on the Hill Bed & Breakfast, 9661 Lake Street, Ellsworth. Call 231-588-6304. Website: thehouseonthehill.com.

Stafford's Perry Hotel, Bay and Lewis Streets, Petoskey. Call 231-347-4000. Website: staffords.com/perry hotel.

The Terrace Inn, 1549 Glendale Avenue, Petoskey. Call 1-800-530-9898. Website: theterraceinn.com.

ATTRACTIONS AND RECREATION

Beaver Island Marina, 25860 Main Street, Beaver Island. Call 231-448-2300. Website: beaverislandmarina .com.

Bier Art Gallery, 17959 Ferry Road, Charlevoix. Call 231-547-2288 or

1-866-880-5624. South of Charlevoix 6 miles on US 31. Open year-round. Website: biergallery.com.

Brownwood Acres. Call 231-544-3910. Website: porkyfarm.com/brown wood.html.

Crooked Tree Arts Center, 461 East Mitchell Street, Petoskey. Call 231-347-3209. Website: crookedtree.org.

Friske's Farm Market, 10743 North US 31, Atwood. Call 1-888-968-3554. Website: friske.com.

Good Hart General Store, 1075 North Lake Shore Drive, Good Hart. Call 231-526-7661. Website: goodhart store.com.

Grass River Nature Area, 6500 Alden Highway, Bellaire. Call 231-533-8576. Website: grassriver.org.

King Orchards, 4620 North MI 88, Central Lake. Call 1-877-937-5464. Website: kingorchards.com.

Lakesports & Paradise Bay Gifts, Beaver Island. Call 231-448-2166.

McLean & Eakin Booksellers, 307 East Lake Street, Petoskey. Call 231-347-1180 or 1-800-968-1910. Website: mcleanandeakin.com.

North Seas Gallery, 237 Bridge Street, Charlevoix. Call 231-547-0422. Website: northseasgallery.com.

Primitive Images and the Good Hart & Soul Tea Room, 1129 North Lake Shore Drive, Good Hart. Call 231-526-0276. Website: primitive images.com.

Riverside Marina, 115 West Cayuga Street, Bellaire. Call 231-533-8559. Website: riverside-marina.com.

Round Lake Books, 216 Bridge Street, Charlevoix. Call 231-547-2699.

Royal Farms, 10445 North US 31, Ellsworth. Call 231-599-3222. Website: royalfarmsinc.com.

Twisted Fish Gallery, 10443 South Bayshore Drive, Elk Rapids. Call 231-264-0123. Website: twistedfishart.com.

Wilderness State Park, 903 Wilderness Park Drive, Carp Lake. Call 231-436-5381. Website: michigan.gov/wilderness.

PETOSKEY STONES

Petoskey Stones are scattered all along the northern shores of the Lower Peninsula. Millions of years ago, when what the geologists call the Devonian seas covered the Great Lakes, these stones were colony corals. Over time the corals were petrified, and when the glaciers receded, these stones were scraped loose and deposited in this region of the state. While similar fossilized coral "stones" can be found around the world, northern Michigan is the only place you will find this particular genus of fossilized coral (*Hexagonaria percarinata*).

In 1965 the stone—or more properly, the fossil—was declared to be Michigan's state stone. The patterns can best be seen when the stones are wet. They can also be polished to reveal their delicate skeletal patterns. Alternatively, children often paint them with clear nail polish to keep them looking wet.

DINING

Classic Pizza, 2461 North MI 88, Central Lake. Call 231-544-5555.

Dalwhinnie Bakery and Deli, 38240 Michigan Avenue, Beaver Island. Call 231-448-2736. Website: mcdonoughs market.com/dalwhinnie.

Legs Inn, 6425 North Lake Shore Drive, Cross Village. Call 231-526-2281. Website: legsinn.com.

Mōka, 102 North Bridge Street, Bellaire. Call 231-533-6262. Website: the techsolvers.com/moka/.

Pearl's New Orleans Kitchen, 617 Ames Street, Elk Rapids. Call 231-264-0530. Website: magnumhospitality .com/pearls.

The Restaurant, 38210 Beaver Lodge Drive, Beaver Island. Call 231-448-2396. Website: beaverislandlodge.com/dining.

Riverwalk Grill, 106 Ames Street, Elk Rapids. Call 231-264-9121. Website: tcgrills.com/riverwalk-grill.

TRANSPORTATION

Beaver Island Boat Company, 103 Bridge Park Drive, Charlevoix. Call 231-547-2311 or 1-888-446-4095. Website: bibco.com.

Fresh Air Aviation, 1520 Bridge Street, Charlevoix. Call 231-237-9482 or 1-888-FLY-RGHT (359-7448). Website: freshairaviation.net.

Island Airways, 111 Airport Drive, Charlevoix. Call 1-800-524-6895. Website: islandairways.com.

OTHER CONTACTS

Bay View Association. Call 231-347-6225. Website: bayviewassociation.org.

The Terrace Inn is tucked in among Bay View's Victorian cottages.

Beaver Island Chamber of Commerce. Call 231-448-2505. Website: beaverisland.org.

Bellaire Chamber of Commerce, 308 East Cayuga Street, Bellaire. Call 231-533-6023. Website: bellaire chamber.org.

Central Lake Chamber of Commerce, 2587 North MI 88, Central Lake. Call 231-544-3322. Website: central-lake.com.

Charlevoix Chamber of Commerce, 109 Mason Street, Charlevoix. Call 231-547-2101. Website: charlevoix.org.

Elk Rapids Chamber of Commerce, 305 US 31 North, Elk Rapids. Call 231-264-8202 or 1-800-626-7328. Website: elkrapidschamber.org.

Petoskey Regional Chamber of Commerce, 401 East Mitchell Street, Petoskey. Call 231-347-4150. Website: petoskey.com.

The Au Sable River meanders lazily from Grayling to Oscoda/Au Sable.

8 The Sunrise Coast: Old Lumber Towns and Lazy Rivers

TAWAS CITY, AU SABLE & OSCODA, HARRISVILLE, ALPENA, PRESQUE ISLE, ROGERS CITY, CHEBOYGAN, AND PIGEON RIVER COUNTRY

Estimated length: 250 miles
Estimated time: 5 hours

Getting there:: The trip begins in Tawas City. From the south, exit I-75 at East Pinconning Road (exit 181). Turn left on MI 13 in Pinconning. In Standish, the road becomes US 23. Stay on US 23 for 35 miles to Tawas City. From Tawas, follow US 23 all the way to Cheboygan, passing through Au Sable, Oscoda, Harrisville, Alpena, Presque Isle, and Rogers City en route.

Highlights: This route begins in Tawas City and East Tawas. Here you will find places to eat and some light shopping. Continue east to Tawas Point State Park, where there's a beach for swimming and the historic Tawas Point Lighthouse. Farther north, following the Au Sable River, the River Road Scenic Byway passes the AuSable River Queen paddle-wheeler, which gives tours of Foote Pond. Farther upstream, next to the Huron National Forest Visitors Center, is the Lumberman's Monument, which commemorates the men who harvested the state's trees. Fewer than 3 miles farther, also part of the national forest, the Iargo Springs Interpretive Site tells the history of these springs, which Native Americans saw as sacred. In Harrisville, take in the sun at the beach at Harrisville State Park or tour the Sturgeon Point Lighthouse. For an interesting detour, stop by the Killmaster Soapworks and purchase handmade, milk-based soaps. In Alpena's Old Town, grab a bite at the John A. Lau Saloon before seeing about a boat tour to the Middle Island Lighthouse. Farther north, tour the Old and New Presque Isle Lighthouses. In Rogers

8. The Sunrise Coast: Old Lumber Towns and Lazy Rivers

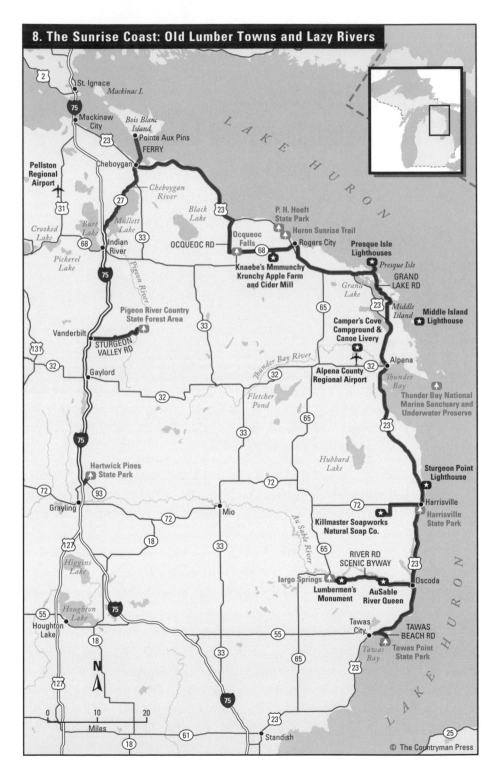

© The Countryman Press

The Sunrise Coast has more morning sun for tanning.

City, take a look at the largest limestone quarry in the world, then head inland for a short hike near Ocqueoc Falls. In Cheboygan, sit along the river and watch boats on the northern portion of the Inland Waterway or grab a snack at the Big Dipper Ice Cream Parlour. Returning home south on I-75, stop at Hartwick Pines State Park, with its stand of old growth pine. An understanding of the region's lumber heritage would not be complete without a visit there.

The northeastern curve of the mitten is punctuated by the mouths of three rivers popular with paddlers and anglers: The Rifle River empties into Saginaw Bay, south of Omer. The Au Sable River, which is possibly the most popular recreational river in the Midwest, empties into Lake Huron near the neighboring villages of Au Sable and Oscoda. The Thunder Bay River winds through Alpena to Thunder Bay. These rivers were the highways of the past. Native American canoes once plied these waters, followed by French trappers and fur traders. They provided the means for moving the land's abundant bounty of old-growth forest from the interior to the sawmills and port towns that sprang up on Lake Huron.

The northeastern half of the Lower Peninsula is not the mirror image of the northwestern part of the state. The predominant winds from the west do not carry

The Tawas Point Lighthouse once stood at the tip of Tawas Point.

Lake Michigan's summer warmth, so farmers have a tougher go of it here. The flow of summer tourists up from Detroit and Chicago follows US 31 and I-75, bypassing the Sunrise Coast. In a real sense, the region remains a backwater, and that is part of its great charm. There are no fudge shops from Oscoda to Cheboygan. There are more antiques shops than art galleries and more mom-and-pop convenience stores than T-shirt outlets.

This route begins in Tawas. The bay that shelters Tawas and East Tawas is formed by Tawas Point. Driving east on US 23, turn right on Tawas Beach Road. Once called Ottawa Point, this barbed spit of land is where you will find **Tawas Point State Park** and the Tawas Point Lighthouse. In the past 150 years, the currents of Lake Huron have continually deposited new sand at the end of the point, increasing its overall length by 1 mile. In 1852, when the original light was erected, the property that is now a state park did not exist. The second light was raised in 1872 near the shore, but today you will notice the point is far from water. Tours of the lighthouse are offered throughout the week in the summer. Check with the park for a schedule.

The park's 2-mile Tawas Point–Sand Hook Nature Trail begins in the parking lot near the lighthouse. The trail follows the north side of the point to the U.S. Coast Guard foghorn and loops on the south side. Swimmers have a choice of beaches, either on Lake Huron or Tawas Bay. Shallower and somewhat protected from the deeper waters of the open lake, Tawas Bay usually has warmer water.

The Au Sable River is one of the most popular rivers in the state for canoeing, kayaking, and tubing. Every year during the last full weekend in July, the **AuSable River Canoe Marathon** has paddlers making the 120-mile route nonstop from Grayling to Oscoda. Race leaders typically make the run in 14 to 19 hours. It's the

The AuSable River Queen tours the Au Sable River's Foote Pond.

longest race of its kind in North America, with competitors beginning the race at 9 PM and paddling through the night.

West of Grayling, the river is less navigable and not as attractive to the thousands of paddlers and tubers who hit the water every summer weekend. This remote section of the river passes within miles of the Manistee River. In centuries past, a short portage connected the two rivers, and Native Americans used the route to travel across the peninsula.

Beginning in Mio, a series of dams create six ponds along the river. For paddlers, these dams create a bit of a nuisance, but portages are clearly marked and well trod. Canoes can be rented all along the stretch of the river—from Grayling to Mio to Oscoda. Coming from US 23 in Au Sable/Oscoda, check out **Oscoda Canoe Rental.** The outfitter shuttles guests to the put-ins throughout the day in the summer. The most popular trip is the 6-mile float from the Whirlpool put-in. It takes about two hours. For a longer trip, they will drop you at the Foote Dam, which is 12 miles upstream.

From Oscoda, the River Road Scenic Byway follows the river west. Along the way, the road passes the *AuSable River Queen*, a restored paddle-wheeler docked on Foote Pond. The patriotically painted, double-decker boat takes passengers on two-hour tours of the river, and it runs all summer and into the fall for the changing of the colors. Anglers will want to take note of the **Dam Store,** just 0.25 mile before

On a bluff overlooking the Au Sable, the Lumbermen's Monument commemorates the hard work of Michigan's lumberjacks.

the riverboat. The shop carries all the fishing gear you forgot, and they forgot more than you'll ever know about fishing this stretch of the Au Sable.

Farther along the scenic byway, stop at the Huron National Forest Visitors Center. The visitors center is situated in a park, the centerpiece of which is the **Lumberman's Monument**, a sculpture sitting on a bluff that overlooks Cooke Pond. The life of a lumberman was no picnic. The job required long hours of muscle-straining work in all sorts of weather. Far from home and hearth, the men that logged the state's forests faced risks unheard of today. A list of 19th-century obituaries from northern Michigan tells of men crushed beneath falling trees, pinned to skids by wayward logs, and drowned in mill ponds and rivers. Quite a few even died from infection following ax wounds.

Erected in 1931, this sculpture commemorates the hard work and sacrifice of the men who provided lumber that fed the growth of the nation in the 19th century.

Also in the national forest, 3 miles up the road, is Iargo Springs. This interpretive site looks at the history of the springs, from the use by Native Americans to the dams created by lumbermen to divert drinking water to their camps. These natural springs burst forth from the sandy soil. Dams, a few logs high, create small waterfalls for two of the springs as they tumble toward the river. A stairway of three hundred steps leads down to the Au Sable, but for those who prefer not to climb, a deck along the bluff provides an easy overlook.

In Oscoda, the **Huron House B&B** is worth a look if you need lodging. Located on the sandy shores of Lake Huron, this bed & breakfast has the perfect view of the lake. The inn has 14 guest rooms on two floors. Many have private decks, some with hot tubs, in-room Jacuzzis, and fireplaces. The rooms are spacious; none is under 400 square feet. A light breakfast is delivered to the rooms each morning.

For dinner, **Wiltse's Brew Pub & Family Restaurant** in Oscoda is just the place for comfort food. The dinner menu is stocked with favorites. The mac and cheese with honey-baked ham is sure to hit the spot after a day on the river. For seafood, they have Great Lake classics like perch and walleyes. The brewpub offers their own ales and lagers, including Blue Ox Stout and Paul Bunyan Ale—or try the sampler.

Coming from the south on US 23, **Harrisville State Park** is on the right, less than 1 mile before the turn for Harrisville. The park is completely wooded, except for the ribbon of sand along Lake Huron. The campground has nearly two hundred sites, all modern, and two cabins.

Harrisville is a small harbor town that thrived during the lumber era. In the summers anglers come for chartered fishing trips on Lake Huron or to take in the annual **Harrisville Arts & Crafts Show** over Labor Day weekend. The festival is often called Harmony Weekend and features a slew of performances by the Society for the Preservation and Encouragement of Barber Shop Quartet Singing in America —or more simply, the Barbershop Harmony Society.

A town named Killmaster once thrived west of Harrisville in the 1800s. Plenty of tall white pine, a swift river, and a sawmill were all that was needed for the settlement to succeed when it was founded in 1850. After the trees were harvested, however, fields were turned into farmland and the town began to decline. Not much remains of Killmaster today—a church that has been converted into a home, a few buildings here and there, and a farmhouse, the latter the home of **Killmaster Soapworks Natural Soap Co.** Casey Makela, the author of *Milk-Based Soaps* and *Making Natural Milk Soap,* and founder of the company, makes soap using milk from the goats, cows, and horses on her eco-friendly farm. Tours of the soap-making process are available if you call ahead. To get there, drive west on MI 72 for 6 miles. Turn left on Somers Road, right on Gustin and then McConnell, and then left on Killmaster. The farm is 1 mile down the road.

North of Harrisville 5 miles is another lighthouse at the Sturgeon Point Scenic Site. Though unseen from land, a reef extends nearly 1 mile out into Lake Huron, just below the waves. The **Sturgeon Point Lighthouse** was built to warn ships of this danger in 1870, and it still operates today. Visitors can climb the tower, tour the museum, and buy a lighthouse souvenir at the gift shop. To get there from US 23, turn right on North Lakeshore Drive, and then right again on East Point Road.

Alpena is 30 miles north of Harrisville, still on US 23. The sand beaches of Lake Huron disappear around Alpena, giving way to long rocky stretches of coastline. Alpena sprang up in the 19th century at the mouth of the Thunder Bay River, where the river pours into Thunder Bay. This part of Lake Huron is notorious for shipwrecks, and the bay was classified as the Thunder Bay State Underwater Preserve in 1981. It has since received national attention and is now the **Thunder Bay**

The Alpena Marina has a nice path along the breakwall.

The exhibits at the museum in Alpena attempt to put you on a ship in a Lake Huron storm.

National Marine Sanctuary and Underwater Preserve. (The name just rolls off the tongue, doesn't it?) Scuba divers come from all around to explore the many wrecks in and around the bay, and there are several charter boats ready to take divers out to these sites.

You don't necessarily need to get wet to explore the Thunder Bay preserve. The Great Lakes Maritime Heritage Center presents the history of these waters with models of ships that have gone down in Lake Huron and a large exhibit that puts you on the deck of a ship in a Great Lakes storm. The center is open year-round, and admission is always free.

For exploring the river, paddlers can rent a canoe at Camper's Cove Campground & Canoe Livery. The campground is 6 miles west of town on Long Rapids Road on Seven Mile Pond. They also rent out kayaks, paddleboats, and pontoon boats. There are even duck blinds for hunters.

When you're ready for a bite to eat, stop at John A. Lau Saloon, in Alpena's Old Town. Known for an exceptional selection of beef (no fewer than 12 choices are on the menu), the restaurant also serves plenty of seafood, pasta, and salads, like the Michigan Fruits and Nuts salad. Pub-grub connoisseurs will appreciate the foot-o-rings and bucket-o-shrimp appetizers. Local legend has it that the historic saloon is haunted by Agnes, John Lau's wife, who died following childbirth.

More lighthouse viewing awaits on Middle Island, 2.5 miles out in Lake Huron, halfway between Thunder Bay and Presque Isle. On the east side of the island is the Middle Island Lighthouse, with the original keeper's quarters. Tours of the island can be arranged through Middle Island Keepers' Lodge and Boat Tours. On Saturday, Captain Mike Theut meets passengers at the Rockport boat ramp and takes them out to the island. The tour can take up to four hours (about an hour of that on the water) and includes commentary on local history, shipwrecks, and the lighthouse. For a secluded getaway, the keeper's quarters have been renovated for overnight guests. You will have to bring your own food and toiletries, but the lodge has nearly everything else you will need.

Presque Isle is 20 miles north of Alpena. Take US 23 north 6.5 miles to Grand Lake Road (it practically forks off to the right). At the four-way intersection, Grand Lake Road continues

One of the best places to eat in Alpena is John Lau Saloon.

with a right-hand turn. Staying on Grand Lake through all the twists and turns, you pass the sign for the Fireside Inn Resort and, later, the John Kauffman Homestead on the way to the Presque Isle peninsula and its two lighthouses.

The two Presque Isle lighthouses are as different as can be. At the southern end of this "almost an island" (the meaning of *presque isle* in French), the **Old Presque Isle Lighthouse** guards the entrance to a natural harbor. Built in 1840, the small whitewashed tower rises a mere 30 feet, with hand-hewn stone steps winding to the top. The matching keeper's home is a quaint cottage with fireplaces at each gabled end, the overall effect not unlike a Thomas Kinkade painting.

Sailors complained the light was hard to see, and it was later deemed only sufficient as a harbor light, so funds were approved by Congress to build a new light at the north end of the peninsula. The **New Presque Isle Lighthouse** was built in 1870. It is nearly four times as high as the old light, reaching 113 feet, making it the tallest lighthouse on Lake Huron. Surrounding the light is a 100-acre township park. Two keeper's quarters have been preserved, and the one connected to the tower is a gift shop. The other, a separate home built in 1905, has been restored and is a lighthouse museum.

For overnight accommodations in Presque Isle, consider lodging on Grand Lake. The historic **Fireside Inn Resort**, which has been taking care of guests since 1908, offers sleeping and housekeeping cabins, and a row of sleeping rooms in the main resort that face the lake. Meals are served on the American plan. There's a small beach, volleyball and tennis courts, and horseshoe pits. With the family dining room, lodge with fireplace, and cabins strategically scattered throughout the wooded property, it's a trip back to the days when Americans first started taking to the roads in earnest.

Just 15 miles north of Grand Lake is Rogers City, home of the world's largest limestone quarry. The Huron Sunrise Trail begins south of town with a view of the harbor and the open pit limestone mine. The path winds through town past a number of sites of interest, including several parks and a historic neighborhood. (Guided tours with commentary on these sites are offered by the parks commission.) North of Rogers City 5 miles, the trail connects with **P. H. Hoeft State Park,** which has one of the prettiest beaches in the state. Low, rolling dunes stretch for nearly 1 mile along the shoreline. The campground is wooded, and 4 miles of trails loop through the forested park.

In the fall, stop by **Knaebe's Mmmunchy Krunchy Apple Farm and Cider Mill.** Northeastern Michigan is not traditionally a region where you find orchards, as growing apples in this area requires giving trees the tenderest of care. The folks at Knaebe's are pretty particular about their trees, and, as such, there's no U-pick. In season apples are sold at their farm store, where they also make fresh apple pies, muffins, cookies, and, of course, delicious cider doughnuts. Grab some doughnuts, a gallon of cider, and sit back and relax while the kids go crazy over the farm animals. To get to the apple farm, drive 4 miles west on MI 68 and turn left on Karsten Road. The farm is 1.5 miles south.

The Old Presque Isle Light enjoys retirement in a thick cedar forest with views of Lake Huron's natural harbor.

Officially there are only two waterfalls in Michigan's Lower Peninsula. The most impressive is **Ocqueoc Falls.** It pales in comparison to the big falls north of the bridge, but its small size means you often find families splashing around Ocqueoc River and playing in the falls. Following MI 68 west, the state highway makes a sharp turn to the south about 11 miles out of Rogers City. Leave MI 68 to continue west on the side road (the Ocqueoc Falls Highway). The parking area is on the right less than 0.5 mile up the road. On the left is the Ocqueoc Falls State Forest Campground. If you enjoy fishing and taking it easy in the woods, this is a quiet place to spend a few nights. It's an easy hike from the parking lot, and the associated Ocqueoc Falls Pathway is a great hike for kids. The trail has several loops, which you can customize into a 3-, 5-, or 6-mile hike. The most scenic portion of the route is along the river, and the shortest loop of 3 miles is an easy hike for the whole family and includes views of the river valley. The falls are 11.5 miles west of Rogers City on MI 68.

East of Mackinaw City 15 miles, Cheboygan is often overlooked by tourists. It's a quiet town with a small but loyal summer crowd. For recreational boaters, the Cheboygan River is the final leg of the 38-mile Inland Waterway that begins in Crooked and Pickerel Lakes and passes through Burt and Mullett Lakes before emptying into

The New Presque Isle Light, at 113 feet, is the tallest on Lake Huron.

Lake Huron. At one time, this water route served as the boundary between the Ottawa Nation to the west and the Chippewa in the east. The town of Indian River (exit 310 on I-75) is squeezed in between Burt and Mullett Lakes. The **Indian River Marina** rents pontoon boats and ski boats for an afternoon of fun on the water.

The Opera House in downtown Cheboygan was built in 1877. It was damaged by fire and rebuilt twice—in 1888 and 1903. In the rough-and-tumble lumber days, the Opera House was a cultural centerpiece. Restored in 1984, the theater's acoustics have made it a popular venue for touring artists, as well as the local community theater.

On a warm summer day, nothing beats a cool treat. Outside the **Big Dipper Ice Cream Parlour** is a large wooden ice cream cone with a cherry on top. Inside they serve hearty portions of hand-dipped ice cream, without the usual tourist markup.

Ocqueoc Falls may not be the most breathtaking in the state, but they make for a fun time in the water.

Rich with history, the **Hack-Ma-Tack Inn** was established well over a hundred years ago on Mullet Lake and the Cheboygan River as a private hunting and fishing lodge. The menu is classic American—steak and seafood, with some signature dishes like whitefish amandine and their excellent bone-in pork chops. From town, take MI 27 south 3 miles and turn left onto MI 33. Take the first right on Carter Road, another right at Hackmatack Road, and yet another right on Beebe.

Returning home from Cheboygan on I-75, you will pass two impressive nature areas. The first is just east of Vanderbilt. When a young Ernest Hemingway headed east for some hunting and fishing, he landed in what is today the **Pigeon River Country State Forest Area**. The Sturgeon, the Pigeon, and the Black Rivers flow north from these woods. This is one of the best places in the state to see Michigan's elk herds. There are observation stations scattered about, and crowds come in the fall to watch the elk mingle.

The second nature area worth visiting is a little further south on I-75. Just off exit 259, north of Grayling, is **Hartwick Pines State Park**. For an appreciation of

BOIS BLANC ISLAND

The largest island in the Mackinac Archipelago is Bois Blanc Island (locals pronounce it BAH-blow, the same as Detroit's Boblo Island). Travelers either catch the ferry to the island or schedule a drop-off by plane or helicopter. With 24,000 acres of forest, 30 miles of shoreline, and four lakes, the island's main attraction for tourists is outdoor recreation. Cars are welcome on the island, though reservations with the ferry must be made in advance.

There are few amenities on the island. Pointe Aux Pins, the island's one village, has a school, a tavern, and a post office, but little else. The island does, however, have an incredible bed & breakfast. The **Insel Haus Bed & Breakfast,** run by Christa and Shelby Newhouse, is full of old-world charm. Many of the inn's rooms have a view of the Straits. The home can hold up to 20 lodgers, which is especially nice for retreats, reunions, and the like.

what this region looked like before it was completely logged over, the state park maintains the largest stand of virgin white pine in the Lower Peninsula. The old-growth forest covers 85 acres. The canopy above blocks much of the sun, so the undergrowth is minimal. Be sure to visit the log chapel in the pines, and round out the trip with a visit to the logging museum.

IN THE AREA

ACCOMMODATIONS

Fireside Inn Resort, 18730 Fireside Highway, Presque Isle. Call 989-595-6369. Located on the east side of Grand Lake, the inn is right off East Grand Lake Road Just look for their sign. Website: firesideinngrandlake.com.

Huron House B&B, 3124 North US 23, Oscoda. Call 989-739-9255. South of Oscoda 4 miles on Lake Huron. Website: huronhouse.com.

Insel Haus Bed & Breakfast. Call 231-634-7393 or 1-888-634-7393. The only lodging on Bois Blanc, this B&B is world class, with views of the Straits. Website: inselhausbandb.com.

Middle Island Keepers' Lodge, 7406 US 23 North, Suite C, Alpena. Call 989-884-2722. The boat for the island meets at the Rockport boat ramp. Website: middleislandkeeperslodge.com.

ATTRACTIONS AND RECREATION

AuSable River Canoe Marathon. Call 989-348-4425. Website: ausable canoemarathon.org.

AuSable River Queen. Call 989-739-7351. Website: ausableriverqueen.net.

Big Dipper Ice Cream Parlour, 106 South Main Street, Cheboygan. Call 231-627-7937.

Camper's Cove Campground &

Canoe Livery, 5005 Long Rapids Road, Alpena. Call 989-356-3708. Located on Seven Mile Pond, the livery rents canoes, kayaks, paddleboats, and pontoon boats. Website: camperscove campground.com.

Dam Store, 1879 River Road, Oscoda. Call 989-739-9979. This is the place for fishing gear and advice.

Great Lakes Maritime Heritage Center, 500 West Fletcher Street, Alpena. Call 989-356-8805. Website: http://thunderbay.noaa.gov/maritime/glmhc.html.

Harrisville Arts & Crafts Show, Harrisville. Website: harrisvillearts council.com.

Harrisville State Park, 248 State Park Road, Harrisville. Call 989-724-5126. Website: michigan.gov/harrisville.

Hartwick Pines State Park, 4216 Ranger Road, Grayling. Call 989-348-7068. Website: michigan.gov/hartwick pines.

Indian River Marina, 3020 Apple Blossom Street, Indian River. Call 231-238-9373. Close to I-75 and on the Inland Waterway, the marina rents boats. Website: indianrivermarina.com.

Killmaster Soapworks Natural Soap Co., 1628 Mill Road, Harrisville. Call 989-736-SOAP (7627). Tours are available if you call ahead to set it up; there's a small gift shop that sells soap. Website: milksoaps.com.

Knaebe's Mmmunchy Krunchy Apple Farm and Cider Mill, 2622

A paved trail winds through the old growth forest in Hartwick Pines.

The chapel amid the old-growth forest in Hartwick Pines is a peaceful sanctuary.

Karsten Road, Rogers City. Call 989-734-2567. In the fall the farm sells apples, apple cider, and cider doughnuts. Website: mmmunchykrunchyapple farm.com.

Lumberman's Monument and Iargo Springs, Huron Shores Ranger Station, 5761 North Skeel Road, Oscoda. Call 517-739-0728. Both of these sites are along the River Road Scenic Byway. The Lumberman's Monument is part of the National Forest Visitors Center, 16 miles west of Oscoda. Iargo Springs is 3 miles farther on.

Middle Island Boat Tours. Call 989-884-2722. The boat for the island meets at the Rockport boat ramp on Saturday in the summer. Website: middleislandkeeperslodge.com.

New Presque Isle Lighthouse, 5324 East Grand Lake Road, Presque Isle. Call 989-595-6979. Call ahead for hours. The lighthouse museum is operated by volunteers and is open fewer hours than the tower and the gift shop. Small fee to climb tower. Website: presqueislelighthouses.org.

Ocqueoc Falls, Ocqueoc Falls Road, Millersburg. Call 989-734-2543. Website: michigan.gov/ocqueocfalls.

Old Presque Isle Lighthouse and Museum, 4500 East Grand Lake Road, Presque Isle. Call 989-595-9917. The keeper's quarters and the 30-foot lighthouse are open to tour for a small charge. Website: presqueislelight houses.org.

The Opera House, 403 North Huron Street, Cheboygan. Call 231-627-5432 or 231-627-5841 (for the box office). Website: theoperahouse.org.

Oscoda Canoe Rental, 678 River Road, Oscoda. Call 989-739-9040. This outfitter rents canoes and tubes for two- and four-hour trips on the Au Sable River. Website: oscodacanoe.com.

P. H. Hoeft State Park, 5001 US 23 North, Rogers City. Call 989-734-2543. Website: michigan.gov/hoeft.

Pigeon River Country, 9966 Twin Lakes Road, Vanderbilt. Call 989-983-4101. Website: michigan.gov/dnr pigeonriver.

Sturgeon Point Lighthouse, 6071 East Point Road, Harrisville. Call 989-724-6297.

Tawas Point State Park, 686 Tawas Beach Road, East Tawas. Call 989-362-5041. Website: michigan.gov/tawaspoint.

Thunder Bay National Marine Sanctuary and Underwater Preserve. Website: thunderbay.noaa.gov.

DINING

Hack-Ma-Tack Inn & Restaurant, 8131 Beebe Road, Cheboygan. Call 231-625-2919. Website: hackmatackinn.com.

John A. Lau Saloon, 414 North Second Avenue, Alpena. Call 989-354-6898. Located in Alpena's Old Town, just north of the bridge. Website: johnalausaloon.com.

Wiltse's Brew Pub & Family Restaurant, 5606 F 41, Oscoda. Call 989-739-2231. Just north of Oscoda, F 41 forks off to the left of US 23. The restaurant is 2.5 miles down. Website: wiltsebrewpub.com.

TRANSPORTATION

Bois Blanc Island Ferry, Plaunt Transportation, 412 Water Street, Cheboygan. Call 231-627-2354 or 1-888-752-8687. The ferry runs a regular schedule of trips throughout the summer. Reservations required to transport a car over to the island. Website: bbiferry.com.

OTHER CONTACTS

Alpena Michigan Convention and Visitors Bureau, 235 West Chisolm Street, Alpena. Call 989-354-4181 or 1-800-4-ALPENA (25738). Website: alpenacvb.com.

Oscoda Area Convention and Visitors Bureau. Call 989-739-0900 or 1-877-8-OSCODA (672632). Website: oscoda.com.

Rogers City Chamber of Commerce, 292 South Bradley Highway, Rogers City. Call 1-800-622-4148. Website: rogerscity.com.

Tawas Bay Tourist and Convention Bureau, 402 East Lake Street (US 23), Tawas. Call 1-877-868-2927. Website: tawasbay.com.

Arch Rock has been a stop of Mackinac Island sightseers for generations. *Kim Forster*

9 Where Great Lakes Meet: The Straits of Mackinac and the St. Mary's River

MACKINAW CITY, MACKINAC ISLAND, HESSEL & CEDARVILLE, THE ISLANDS OF THE ST. MARY'S, AND SAULT STE. MARIE

Estimated length: 150 miles

Estimated time: 3 hours (plus another 30 minutes for the round-trip ferry to Mackinac Island)

Getting there: Our route starts in the Lower Peninsula in Mackinaw City. Take I-75 north to exit 339, the last exit before the Mackinac Bridge. Continuing north across the Straits of Mackinac, exit I-75 at North Huron Shore Drive (aka MI 134), heading east. Passing through the town of Hessel, turn north in Cedarville on MI 129. (Or continue east to visit De Tour State Park and Drummond Island.) Sault Ste. Marie is 34 miles north of Cedarville (about an hour's drive). Portage Avenue along the river is where all the sights on the U.S. side are. Cross the bridge for Canada's Sault Ste. Marie.

Highlights: The early history of Europeans in North America is told at several sites around the historic Straits of Mackinac. Near Mackinaw City, on the south shore of the passage is Colonial Michilimackinac, a military outpost and trading center occupied by the French and later the British. The Historic Mill Creek centers on a reconstructed mill, first built in 1790. Also in Mac City, you can tour the recently restored Old Mackinac Point Lighthouse. Take the ferry ride out to Mackinac Island for more history and tour Fort Mackinac and downtown Mackinac. You can also take in the Grand Hotel, grab a bite in town, or take a leisurely carriage or bike-ride tour of the island. And, of course, be sure to pick up some Murdick's Fudge. Crossing the Mackinac Bridge (or Big Mac) and heading east along Lake Huron's northern shoreline, explore the little towns of Hessel and Cedarville, both of which

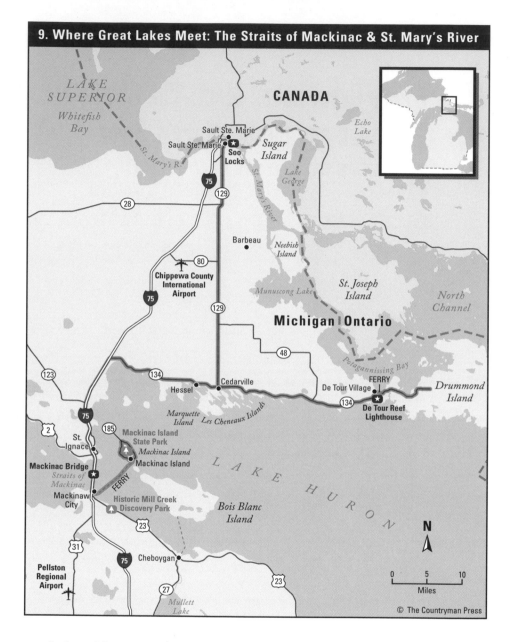

9. Where Great Lakes Meet: The Straits of Mackinac & St. Mary's River

are sheltered from the vagaries of the open lake by Les Cheneaux Islands. These 36 islands can be explored by kayak; rentals and guided trips are available through a local outfitter. From Cedarville, continue east for a side trip to De Tour Village and Drummond Island, or head directly to Sault Ste. Marie to explore the Soo Locks. On the Canadian side of the border there's shopping in Sault Ste. Marie, Ontario, and a popular train excursion to Canada's Agawa Canyon.

Mackinaw City can be a frantically paced tourist town with T-shirt shops, restaurants, a row of hotels one after the other along the lake, and plenty of places to buy fudge and ice cream. On summer weekends, the sidewalks are as packed with pedestrians as the streets are with cars and RVs, and if this town was much bigger than a few blocks, the traffic would be overwhelming. Since everything is so close and there's really nowhere to go that you can't walk to, traffic tends to be just a short-lived frustration.

Behind the endless entrepreneurial efforts to snag your tourist dollars, Mackinaw City offers many opportunities for visitors to learn about and experience the history of the Straits of Mackinac. (You should know that *Mackinaw* and *Mackinac* are two ways of spelling the same word. They're both pronounced with *aw* at the end. The latter seems to be used more often when referring to historic sites.) As Henry Rowe Schoolcraft said in his field report in 1820, "The island of Michilimackinac, and the adjacent coasts, have been the theatre of some of the most interesting

Fort Michilimackinac sits above town on the island's high ground.

Reinactments are a big draw at Fort Michilimackinac.

events in the history of the settlement of the northwestern regions of our continent."

The first known European to pass the Straits was French explorer Jean Nicolet, who in 1624 was searching for the fabled Northwest Passage. The land he discovered, however, was teeming with beaver, not the Chinese. He was followed by trappers and traders looking to cash in on Europe's sudden keenness for beaver pelts and other furs. These voyageurs and *coureur des bois* (literally, "runner of the woods") were often the first Europeans to interact with Native Americans.

Recognizing the strategic importance of the Straits of Mackinac, the French built Fort St. Phillippe de Michilimackinac near an Ottawa village and its Jesuit mission on the south side of the Straits in 1715. The settlement soon became the center of the Great Lakes fur trade. The fort was taken over by the British in 1761 and moved to Mackinac Island in 1780. They used what parts of the fort they could for the new **Fort Mackinac,** and the rest was burned. Since the 1950s, archaeologists have been excavating the site, and they have built a reasonably accurate reconstruction of the original fort.

Today's Colonial Michilimackinac represents this important trading post and military settlement as it existed in the 1770s. Part of **Michilimackinac State Park,** the reconstructed fort overlooks the Straits. In the summer, historical interpreters play the parts of soldiers and civilians who would have lived and worked here over two hundred years ago. The park is on the west end of Huron Avenue, past I-75. Once you see the palisade walls, you know you've arrived.

Another historic site is about 7 miles southeast of Mackinaw City on Mill Creek. In the 1780s, Robert Campbell built a sawmill on the creek, and for 40 years the mill cut planks for Mackinac Island. Over time the mill was forgotten and lost to history. Then, in 1972, the site was discovered by an amateur archaeologist. Since then the area has been painstakingly excavated, and a reproduction of the mill has been built. Inside, guests can watch as timber is processed into lumber, as it was done in the 18th century. Be sure to check out the Millwright's House for a look at the mill stones. They are central to the story of how the Mill Creek site was discovered.

If that were all she wrote, the state park would certainly be worth a visit, but the **Historic Mill Creek Discovery Park** is so much more than a historical attraction. In addition to the human history, natural history is explored with the Adventure Tour. Guests cross a canopy bridge through the trees, tackle a climbing wall that serves as a vertical nature trail, and get an eagle's-eye view of the creek on the Eagle's Flight Zip Line.

Back in Mackinaw City, be sure to tour the **Old Mackinac Point Lighthouse.** Originally built in 1892, the lighthouse featured a sprawling residence that housed two keepers and their families. The architecture, with its towers and battlements, is unlike any other lighthouse on the Great Lakes. To some, it resembles a miniature castle. The light has been restored to its appearance in 1910. Guests can take a tour that includes a trip up the tower and into the lantern room. On the first floor, exhibits and hands-on demonstrations let visitors experience the life of a light keeper.

For dining, downtown Mackinaw City has plenty of options. For simple family dining, **Darrow's Family Restaurant** has been taking care of visitors for over 50 years. They make everything from scratch, from the whitefish dinner to the burger basket. In true diner style, there are stacks of homemade pies for dessert. Serving breakfast, lunch, and dinner, Darrow's is west of I-75 on Louvingney Street at the corner of James. In my experience, some of the fancier places in town aren't worth the extra money.

From Mackinaw City, **Shepler's, Arnold's,** and **Star Line** all offer ferry service to Mackinac Island. They also make runs from St. Ignace north of the bridge. Shepler's has several lighthouse cruises that explore lighthouses you simply can't

In addition to thrilling exploration, Old Mill Creek offers some historical perspective as well.

The Round Island Lighthouse greets ferries from the mainland.

Horses and bikes share the road on Mackinac Island.

drive to. Their two-day "Grand" Lighthouse Cruise includes a night at the Grand Hotel on Mackinac Island. The other ferry services, Arnold's and Starline, have regularly scheduled sunset cruises, and on Sunday evenings Arnold's has a Vespers Service.

Mackinac Island has been a tourist destination since the 19th century. Early on, the local carriage operators lobbied to have automobiles banned from the island, and Mackinac has remained car-free ever since. Most everything on the island is delivered by horse-drawn carts, and seeing the UPS delivery driver behind the reins never ceases to get a chuckle from first-time visitors.

For those who limit their visit to a few hours on the main drag, Mackinac Island can be discouraging. All the advertising would have you believe the island is an idyllic throwback to the 19th century, but all you see are thousands of tourists jostling for a place in line at any one of the half dozen fudge shops on Main Street. But there is much more to Mackinac Island than this strip of whitewashed storefronts. Walk just a few blocks in any direction, and the scene changes dramatically.

Interspersed in between private homes, galleries, and bed & breakfasts, the buildings of Mackinac's historic downtown offer a unique look at the island's history. On Market Street, one block back from Main (aka Huron Street), the Biddle House and the

Benjamin Blacksmith Shop are great places to start your tour. Edward Biddle moved to the island after the War of 1812 from the east and married a local woman. This is their home. The McGulpin House on Fort Street is one of the oldest buildings on Mackinac, dating from the 1780s. The steep roof and unique way the log walls are joined set it apart from most other historic buildings in Michigan.

There are plenty of bikes to rent if you didn't bring your own.

Across from the Bark Chapel, which is a replica of the one once used on the island by a Jesuit missionary in 1670, is the Dr. Beaumont Museum. William Beaumont was a doctor on the island in the early 19th century. In 1822 Alexis St. Martin, a voyageur working for the American Fur Company, was accidentally shot in the stomach with a musket. Drive Beaumont treated the wound but expected the man to die. St. Martin didn't die, and neither did his wound completely heal over. Off and on over the next 11 years, Beaumont used this "window" into St. Martin's stomach to learn about digestion. St. Martin would go on to live until the age

The best way to get around the island is on a bike.

of 86—an exceptional bout of longevity in those days.

As the ferry passes the Round Island Passage Light into Mackinac Island's Haldimand Bay, visitors see the most prominent structure on the island, **Fort Mackinac,** which stands guard high on the bluff above town. The fort was built by the British in 1779 during the American Revolution, and they occupied the fort until 1796. During the War of 1812, the British surprised the American troops stationed on the island: Under the cover of night, they had moved artillery onto the higher ground behind the fort. Without argument, the Americans surrendered, and the British took possession of the island once again. In 1814, the Treaty of Ghent returned Mackinac to the Americans, and the Brits left for good.

The fort is a very active historic site. Visitors can walk the walls, tour the buildings, and witness regular musket-firing demonstrations. A museum in the fort traces Mackinac Island's history back before the arrival of Europeans. Live historical interpreters play the roles of the fort's one-time residents.

In the 1820s, the island became the central fur trading post for the American Fur Company, and as the fur trade petered out, fishing became an important local industry. In 1875, Mackinac Island became the country's second national park, just a few years after Yellowstone was established. Soldiers at Fort Mackinac served as park caretakers. **Mackinac Island State Park,** which is Michigan's first state park, was established when Michigan leaders moved to have the national park transferred to state control. The park covers about 80 percent of the island.

Another way to see what Mackinac has to offer is to ditch town altogether and make a tour along MI 185. This highway makes an 8-mile loop encircling the island —it's the only state highway in Michigan that doesn't permit motorized vehicles. In the summer, it's a short walk east from downtown for the view of Arch Rock. A steep staircase leads to Arch Rock Road above, which in turn leads to the back entrance of the fort.

On warm summer days the road is used by couples on tandem bicycles and parents biking with little ones in tow. From time to time a horse-drawn cart or a group on horseback will pass by. The entire trip can take an hour by bike if you don't make any stops. Plan on two hours if your itinerary includes visiting some of the roadside parks, checking out the British Landing Nature Center, or grabbing a bite at the Cannonball Drive-In (a small concession stand at British Landing).

The road is level all the way around, and at least half of it is always in the shade. Away from the shore, roads and bike trails crisscross the island. From lake level, it's a steep climb inland, but that's where you will find some of Mackinac's less frequented spots, like the remains of Fort Holmes or the Battlefield of 1814.

For a nice introduction to Mackinac Island, consider a ride with **Mackinac Island Carriage Tours.** The tour itself takes no more than 90 minutes, but it makes good sense to extend the tour by spending some time at the midpoint. The carriage ride begins downtown, passing the Grand Hotel on its way to a change of carriages at the Surrey Hills Museum. When you purchase tickets in town, you can pay a little more to access the **Wings of Mackinac Butterfly Conservatory.** Much smaller than most butterfly conservatories, this one makes up for its size with an abundance of butterflies. With little effort, kids will soon have butterflies landing on their fingers.

From the museum stop, the tour takes you through portions of the state park.

You pass the old island cemetery, Arch Rock, and the Avenue of Flags up to the back entrance of Fort Mackinac.

Downtown has plenty of T-shirt shops and candy stores. Murdick's Fudge is a regional favorite, with shops all over northern Michigan—several right on Mackinac Island. The **Island Bookstore** has one of the best selections anywhere of books about Michigan and by Michigan authors—especially those about northern Michigan and Mackinac Island. The bookstore is located in the entrance for the Lilac Tree Inn off Main Street.

Wings of Mackinac is located on Surrey Hill.

For a quick lunch with a great view, visit the **Windermere Doghouse**, the yellow-and-white concession stand southwest of town next to the public library. They serve Koegel Polish sausages, brats, and hot dogs (with or without chili). You can enjoy your meal at one of the yellow-umbrellaed picnic tables across from the Windermere Hotel, on the point. This spot is reserved for hotel guests and Doghouse patrons.

The **Village Inn,** right across from the Shepler's Ferry docks at Huron Street and Hoban, is one of the nicest restaurants in town. In fact, the readers of the *Detroit Free Press* ranked the restaurant the Best in Northern Michigan. They serve breakfast, lunch, and dinner. The dinner menu features steak and their famous planked whitefish. For lunch try their Great Lakes fish and chips. Open year-round, the V.I. serves a pared-down menu in the winter (with pared-down prices to match).

A newer addition to the lodgings on Main Street is the **Bicycle Street Inn & Suites.** Street-side rooms overlook the ferry docks and bustling carriage traffic. In the lobby, guests eat a complimentary breakfast at the small sandwich shop, and there's a Sanders' Fudge right next to reception. Perfect for after-tour snacking.

The best-known hotel on the island is the **Grand Hotel,** which was built in 1887

AN ISLAND PHENOMENON: *SOMEWHERE IN TIME*

In 1979, Christopher Reeve and Jane Seymour filmed *Somewhere in Time* at the Grand Hotel. In the movie, modern-day Richard Collier (played by Reeve) travels back to Mackinac Island, circa 1912, to fall in love with Elise McKenna, a famed actress (played by Seymour). Though the movie bombed at the box office, it later earned a following with the VHS release and plenty of play on the cable channels. It's hard to say whether it's passion for the movie that brings fans to the island, or a passion for the island that has created interest in the movie. In either case, there are souvenirs aplenty on the island—everything from lobby posters to T-shirts to replica props used in the film.

---

in high Victorian style. The front lawns are painstakingly landscaped, and over a hundred rocking chairs line the long front porch, which overlooks the Straits. In an effort to promote the values travelers cherished a hundred years ago, a dress code is enforced in the evenings (coat and tie for gentlemen and dresses or pantsuits for women), and even day visitors who pay for a peek at the lobby must conform to certain standards. Breakfast and dinner are included in the price of a room, but nonguests are also welcome to eat in the hotel's many restaurants.

Just down the street from the Grand is the **Hotel Iroquois on the Beach.** Built as a private home in 1900, it was transformed into a hotel in 1904. Banks of windows let light into every room and offer guests views of the Straits. Close to downtown, the hotel nonetheless provides a quiet retreat from the bustling crowds of tourists. The docks are right next door, and the ferry captains regularly sound the ships' horns to announce their arrival (not a problem at night because ferry service ends rather early). The hotel's Carriage House dining room has an excellent reputation

Across town from the Grand Hotel is the beautiful Misson Point Resort.

The Mackinac Bridge *Kim Forster*

for breakfast, lunch, and dinner. Guests dine with a view of the water from the enclosed dining room or from one of the waterfront verandas.

Bogan Lane Inn is one of the few lodgings open year-round on Mackinac Island. Located east of the fort on a quiet street, the inn has four rooms that can sleep up to 11 guests. Each room shares a bath with one other room. A continental breakfast is served each morning, and the fireplace in the living room is a welcome treat on chilly rainy days. The owner of the inn, a lifelong island resident, is happy to share her experience. All this, and the inn is one of Mackinac's most affordable accommodations.

Having explored the Straits, cross the Mackinac Bridge to Michigan's Upper Peninsula. Folks in the U.P. call themselves "yoopers." They call tourists "fudgies" (since area tourists tend to spend a lot of time in the fudge shops), and folks from below the bridge are kindly referred to as "trolls." Before the Mackinac Bridge was built in 1957, Michigan was a divided state. Ferry service was first established in 1881 with the *Algomah,* which brought passenger and freight across the Straits, towing a barge that could hold four railroad cars. As automobile traffic increased, ferries carried passengers and their cars from peninsula to peninsula. Though nine ferries were at one time moving nine thousand cars a day, traffic would often back up 15 to 20 miles (especially during hunting season).

The view from Hessel

The Mackinac Bridge (often called "Mighty Mac" or "Big Mac") changed all that. For a culture obsessed with being the biggest or the best or the first, the bridge had the interesting distinction of being the longest suspension bridge between two anchorages in the world. Over the years, some doozies have apparently been built in the Eastern Hemisphere, because the Mackinac Bridge is now officially the longest bridge with two towers between anchorages in the Western Hemisphere. It is, nonetheless, quite impressive. At its highest, cars are 200 feet above the Straits, and the bridge's two towers rise 552 feet above the water. From end to end, counting the long run-ups on either side, the bridge is 5 miles long.

For three years, 2,100 men worked on building the bridge. In the process five men died. The **Mackinac Bridge Museum** in Mackinaw City tells the story of the iron workers whose labor made the bridge possible. The museum, which was above Mama Mia's, was destroyed along with the restaurant by fire in 2005. In 2007, the museum returned to its post above the rebuilt Mama Mia's. The museum has a 30-minute video showing images of the bridge being built.

Mighty Mac is closed to pedestrians except for the annual Mackinac Bridge Walk. Each Labor Day, tens of thousands of walkers make the one-way trek along the two northbound lanes, which are closed to traffic. It's a festive event, with the governor and other politicians in attendance for a hearty round of glad-handing with their constituents.

North of St. Ignace, North Huron Shore Drive makes its way east around St. Martin Bay to the villages of Hessel and Cedarville. Along the way, you get stunning peeks of Lake Huron when the trees clear. On a good day you can see the towers of the Mackinac Bridge in the far distance.

Les Cheneaux Islands—nicknamed "the Snows"—are a paddler's paradise. These 36 islands are scattered along 12 miles of Lake Huron, and the countless channels and bays act as a buffer against the wiles of the greater lake. Hessel and Cedarville have long been the unofficial gateways to the islands. Though summer is the tourist season, the towns remain laid-back and unpretentious. Summer homes and rental cottages dot the shore, and boathouses, small marinas, and long-reaching wooden docks provide access to the water.

Though there are places to camp out on the islands—Government Island, for example, is part of the Hiawatha National Forest and has primitive facilities—many of the islands are privately owned. To get oriented, consider a paddling expedition with **Woods & Water Ecotours** in Hessel. This outfitter tours all over the region—from nature hikes on Bois Blanc Island near Cheboygan to snowshoeing along the coast of Lake Superior. Regularly scheduled kayak trips in the summer explore Les Cheneaux Islands and Drummond Island.

The **Les Cheneaux Historical Museum** in Cedarville tells about the region's history with artifacts like Native American tools and crafts displayed alongside a logging-camp diorama and model ships representing those that have sailed the local waters. The museum is maintained by the Les Cheneaux Historical Association and is housed in a log cabin (with a hearty addition) on South Meridian Street. Also run by the historical association is the **Les Cheneaux Maritime Museum**, on MI 134 east of the Cedarville light. This museum, housed in the O. M. Reif Boathouse (circa 1920), displays vintage boats and antique outboard motors, and in the summer offers a boatbuilding workshop.

Les Cheneaux Islands Art Gallery in Hessel features the art of Diana Windsor Grenier. Diana and her husband, John, began their business, Up North Studio, in 1994. Her paintings

For exploring the Les Cheneaux Islands, check in with Hessel Woods & Water Ecotours

Les Cheneaux Historical Museum in Cedarville

The view from Cedarville

and pastels document the imagery of the entire region. Boats docked in Cedarville, the Round Island Light, a classic boathouse on the lake—all of these are captured by Grenier's artistry and celebrated. The gallery is right on MI 134, just east of the blinking light in Cedarville.

For food, the **Hessel Bay Inn** serves breakfast, lunch, and dinner. The restaurant, with its patio seating overlooking the Hessel marina, is a popular nightspot. Locals and regular summer folk love the menu, which features made-from-scratch cooking.

The next stop is Sault Ste. Marie. Follow MI 129 north from Cedarville for 35 miles. The highway ends in the Soo.

The Hessel Bay Inn is the place to eat in Hessel.

Sault Ste. Marie is the northern terminus of I-75, which stretches 1,700 miles south and ends just northwest of Miami, Florida. With over sixteen thousand residents, it is the largest city in the eastern part of the peninsula and a main driver of the region's economy.

In 1671, a group of French officials called together Native Americans from 14 different nations to meet them beside the St. Mary's River, a favorite fishing ground because of the nearby rapids. There, in an elaborate cere-mony, later to be known as the Pageant of the Sault, the French raised a huge cross and claimed the territory for the king of France. Sault Ste. Marie, the oldest European settlement in the Mid-west, has long been a meeting ground; French missionaries settled at the Soo in 1668 because they wanted to be close to the large number of Chippewas en-camped by the rapids.

Visitors can get up close as towering freighters pass through the Soo Locks.

Nowadays, people gather at Sault Ste. Marie to explore the Soo Locks and watch the freighters as they pass. From Lake Superior to Lake Huron, the St. Mary's River drops 21 feet, creating the St. Mary's Rapids. For centuries, travelers had to portage around the rapids if they wanted to make their way between the lakes. After the U.P.'s vast mineral resources were discovered in the 19th century, there needed to be a way to open Lake Supe-rior to Great Lakes shipping, and the locks were born. In 2005, the city celebrated the 150th anniversary of the first lock, which was completed in 1855.

The locks are best viewed from the **Soo Locks Park.** The visitors center has displays telling about the history of the locks and a model showing how they work. There's also a screen that tracks freighters as they cross the Great Lakes and ap-proach the St. Mary's River. Outside, a two-story platform allows visitors a bird's-eye view of the locks as ships pass through.

The locks, however, are not all that Sault Ste. Marie has to offer. In recent years, more and more visitors have been coming to Sault Ste. Marie to explore the surrounding countryside, play a little golf, and visit the Kewadin Sault Casino just south of town. One popular stop is the **Museum Ship** *Valley Camp,* which is part of the Sault Historic Sites. Once a freighter that plied the Great Lakes, the *Valley Camp* now serves as a maritime museum. Inside there are over a hundred exhibits, includ-ing four aquariums that are stocked with regional species of fish and two lifeboats from the *Edmund Fitzgerald.* Another museum is the **Tower of History.** Once the beginning of a poorly conceived Catholic shrine, the 210-foot tower offers visitors a view of the entire Sault. Exhibits tell the story of the first missionaries, who were an important part of the European settlement of this part of the world.

For a bite to eat, Sault Ste. Marie has two drive-ins. Near the dock for the Sugar Island Ferry, **Clyde's Drive-In** customers rave about the C-burger. Diners have

DRUMMOND ISLAND AND THE ISLANDS OF ST. MARY'S

At the eastern tip of the Upper Peninsula, De Tour Village is the last stop before stepping on the ferry and crossing the De Tour Passage to Drummond Island. There used to be a state park here, but it has become part of the Lake Superior State Forest. Still, there are some campsites for those who prefer a low-amenity camping experience (we're talking vault toilets and a hand pump). There are also nice picnic grounds and swimming.

The Drummond Island ferry leaves hourly during the season and makes the crossing in 10 minutes. Once on the island, you will have to make your own fun. Most summer tourist activities involve fishing or paddling around the island's rocky shoreline. In the winter, snowmobiling is a popular activity. Drummond Island is the biggest island in the St. Mary's River and the largest freshwater island in the United States. It sits in Lake Huron at the mouth of the St. Mary's River.

The De Tour Reef Lighthouse was built in 1931 on the reef 1 mile from shore. To access the light, visitors are brought out by boat. For safety reasons,

their choice of eating in or eating in their car. The **West Pier Drive-In** is located at the far west end of Portage Avenue, underneath the bridge to Canada. The servings are huge: The burger is a 1-pounder. They also have a neat way of serving hot dogs on a hamburger bun. Both drive-ins are next to the river, great for watching freighters while you eat.

For a unique-to-the-Soo experience, consider dining at **The Antlers.** Their appetizers alone are worth the stop—whitefish dip, beer cheese, fried pickle chips, and cheese skewers. Their version of the Canadian dish *poutine* is a pile of fries topped with mozzarella and gravy, and they serve stews in bread canoes. The decor is strictly Yooper, and the restaurant gets its name for all the antlers lining the walls, ceilings, etc.—and kids love the loud bells and horns that go off at random intervals.

IN THE AREA

ACCOMMODATIONS

Algoma's Water Tower Inn, 360 Great Northern Road, Sault Ste. Marie, Ontario, Canada. Call 705-949-8111 or 1-800-461-0800. Website: watertower inn.com.

Bicycle Street Inn & Suites, 7416 Main Street, Mackinac Island. Call 906-847-8005. Website: bicyclestreet inn.com.

guests are then strapped into a harness before they begin climbing the ladder up to the main platform.

If a short tour of the lighthouse doesn't sound like enough, you can make arrangements to serve as a temporary lighthouse keeper. For one weekend you can live in the lighthouse, bake cookies for visitors, and staff the gift shop. Of course you have to pay for the opportunity, but it's a once-in-a-lifetime experience.

Farther upriver, there are many islands—Lime Island is the first of any real size, then Neebish and Sugar Islands nearer to Sault Ste. Marie. You can catch a ferry in the Soo that will take you to Sugar Island, and the ferry to Neebish is out of Barbeau. These islands are not well populated, though Sugar Island (the larger, with seven hundred residents) does boast an ice cream shop and a bar. Each island has a growing number of resorts—typically someone with a cabin or two to rent—where you can stay and fish. A boat is usually included in the package.

Bogan Lane Inn. Call 906-847-3439. Website: boganlaneinn.com.

Brockwell Chambers B&B, 183 Brock Street, Sault Ste. Marie, Ontario, Canada. Call 705-949-1076. They don't accept credit cards. Website: brockwell .biz.

Grand Hotel, 1 Grand Avenue, Mackinac Island. Call 1-800-33-GRAND (47263). Website: grandhotel.com.

Hotel Iroquois on the Beach, 7485 Main Street, Mackinac Island. Call 906-847-3321. Website: iroquoishotel .com.

ATTRACTIONS AND RECREATION

Agawa Canyon Tour Train, 129 Bay Street, Sault Ste. Marie, Ontario, Canada. Call 705-946-7300 or 1-800-242-

9287. Website: agawacanyontourtrain .com.

De Tour Reef Lighthouse, Drummond Island. Website: drlps.com/ Lighthouse.aspx.

Fort Mackinac, 7127 Huron Road, Mackinac Island. Call 906-847-3328 (May–Sept.) or 231-436-4100 (Oct.–Apr.). Website: mackinacparks.com.

Historic Mill Creek Discovery Park, 9001 US 23, Mackinaw City. Call 231-436-4100. Website: mackinacparks .com.

Island Bookstore. Call 906-847-6202. Inside the Lilac Tree Inn entrance off Main Street. Website: islandbookstore .com.

Les Cheneaux Historical Museum. Call 906-484-2821. Look for the dark brown log cabin south of the light

THE CANADIAN SIDE OF THE SOO

Though the larger locks used for the big freighters are located on the Michigan side of the border, the Ontario side has become the center of tourist activity and offers plenty of options for travelers when it comes to lodging, dining, and shopping. It is also where people go to catch the Agawa Canyon Tour Train, operated by the Algoma Central Railway. This train makes regular runs north for a sight-seeing tour that passes through 114 miles of Canada's most pristine wilderness. The trip is especially popular in the fall.

The Algoma's Water Tower Inn in downtown Sault Ste. Marie caters to every kind of guest, from the business traveler to the spa seeker to the outdoor adventurer. For the latter, the hotel offers packages that include everything from arranging for your lodgings to getting you in touch with businesses that can outfit your entire trip, be it backpacking, mountain bike riding, fishing, ice climbing, or whatever.

The Brockwell Chambers B&B has four rooms, which all include a private bath, cable TV, air-conditioning, and high-speed Internet access. Two of the rooms have Jacuzzis. Breakfast is served at individual tables in the dining room, and the rotating menu includes French toast and omelets. In the sitting room, you can relax by the fireplace and enjoy complimentary wine while playing a game of chess or reading a book.

on Meridian Road. Open in the summer; see Website for hours. Website: lchistorical.org.

Les Cheneaux Islands Art Gallery, 2960 West MI 134, Hessel. Call 906-322-2886 or 906-484-3949. The gallery is on MI 134, just east of the blinking light. Website: lescheneauxislandsart gallery.com.

Les Cheneaux Maritime Museum. Call 906-484-3354. The museum is on MI 134, two blocks east of the light. Open in the summer; see Website for hours. Website: lchistorical.org.

Mackinac Bridge Museum, 231 East Central Avenue, Mackinaw City. Call 231-436-5534. Open May through Oct. Website: mightymac.org/bridge museum.htm.

Mackinac Island Carriage Tours, 7278 Main Street, Mackinac Island. Call 906-847-3307. Website: mict.com.

Mackinac Island State Park, Mackinac Island. Call 906-847-3328 (May–Sept.) or 231-436-4100 (Oct.–Apr.). Website: mackinacparks.com.

Michilimackinac State Park, 102 West Straits Avenue, Mackinaw City. Call 231-436-4100. Website: mackinac parks.com.

Museum Ship *Valley Camp*, 501 East Water Street, Sault Ste. Marie. Call 906-635-3658 or 1-888-744-7867. The Tower of History, one of the other Sault museums, is just southeast of town on Portage Avenue. The Museum Ship is one block closer to the river on Water Street. Website: saulthistoric sites.com.

Old Mackinac Point Lighthouse, 526 North Huron Avenue, Mackinaw City. Call 231-436-4100. Website: mackinacparks.com.

Soo Locks Park, Sault Ste. Marie. Call 906-253-9101. Website: saultstemarie.com/soo-locks-46.

Tower of History, 326 East Portage Avenue, Sault Ste. Marie. Call 906-632-3658 . Website: saulthistoricsites.com/tower-of-history-4.

Wings of Mackinac Butterfly Conservatory, Surrey Hill, Mackinac Island. Call 906-847-9464. Website: wingsofmackinac.com.

Woods & Water Ecotours, 20 Pickford Avenue, Hessel. Call 906-484-4157. Website: woodswaterecotours.com.

DINING

The Antlers, 804 East Portage Avenue, Sault Ste. Marie. Call 906-253-1728. Website: saultantlers.com.

Clyde's Drive-In, 1425 Riverside Drive, Sault Ste. Marie. Call 906-632-2581. Located east of town near the Sugar Island Ferry.

Darrow's Family Restaurant, 303 Louvingney Street, Mackinaw City. Call 231-436-5514. Located at the corner of Louvingney and James. Open May through Oct. Website: darrowsrestaurant.com.

Hessel Bay Inn, 186 South Pickford Avenue, Hessel. Call 906-848-2460. Open daily in the summer; call for off-season hours.

Village Inn. Call 906-847-3542. Open year-round; located across from the Shepler's Ferry dock. Website: viofmackinac.com.

West Pier Drive-In, 601 West Portage Avenue, Sault Ste. Marie. Call 906-632-0444. This drive-in is under the bridge to Canada at the west end of Portage Avenue.

Windermere Doghouse. Call 1-800-847-3125. Website: windermerehotel.com/doghouse.htm.

TRANSPORTATION

Arnold Mackinac Island Ferry, 801 South Huron Street, Mackinaw City. Call 906-847-3351. Website: arnoldline.com.

Shepler's Mackinac Island Ferry, 556 East Central, Mackinaw City. Call 231-436-5023. Website: sheplersferry.com.

Star Line Mackinac Island Hydro-Jet Ferry, 711 South Huron, Mackinaw City. Call 1-800-638-9892. Website: mackinacferry.com.

OTHER CONTACTS

Les Cheneaux Islands Chamber of Commerce, 680 West MI 134, Cedarville. Call 906-484-3935 or 1-888-364-7526. Website: lescheneaux.net.

Mackinac Island Tourism Bureau. Call 1-877-847-0086. Website: mackinacisland.org.

Mackinaw City Chamber of Tourism. Call 1-800-577-3113. Website: mackinaw-city.com.

St. Ignace Visitors Bureau, 6 Spring Street, Suite 100, St. Ignace. Call 1-800-338-6660. Website: stignace.com.

Sault Ste. Marie Chamber of Commerce, 2581 I-75 Business Spur, Sault Ste. Marie. Call 906-632-3301. Website: saultstemarie.org.

The power of Lake Superior cuts arches into the cliff walls.

10 Superior's Scenic Shoreline

POINT IROQUOIS LIGHTHOUSE, WHITEFISH POINT, NEWBERRY, GRAND MARAIS, MUNISING & AU TRAIN, AND MARQUETTE

Estimated length: 200 miles

Estimated time: 7 hours

Getting there: From the Mackinac Bridge, drive north on I-75 about 8 miles to exit 352 and MI 123. Take MI 123 north 55 miles to Paradise. This portion of the trip will take about two hours. From Paradise, take MI 123 to Newberry and south to MI 28. Cut north to Grand Marais on MI 77. Back on MI 28, drive to Munising, Au Train, and Marquette. To add a couple-hour side trip to Big Bay, continue north of Marquette on Big Bay Road.

Highlights: Beginning at the historic Point Iroquois Lighthouse on Whitefish Bay, you follow the shoreline around the bay west and north until you reach Whitefish Point, where you can take in the beauty of Lake Superior from the beach. Tour the Whitefish Point Lighthouse and the Coast Guard Station, and get an idea of how dangerous the Great Lakes can really be at the Great Lakes Shipwreck Museum. Heading south and inland a bit, take in the Tahquamenon Falls at Tahquamenon Falls State Park. The park boasts the most moose sightings in the state. From Newberry, you can travel north for fishing or paddling on the famous Two Hearted River. In Grand Marais, visit the Au Sable Point Light Station. Then it's on to Munising to witness Lake Superior's breathtaking Pictured Rocks. The best way to see these sandstone cliffs is to take a tour with Pictured Rocks Cruises. Also interesting are the glass-bottom boat trips offered by Shipwreck Tours. While in Munising, make an excursion into the Pictured Rocks National Lakeshore and hike to some waterfalls or one of the hidden beaches. Grab a bite at the Brownstone Inn in Au Train before continuing to Marquette, a great home base for fall-color tours or winter sports in the surrounding wilderness.

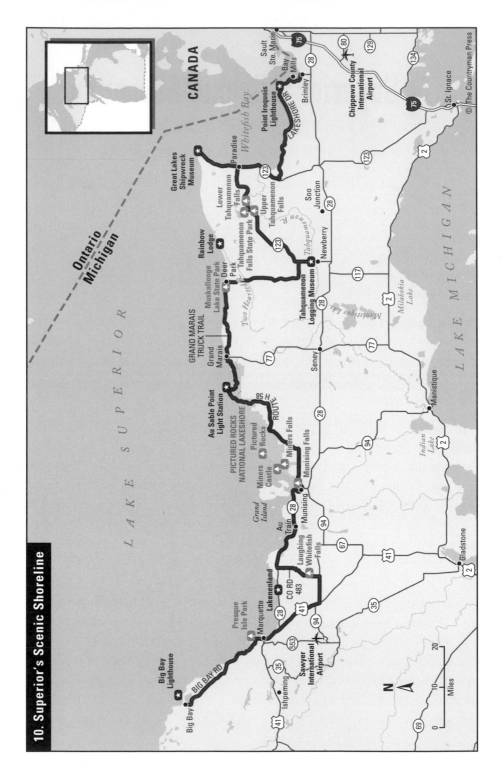

10. Superior's Scenic Shoreline

The Song of Hiawatha by Henry Wadsworth Longfellow was inspired by the stories Henry Rowe Schoolcraft was told by his Ojibwa wife. The epic poem tells of an Ojibwa chieftain who lived "By the shores of Gitche Gumee / By the shining Big-Sea-Water" and welcomed the first French explorers. The driving meter of the poem is reminiscent of the Kalevala, the epic poems of the Finnish people, whose sons and daughters would later join thousands of European immigrants bound for Michigan's Upper Peninsula to work in the mines by the shores of Gitche Gumee.

The Great Lake was called *le lac supérieur* by the French, or simply Lake Superior—so named because it was originally believed to be the most northerly of two large lakes. However, the lake is superior in ways other than geography. The deepest of the five Great Lakes, Superior has enough volume to cover both North and South America in a foot of water. The bottom of the lake is 700 feet below sea level, the deepest spot in North America. Its average temperature is 40 degrees, and it doesn't warm much in the summer.

The northern shore of the Upper Peninsula is a rugged place; it's not the gentrified wilderness of the northern Lower Peninsula. Roads are often less traveled, the weather can be harsh, and black flies and mosquitoes are difficult in early and midsummer. But there is a beauty in this wilderness: Short summer days explode with green and then give way to autumn's vibrant color show, Lake Superior grows restless and leaves you short of breath as its waves beat against rocky shore, and it is a grand spectacle to watch nature surviving in this often hostile environment.

This route begins at the **Point Iroquois Lighthouse** on **Whitefish Bay**. The lighthouse, 7.5 miles north of Brimley, guides ships entering the St. Mary's River from Lake Superior. In 1662, the local Ojibwa discovered a group of invading Iroquois encamped on the point. After a day of fighting, the Iroquois were completely wiped out. This battle was the last in a long war, which essentially stopped the Iroquois from encroaching westward into Ojibwa territory. The point was named for the massacre.

This lighthouse, built in 1870, is the second on the point.

The first lighthouse on the point was lit in 1857, and its tower and small keeper's home were replaced in 1870 with the lighthouse and residence you see today. The Bay Mills–Brimley Historical Research Society maintains the light, and they have restored much of the property and created a maritime

Monocle Lake makes this a popular campground for anglers.

museum. The museum is open daily throughout the summer and into October.

Following Lakeshore Drive westward, you can catch glimpses of the lake on your right. Much of this land is part of the Hiawatha National Forest, and along the route are a day-use park and a few national forest campgrounds. In fact, just east of the Point Iroquois Lighthouse is a quiet national forest campground on **Monocle Lake.** The site features a hike high up a bluff with views of Lake Superior.

It is 36 miles from the lighthouse to Paradise. Along the way you will pass the mouth of the Tahquamenon River and its accompanying state park campground.

Paradise benefits from its proximity to Whitefish Point and the Tahquamenon Falls. Paddling, fishing, and camping are common summer activities, and in the winter snowmobilers ride the backwoods trails. With the exception of several independently owned motels (and some places that rent cottages), most of the businesses in town—a general store/gas station, a few gift shops, the grocery store—seem to exist for the convenience of locals and a few folks who are just passing through. From Paradise, the shore makes a graceful curve into Whitefish Bay, terminating 11 miles to the north at the point.

The Whitefish Point Lighthouse stands at the tip of Whitefish Point surrounded by a complex of buildings that was once a Coast Guard Station. The light marks

WHEELS OF HISTORY MUSEUM

At one time, the towns of Brimley and Bay Mills in the U.P. were connected by train. The railroad is gone and Bay Mills is no more, but the Wheels of History Museum keeps the memory of both alive.

Most likely you'll pass through Brimley on the way to the Point Iroquois Lighthouse. If you have time, and the museum is open, it's worth a stop. The museum itself is housed in an old train car and caboose. The Bay Mills–Brimley Historical Research Society, which runs the museum, helped restore the Point Iroquois Lighthouse, so they know what they're about. In the summer, the museum is open Wednesday through Sunday.

the way into the bay where Lake Superior is funneled into the St. Mary's River. It is the oldest operating light on Lake Superior, marking the eastern end of the lake's treacherous "Shipwreck Coast." The site is the perfect spot for the **Great Lakes Shipwreck Museum.** Stepping into the museum feels like a journey to the depths of the Great Lakes. Against the backdrop of enlarged underwater photographs of various wrecks, displays of recovered artifacts are complemented by haunting music and light that seems filtered through darkling water. Models of sunken ships help put the artifacts in context.

One exhibit serves as a memorial for the men who died on the *Edmund Fitzgerald.* In 1975, the freighter sank with all hands a mere 17 miles from Whitefish Bay. The ship's 200-pound bronze bell is displayed at the museum.

With several buildings to explore, visitors can get quite an education. At the Whitefish Point Light Station, built in 1849, you can see what the day-to-day life of a 19th-century lighthouse keeper and his family was like. The Coast Guard's Lifeboat Station was added to the complex in 1923, and there's also the classy Shipwreck Coast Museum Store.

Guests can spend the night in the Crews Quarters. Built in 1923 and used by the Coast Guard lifeboat station crew, the quarters have been restored. Five guest rooms have queen beds, private

The Whitefish Point Light Station has guided ships on Lake Superior since 1849.

A freighter prepares to enter the lock in Sault Ste. Marie.

THE *EDMUND FITZGERALD*

On June 8, 1958, the freighter SS *Edmund Fitzgerald* was launched at the Great Lakes Engineering Shipyard on the Detroit River. Named for the president of the company that had commissioned the ship, it is often superstitiously noted that the christening was only carried out with some difficulty, the bottle of champagne refusing to break.

When the 729-foot freighter hit the water, it was the longest ship to ever sail the Great Lakes. (It would be over a decade before 1,000-foot freighters became a common sight on the water.) For 17 years, the *Fitzgerald* carted taconite from mines near Duluth to Detroit and Toledo ironworks.

A view of Lake Superior's Whitefish Bay

Making a late season run in 1975, captained by Ernest McSorley, the *Fitzgerald* was bound for Detroit with another load of taconite. Encountering a winter storm on Lake Superior, the ship sought shelter along the Canadian coast, north of Whitefish Bay. At 7:10 in the evening on November 10, another freighter, the Anderson, radioed the *Fitzgerald* to warn of rogue waves and to get the ship's status. McSorley's response, "we're holding our own," was the last word from the ill-fated ship. It is believed to have sunk just moments later. There were no survivors.

The next day, at the Mariner's Church in Detroit, church bells tolled 29 times, once for each of the men lost. The tragedy was immortalized by Gordon Lightfoot's haunting ballad, "Wreck of the *Edmund Fitzgerald*."

The ship's bell, which was recovered in 1995, can be seen at the Great Lakes Shipwreck Museum on Whitefish Point. Other artifacts from the freighter, including two of the lifeboats, are on display at the Museum Ship Valley Camp in the Soo (see Chapter 9).

bathrooms, and TVs. The museum is open seasonally from May through October, but the overnight accommodations are open from April through November—the perfect chance to spend more time on the lake when the skies of November turn gloomy.

West of Paradise, the water of the Tahquamenon River is the rich color of tea, not uncommon in the north woods of the Great Lakes. Steeped in cedar marshes, the river springs up from the Tahquamenon Lakes and flows east to Whitefish Bay.

Along the way, a series of waterfalls add significant drama to an otherwise easygoing flow. The Upper Tahquamenon Falls is the most dramatic and attracts thousands of sightseers every year. During the spring melt, it was once recorded that 50,000 gallons poured over the 50-foot drop every second. (After a dry summer, that number is dramatically lower, though the falls are no less impressive.)

As the falls is surrounded by **Tahquamenon Falls State Park,** a trip there is certainly no hardship. You can expect to find a large parking lot, convenient restrooms, a snack counter, full-service restaurant and bar, and a wide path to the river. Several vantage points along the trail allow a peek at the falls before you descend the Brink

The tea-brown water of the Tahquamenon River drops 50 feet from the crest of Upper Tahquamenon Falls.

Stairs to see them up close. The Gorge Stairs downstream offer even another view.

The 4-mile River Trail connects the upper and lower falls, or you can simply drive to the lower falls parking area. The Lower Tahquamenon Falls cascades down a series of ledges, and the pools above and below the falls are great spots to fish for brown trout, pike, and walleyes. Early in the morning, you might even see bald eagles hunting for fish in the river's rapids.

The state park, interestingly enough, is one of the best places in the area for dining out. The **Tahquamenon Falls Brewery & Pub** serves the usual burgers, fries, and other family fare, with a couple of surprises. Appetizers like mozzarella sticks sit on the menu alongside sautéed wild forest mushrooms. There's also a yellowfin tuna sandwich and a buffalo burger, or you can settle in beside their stone fireplace with nachos and a steak. Open year-round, the restaurant caters to the winter crowd that comes for snowmobiling and cross-country skiing.

For seafood, a local commercial fisherman, Buddy Brown, runs **Brown's Fish House** in Paradise. In addition to a fish market, the place offers fried whitefish with the usual assortment of sides (coleslaw, fries, and so on). The place is laid-back and only open when the owner has fresh fish. A local favorite.

Located between Paradise and Newberry, the **North Star Brick Oven Bakery** is not a place for a meal, but they make excellent artisan breads in their wood-fired oven. The shop is just south of the entrance to the Upper Tahquamenon Falls on MI 123. For campers, a hearty loaf of their bread goes well with almost anything you might be cooking up on the fire.

In Paradise, MI 123 turns into the wind and bends southwest to Newberry, the self-proclaimed Moose Capital of Michigan. More moose are sighted here in Luce County than any other county in the state, the majority seen in Tahquamenon Falls State Park.

The town has several chain restaurants, like a Pizza Hut and a McDonald's. And south of Newberry, there are a few smaller chain hotels as well as a handful of independent hotels and motels. On the other side of the state park, Newberry is a popular home base for folks exploring the falls. In the winter, businesses switch gears and cater to the crowds of snowmobilers who come for the U.P.'s legendary trails.

The **MacLeod House Bed & Breakfast** is 1.5 miles south of downtown. This ornate Victorian home was built in 1898. With a grand red oak staircase, a copper fireplace with oak mantle, and hardwoods throughout, the home celebrates Newberry's heyday as a lumber town. There are three guest rooms with private bath, each decorated in grand style reflecting the historic character of the inn. To get there, head west on Cherry Hill Drive south of Newberry. The inn is just past the curve, 0.5 mile in, where the road turns into County Road 441 (CR 441).

A unique way to experience the falls is to take the **Tahquamenon Falls Wilderness Excursion** on the Toonerville Trolley in Soo Junction. The trip begins with a 5.5-mile train ride through the U.P. wilderness. At the end of the tracks, passengers board the Hiawatha Riverboat for a 21-mile cruise down the Tahquamenon River to the Upper Falls. The entire trip takes 6 1/2 hours, and guests get over 1 hour to view the falls from a private vantage point. To get to the depot in Soo Junction, take MI 123 south out of Newberry to MI 28, turn east, and drive 12 miles. Turn left on County Road 381 (CR 381), and your destination is fewer than 2.5 miles north of the highway. Reservations are helpful, but they take walk-ins.

North of Newberry 1.5 miles on MI 123, the **Tahquamenon Logging Museum** celebrates the region's logging heritage. The museum's 29 acres include a building constructed by the Civilian Conservation Corps, a logging camp cook shack, and a nature trail that winds through the woods. In the summer, an authentic lumberjack's breakfast is served from the museum cook shack (call ahead for schedule).

Ernest Hemingway's collection of short stories *In Our Time* ends with a two-part Nick Adams story, "Big Two-Hearted River." The name of the river, he said, was poetry. Though he used the name to suit his artistic inclinations and was most likely describing the Fox River in his story, the poetic associations with the Two Hearted River have become ingrained in the public's imagination.

The **Rainbow Lodge** at the mouth of the Two Hearted organizes canoe trips down the river. One-day paddles are the most popular, but more involved two- and three-day trips are also possible. The lodge has motel rooms and rental cabins, which are spare but cozy and clean. The folks there also know a lot about fishing local waters, and they're happy to offer advice.

From Newberry, it's 27 miles north to the town of Deer Park and **Muskallonge Lake State Park**, wedged between Muskallonge Lake and Lake Superior. At one time the lake was used as a mill pond for the lumber industry in Deer Park, but today the park is simply a popular recreation destination.

Continuing west on County Road H58 (CR H58), it's another 19 miles to Grand Marais. This route is along the Grand Marais Truck Trail. Though patches east of Deer Park might require four-wheel drive, the route west is a regularly graded county road. Like any dirt road, there's always a chance of washboard bumps and minor ruts, but a car can get through fine.

Once connected by train to Marquette, Grand Marais was a frontier town in the grand tradition. Back when lumber was king, ships lined the docks and saloons lined the streets—30 of them, no less. Visiting Grand Marais today, it's hard to imagine it was once a bustling town with a half-dozen hotels. For a quiet retreat, you can't beat this low-key backwater on the eastern edge of the Pictured Rocks National Lakeshore.

The harbor of refuge, West Bay, was created by the construction of a breakwall in 1880. The wall prevented the northeast winds from filling the bay with sand. Since World War II, the breakwall was left to fall into disrepair and eventually disappeared altogether. Today, thousands of tons of sand pour into the bay each year, and the community is working hard to secure funding to rebuild the breakwall. Without a harbor, the town will have an even harder time attracting tourists.

West 12 miles from Grand Marais, the Au Sable Point Light Station sits atop an 87-foot tower on a bluff. The fixed light shines 150 feet above Lake Superior, providing the only light on this 80-mile stretch known as the Shipwreck Coast. When the lighthouse and its rather spacious keeper's quarters were built in 1874, it was an exceptionally lonely place to live. It was 12 miles from Grand Marais, and the keeper and his family could only get to town by a trail through the woods or by boat. Imagining the winters here, neither seems an attractive option. The light was automated in the 1950s and given over to the National Park Service. To explore the lighthouse, take CR H58 west into the Pictured Rocks National Lakeshore; 12 miles in is the Hurricane River Campground. From there it's a 1.5-mile hike to the lighthouse. In the summer, a ranger is on hand to help visitors appreciate the site.

Walking the shores of Lake Superior, people often stumble upon agates. These

THE PICTURED ROCKS

The centerpiece of the Pictured Rocks National Lakeshore is the Pictured Rocks, 15 miles of sandstone cliffs that rise dramatically over the surface of Lake Superior. Over the centuries, the relentless waves, wind, and weather have sculpted the cliffs in ways that spark the imagination. The effect is amplified by the varied color of the rocks, stained by the action of water and minerals. Arches, caves, and distinguished promontories—rust red cliffs against which emerald green water slaps—attract thousands of visitors every year.

The French called the cliffs Les Portails, or "The Gates." For voyageurs who traveled by canoe without the benefit of regular weather reports, the cliffs must have been viewed with some apprehension. A sudden storm would most certainly batter a boat to pieces against the tall stone walls, and for 12 miles at least, harbor is not readily available.

The tourism potential of the cliffs was recognized early on. Harper's Magazine reported in 1867 that the Pictured Rocks area made for the perfect summer retreat, with the only real disadvantage being "the appalling fact

that it is about two or three days' canoe journey, either way, to a beef-steak."

In 1966, President Johnson signed the act that created the Pictured Rocks National Lakeshore, which extends 42 miles along the shore of Lake Superior. Most visitors will want to experience the cliffs by boat, but don't miss out on the park's other opportunities for recreation and exploration. The North Country Trail, which crosses from eastern New York to North Da-

colorful rocks were formed millions of years ago by volcanoes and lava flows. Lake Superior agates are unique for their red, orange, and yellow hues—the result of oxidized iron. The **Gitche Gumee Agate & History Museum** has an excellent collection of agates and other rocks, including a display on U.P. mining. The museum also tells about life in Grand Marais a hundred years ago, when the industries were fishing, mining, and logging.

The **Campbell Street Gallery** in Grand Marais carries oil paintings by gallery owner Maeve Croghan, as well as the work of other local artists and artisans. Croghan's expressionist land and waterscapes represent the local area, as well as Tuscany and vineyards in California, where she lives part time.

kota, passes through the park, following the Lakeshore Trail.

While there's plenty of camping and hiking, there are also day trips and short hikes that allow visitors to see many of the park's best features. Close to town, for example, is Munising Falls. To get there, take East Munising Avenue 1.3 miles east to Washington Street. Turn left. The Munising Falls Interpretive Center is about 0.5 mile down the road. From there an 800-foot path leads to Munising Falls. The path leads up a sandstone canyon to the 50-foot waterfall, and there is a staircase to climb to get to the viewing platform.

Another easy way to explore the park is to see the sights along the Miners River. Continue 4 miles past Washington Street on East Munising Avenue and turn left onto Pictured Rock Trails (also called Miners Castle Road or CR H11). Follow the signs to Miners Falls. From the trailhead, it's a little over 0.5 mile to the waterfall. Continue north to Miners Castle, where there's an information center and an overlook with stunning views of Lake

Munising Falls

Superior and a portion of the Pictured Rocks. From the information center/ picnic area, it's a 1 mile hike to Miners Beach, a beautiful 1-mile-long run of sand.

For a bite to eat, a good bet is **Lake Superior Brewing Co.** No tourist trap, this place is a real townie bar with wood-paneled walls and a true up-north feel. In addition to a line of microbrews, there's a decent menu.

From Grand Marais, take MI 77 south to Seney, and then pick up MI 28 west to Munising. A more direct scenic route cuts through the **Pictured Rocks National Lakeshore.** However, the dirt road is marked with ruts and potholes, and even in the best conditions it will take much longer to make it to your destination. To take the scenic drive, head west from Grand Marais via CR H58 and pick up a map at the park's Grand Sable Visitors Center.

Munising has become the spring pad for enjoying the Pictured Rocks. The most

Once called Indian Head, this promontory, part of the Pictured Rocks, has eroded over the years.

popular way to view the cliffs is to take a trip with **Pictured Rocks Cruises,** which offers a regular schedule of tours daily in the summer. As the boat pulls out into Munising Bay, the narration begins. Throughout the trip, the captain will point out rock formations— Indian Head, Miners Castle, the Great Caverns—and talk about the history of the cliffs. The company was begun by Captain Everett Morrison, who took passengers out to view the rocks in a wooden boat after World War II, a year before the national lakeshore was even established.

The entire tour takes up to three hours, and boats leave from City Dock right in town (you can hardly miss it). The light for photographs can be tricky, but fortunately, the boat passes the entire stretch of Pictured Rocks again on the return to the dock. Personally, I think the Pictured Rocks are wonderfully photogenic in the late-day sun, so I like to aim for an afternoon outing there.

Shipwrecks are many along the southern shore of Lake Superior, and three in Munising Bay can be seen from the glass-bottom boats of Munising's **Shipwreck Tours.** The tour takes passengers out to see the remains of the *Bermuda,* the *Herman H. Hettler,* and a scow (the name of which remains a mystery). The Bermuda, a wooden schooner that sank in 1870, rests only 12 feet below the surface, so you can see where the masts should be. The shipwreck tour takes about two hours and passes close to the unique East Channel Lighthouse. Though clad in bare wood today, the lighthouse was painted white back when it guided ships into Munising Harbor.

The weathered East Channel Lighthouse used to guide ships into Munising Harbor.

For a self-guided tour of Munising Bay, you can rent a pontoon boat at **Seaberg Pontoon Rentals.**

Grand Island, out in the bay, is part of the Hiawatha National Forest. Set aside as a national recreation area, it has trails and rustic campsites. Visitors are required to follow a leave-no-trace policy. If you are intrigued by Grand Is-

land, **ALTRAN Bus Service** offers three-hour narrated tours with plenty of stops to get out and take in the scenery. The bus takes you over to the island via the **Grand Island Ferry.** Or you can rent mountain bikes, ride over on the ferry, and explore the old dirt roads that circle the island. Check the Grand Island National Recreation Area website for more information.

One of the nicest family-friendly places to eat in Munising is the **Dogpatch.** Named for the hometown of comic strip hero Li'l Abner, the restaurant is decorated in an all-out tribute to Abner, Daisy Mae, and Mammy and Pappy Yokum. They serve burgers and fries, steaks, fish dinners, and a full salad bar. For a Yooper tradition, stop by **Muldoon's Pasties** just west of town. They have chicken, beef, and dessert pasties, as well as a nice gift shop.

West on MI 28 in Au Train, the **Brownstone Inn** serves Lake Superior whitefish, steaks, and a few imaginative dishes like the Jamaican whitefish, the brown rice lentil sandwich, and almond breaded duck tenders. The restaurant has been there for more than 50 years, built with a hodgepodge of local materials—rocks from the beach, hewn logs, windows from a demolished Ford plant. The current owners took over the restaurant in 1991, and it continues to be one the area's best places to eat.

If you stay on MI 28, you eventually pass **Lakenenland**—several acres of whimsical art designed to be a drive-through sculpture park of sorts. Completely crafted and developed by one man, the park is open and free to visitors. Local zoning officials, however, need to obey the NO TRESPASSING signs. Roadside attractions of this kind used to be more common, but they also used to be money-makers, and few were ever as well-done as this one.

South of the highway into Marquette is one of the more legendary waterfalls in the Upper Peninsula. Laughing Whitefish Falls drops 100 feet from top to bottom. The water cascades down an incline and is best viewed when water levels are running high. A long staircase leads to the base

The sculptures at Lakenenland are full of a particularly American style of individualism.

It's a hike to Laughing Whitefish Falls, but the falls are worth it.

The ore dock is the one Marquette landmark you won't miss.

of the falls and visitors get a view from both angles. It's a short hike back to the river, so you need to be prepared with decent walking shoes, a hat, and bug spray. The falls are named for the river. The mouth of the river apparently looked like a laughing whitefish to the Ojibwa on Lake Superior.

Marquette is 30 miles west of Au Train on MI 28. With 20,000 people living in Marquette, and another 45,000 in the surrounding area, the Queen City of the North, as it is called, is by far the largest city in the Upper Peninsula. The town sprang to life in the 1840s when, with the discovery of iron ore nearby, two brothers from Massachusetts established an iron mining company. As people began to make money, a building boom resulted in the fine examples of 19th-century architecture you see today, many constructed with the local Lake Superior sandstone.

Freighters once lined up at the town's ore dock and were part of the driving force behind the city's growth. While freighters still dock north of town to fill their holds with ore, the city's economy has shifted to service industries, the largest employers being the university, public schools, the hospital, and the state prison. In recent years, it has grown considerably with stores, restaurants, and hotels multiplying along US 41. Northern Michigan University brings nearly nine thousand students to Marquette, which translates into an active bar scene and plenty of good pizza.

Every year, this region gets hit with 170 inches of snow. Winter sports are popular—snowmobiling, cross-country and downhill skiing, snowshoeing. On the third weekend in February, thousands of people gather in the cold along Washington Street to watch the start of the U.P. 200, Michigan's premier dog-sledding race. While mushers and their teams make the 240-mile round-trip to Grand Marais, other dogsled races and events keep the festive momentum of the weekend alive.

Snowbound Books, a great source for books on local subjects, as well as everything else

Snowbound Books on Third Street is one of the nicest bookstores you will find anywhere. Opened in 1984 with a mere ten thousand books, the store had to expand to a second location (called Chapter Two) just down the street to carry all of its stock. In recent years the used book trade has taken some hits. Snowbound is back to their one location, and they primarily deal in new books these days—though you will find used books here and there. There's an especially fine assortment of books on Michigan history, geography, and more, as well as fiction by Michigan authors. If you have a particular passion for the works for Robert Traver, they typically have a shelf of collectible editions available.

For breakfast, lunch, or dinner, you can't go wrong at the **Sweet Water Café**. The menu is a comforting selection of family dining favorites with a few house specialties thrown in for variety. They serve fresh baked goods for breakfast, and there's a full bar in the evenings. The walls are tastefully adorned with the work of local artists.

For more of a treat, head downtown to **Donckers**. This classic soda fountain dishes up all sorts of delights—from ice cream floats to old-fashioned phosphates. Donckers is not a retroesque experiment. This place is the real deal. In 1895, Fred Donckers began a small confectionary of sorts, a cart selling popcorn and candy and a few sundries. In 1914 he moved the business into its present location. Over the years, a soda fountain was added and then a restaurant. The restaurant is upstairs, and the sandwiches are excellent; just remember to save room for dessert.

Of course, if you want to try a little of everything, there's more ice cream to be had over at the **Jilbert Dairy.** Heading west on Washington, the dairy is off on a side street just before you reach US 41. The dairy supplies most of the U.P. with milk and other dairy products. Located in Marquette since 1983, they also run a nice ice

For ice cream, be sure to visit Jilbert Dairy and its giant cow. *Kim Forster*

North of town, the Presque Isle Park is one of the most scenic parks in the U.P. *Kim Forster*

cream business right on the premises. A gigantic cow overlooks the picnic tables where thousands have enjoyed a warm-weather snack.

For lodging, the historic **Landmark Inn** was the classiest hotel in Marquette when it opened downtown in the 1930s. Guests included the pilot Amelia Earhart and comedians Abbott and Costello. For some years it fell into disrepair, closing in the 1980s. It was purchased in 1997, and the hotel has been restored to its former glory. The inn has 62 rooms, a bar, a restaurant, and a penthouse cocktail lounge with spectacular views of Lake Superior.

The best place to take in the natural beauty of Marquette is at **Presque Isle Park,** a few miles north of town. *Presque* is French for "not quite a," and this 323-acre park is just what the name suggests: not quite an island. Nearly surrounded by Lake Superior, the shoreline of Presque Isle is rocky, at times soaring above the water below. At other times, the rocky shore descends close enough for kayakers to launch into the great lake.

The park itself is thickly forested and features several trails. In the warmer months, you will see joggers, cyclists, paddlers, and the occasional group of cliff jumpers (you'll have to ask them yourself if you want to find a safe place to jump). There are also picnic areas, a venue for summer concerts, and concessions.

Just across from the entrance to Presque Isle Park, you will find the studio for **Risak Pottery & Gallery.** Ed Risak combines local elements into his art, creating pieces with a naturally indigenous look and feel. There you will also find work by his wife, Julie Risak, and their daughter, Thea.

IN THE AREA

ACCOMMODATIONS

Big Bay Point Lighthouse B&B, 3 Lighthouse Road, Big Bay. Call 906-345-9957. Website: bigbaylighthouse.com.

The Landmark Inn, 230 North Front Street, Marquette. Call 906-228-2580 or 1-888-752-6362 (for reservations). Website: thelandmarkinn.com.

MacLeod House Bed & Breakfast, 6211 CR 441, Newberry. Call 906-293-3841. Website: macleodhouse.net.

Monocle Lake Campground, 1 mile south of the Point Iroquois Lighthouse, Brimley. Website: www.fs.usda.gov/recarea/hiawatha/recarea/?recid=13289.

Rainbow Lodge, 32752 CR 423, Newberry. Call 906-658-3357. At the mouth of the Two Hearted River, the lodge offers rooms and canoe rental. Website: exploringthenorth.com/twoheart/rainbow.html.

ATTRACTIONS AND RECREATION

ALTRAN Bus Service, 530 East Munising Avenue, Munising. Call 906-387-4845. The company offers bus tours of Grand Island. Website: altranbus.com.

Campbell Street Gallery, 14281 Campbell Street, Grand Marais. Call 734-395-3288. Website: sites.google.com/site/campbellstreetgallerygrandmarais/.

Gitche Gumee Agate & History Museum, E21739 Braziel Street, Grand Marais. Call 906-494-2590. Website: agatelady.com.

Grand Island Ferry Service. Call 906-387-3503. Website: grandislandmi.com/transportation.html

The arena at Northern Michigan University

Close to Presque Isle Park is the town's working ore dock. *Kim Forster*

Great Lakes Shipwreck Museum, 8335 North Whitefish Point Road, Paradise. Call 1-877-635-1742 or 1-888-492-3747 (for accommodations). Website: shipwreckmuseum.com.

Lakenenland, 2800 MI 28, Chocolay Charter Township. Call 906-249-1132. Website: lakenenland.com.

Muskallonge State Park, 30042 CR 407, Newberry. Call 906-658-3338. Website: michigan.gov/muskallonge.

North Star Brick Oven Bakery,

> ## BIG BAY
>
> **T**he small town of Big Bay is 28 miles north of Marquette, and unless you have a truck or four-wheel drive, it's the end of the road.
>
> The town is best known for an event that transpired in 1952: An army lieutenant walked into the Lumberjack Tavern and murdered the bar owner. The story was retold in the book Anatomy of a Murder by Robert Traver (the pen name for local lawyer John Voelker). In the book, the town's name was changed to Thunder Bay, and eight minutes of the Otto Preminger movie adaptation, starring Jimmy Stewart and Lee Remick, were filmed in town in a tavern built in the Thunder Bay Inn by the movie crew.
>
> Voelker was an angler with a philosopher's appreciation for the sport. He eventually served on the Michigan Supreme Court, but he retired in his 50s to spend time fishing and writing in the U.P. His Anatomy of a Fisherman is considered a classic of fishing literature, and his Laughing Whitefish is another compelling legal drama.
>
> The Lumberjack Tavern is still in Big Bay. The Thunder Bay Inn, however, closed its doors in 2008, depriving the town of a significant landmark.
>
> Northeast of town, on the point that forms the bay, the Big Bay Point Lighthouse has been repurposed as a bed & breakfast. Seven guest rooms all feature private baths; five have a view of the lake, and the remaining two face the woods. Common areas include a living room with a fireplace, and guests are welcome to climb the 60-foot tower for stunning views of Lake Superior.

19639 MI 123, Newberry. Call 906-658-3537.

Pictured Rocks Cruises, 100 City Park Drive, Munising. Call 906-387-2379 or 1-800-650-2379. Website: picturedrocks.com.

Pictured Rocks National Lakeshore, N8391 Sand Point Road, Munising. Call 906-387-3700 or 906-494-2660 for the Grand Sable Visitors Center (E21090 CR H58, Grand Marais), which is open only in the summer. Website: nps.gov/piro.

Point Iroquois Lighthouse & Maritime Museum, 12942 West Lakeshore Drive, Brimley. Call 906-437-5272. The lighthouse is 7.5 miles north of Brimley on Lakeshore Drive.

Presque Isle Park, north end of Lakeshore Boulevard, Marquette. Call 906-228-0460. Website: mqtcty.org/parks_presque_isle.html.

Risak Pottery & Gallery, 2909 North Lakeshore Boulevard, Marquette. Call 906-228-6003. Website: risakpottery.com.

Seaberg Pontoon Rentals, 1330 Commercial Street, Munising. Call 906-387-2685. Pontoon boats are available for three-hour, half-day, and full-day rental.

Shipwreck Tours, 1204 Commercial

Street, Munising. Call 906-387-4477. Website: shipwrecktours.com.

Snowbound Books, 118 North Third Street, Marquette. Call 906-228-4448. Website: snowboundbooks.com.

Tahquamenon Falls State Park, 41382 West MI 123, Paradise. Call 906-492-3415. Website: michigan.gov/tahquamenonfalls.

Tahquamenon Falls Wilderness Excursion, Soo Junction. Call 906-876-2311 (for the depot) or 1-888-77-TRAIN (87246). The Toonerville Trolley takes you to the Tahquamenon Riverboat for a tour of the falls. Website: superiorsights.com/toonerville.

Tahquamenon Logging Museum, 1 mile north of Newberry on MI 123. Call 906-293-3700. Website: superiorsights.com/loggingmuseum.

DINING

Brown's Fish House, 0.5 mile west of blinking light on MI 123, Paradise. Call 906-492-3901.

Brownstone Inn, E4635 MI 28 West, Au Train. Call 906-892-8332. Open for lunch and dinner. Closed Mon. Website: brownstoneinn.net.

Dogpatch Restaurant, 325 East Superior Street, Munising. Call 906-387-9948. Website: dogpatchrestaurant.com.

Donckers, 137 West Washington Street, Marquette. Call 906-226-6110. Website: donckersonline.com.

Jilbert Dairy, 200 Meeske Avenue, Marquette. Call 906-225-1363. Website: jilbertdairy.com.

Lake Superior Brewing Co., N14283 Lake Avenue, Grand Marais. Call 906-494-BEER (2337). Website: grandmaraismichigan.com/LSBC.

Muldoon's Pasties, 1246 MI 28 West, Munising. Call 906-387-5880. Website: muldoonspasties.com.

Sweet Water Café, 517 North Third Street, Marquette. Call 906-226-7009. Open daily for breakfast, lunch, and dinner. Website: sweetwater.org.

Tahquamenon Falls Brewery & Pub. Call 906-492-3300. Located next to the upper falls parking lot at Tahquamenon State Park. Open year-round, with a few weeks off in the late fall and early spring off-season. Website: tahquamenonfallsbrewery.com.

OTHER CONTACTS

Alger County Chamber of Commerce, 129 East Munising Avenue, Munising. Call 906-387-2138. Website: algercounty.org.

Grand Island National Recreation Area, Munising Ranger District, 400 East Munising Avenue, Munising. Call 906-387-2512 or 906-387-3700. Website: grandislemi.com.

Grand Marais Chamber of Commerce. Call 906-494-2447. Website: grandmaraismichigan.com.

Marquette County Convention & Visitors Bureau, 337 West Washington Street, Marquette. Call 906-228-7749 or 1-800-544-4321. Website: travelmarquettemichigan.com.

Munising Visitors Bureau, P.O. Box 42, Munising, MI 49862. Website: munising.org.

Newberry Area Tourism Association, 4947 East CR 460, Newberry. Call 906-293-5739. Website: newberrytourism.com.

Paradise Chamber of Commerce. Call 906-492-3219. Website: paradisemichigan.org.

The Gorge Falls on the Black River

11 Waterfalls & Big Snow, Iron & Copper: The Porkies to the Keweenaw Peninsula

IRONWOOD & BESSEMER, THE PORCUPINE
MOUNTAINS, HOUGHTON-HANCOCK,
LAC LA BELLE, COPPER HARBOR,
EAGLE RIVER, CALUMET & LAURIUM,
L'ANSE, AND MICHIGAMME

Estimated length: 300 miles

Estimated time: Close to 7 hours

Getting there: Ironwood is the farthest west you can go in Michigan. From the Mackinac Bridge, drive 317 miles west on US 2. From the Chicago area, take I-90 west to I-39 north in Rockford; in Portage, continue driving 230 miles north on US 51 to Ironwood. From Minneapolis, drive north on I-35 to Duluth, continuing east on US 2 for 103 miles.

From Ironwood, drive east on MI 28 to Bergland, and then head north on MI 64 to the Porcupine Mountains Wilderness State Park. Continue east on MI 64 to Ontonagon, where the route to Houghton follows MI 38 and MI 26. In Houghton, US 41 crosses the bridge to Hancock. Drive north along the east shore of the Keweenaw Peninsula through Lake Linden, Gay, and Lac La Belle on the way to Copper Harbor. Take MI 26 south through Eagle Harbor and Eagle River, finally landing in Calumet and Laurium.

The final stretch of the loop returns through Houghton and follows the river east to L'Anse and eventually ends in Michigamme.

Highlights: The tour begins in Ironwood, where the Stormy Kromer cap is now made. In the winter, there's downhill skiing at Big Powderhorn Mountain, and for kitschy fun, check out the Statue of Hiawatha near town. Waterfall hunters will enjoy the nearby Superior Falls and Gabbro Falls, and the Black River Scenic Byway

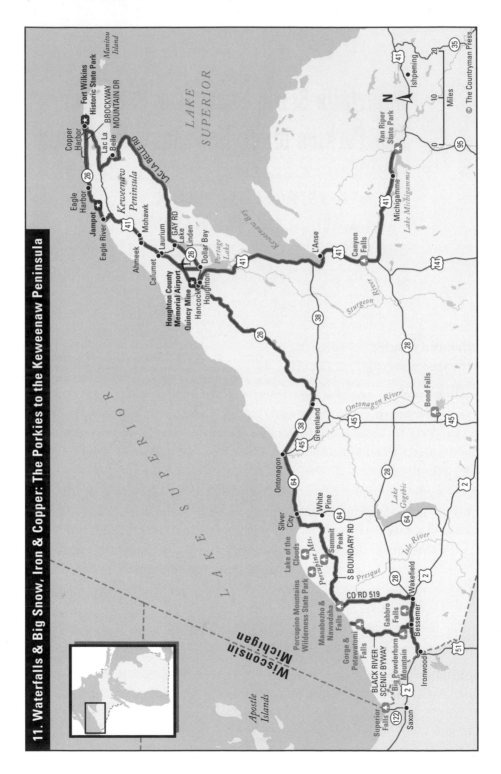

11. Waterfalls & Big Snow, Iron & Copper: The Porkies to the Keweenaw Peninsula

has an afternoon's worth of waterfalls to explore. The Porcupine Mountains Wilderness State Park is to the north. Stop and view the Lake of the Clouds or take a short scenic hike on the Summit Peak Side Trail. For a multiday adventure, consider hiking the park's Lake Superior Trail. In Greenland, stop for an introduction to U.P. mining with a tour of the Adventure Mining Company. The education continues in Houghton-Hancock with a tour of the Quincy Mine. Then follow the back roads for a scenic tour up the eastern edge of the Keweenaw Peninsula. Stop for lunch, or maybe lodging, in Lac La Belle, before continuing on to Copper Harbor and tours of Fort Wilkins and the Copper Harbor Lighthouse. Head back south along the western shore of the peninsula. Purchase monk-made jam at The Jampot and check out the Eagle River Timber Bridge in Eagle River. The historic town of Calumet has plenty of ways to explore this area's history of copper mining. There is also some good shopping and dining. In nearby Laurium, you can drive past historic mansions, or stay the night in one at either the Laurium Manor Inn or Victorian Hall. For a night close to Lake Superior, the Sands Hill Lighthouse is now a cozy bed & breakfast. On your way home, be sure to stop by L'Anse for a sweet roll at the Hilltop Restaurant and tour some of the local waterfalls before ending the trip in Michigamme.

I t's here at the westernmost part of the state that you really get a sense of how big Michigan is. The drive from Detroit to Ironwood, on the Wisconsin border, is 100 miles farther than the distance from Detroit to Washington, DC. Ironwood, together with Hurley across the border in Wisconsin, was once the center of iron mining in the Gogebic Range. The town sprang up in the 1880s after ore was discovered in the nearby mountains. A true frontier settlement, Hurley once boasted a street with 30 saloons and was known far and wide as the place where a miner could come for a little debauchery. So prolific was the flow of spirits that when Prohibition was made law in 1920, folks didn't seem to notice. This reputation brought gangsters from Chicago, and Al Capone's brother retired to Hurley, dying late in life in a local nursing home.

The town fell on hard times when the mines closed, and tourism has become a necessary mainstay for both Ironwood and nearby Bessemer and Wakefield. For visitors, the big attractions are what lay outside the city limits. The region bills itself as a winter playground—lots of snow, local ski hills, cross-country skiing and snow-shoeing trails, and plenty of country for snowmobiling are a big draw. The towns of Ironwood and Bessemer offer ready access to the Porcupine Mountains Wilderness State Park, and there are enough waterfalls to keep a family driving around for days. The falls, which swell with the melting snow, are best in the spring. In autumn, fall colors are so bright that you might think the hills have caught fire.

Throughout Ironwood, several large fiberglass sculptures hark back to a day

BOND FALLS

Driving into Ironwood from the east, you pass the most impressive waterfall in the Upper Peninsula, the Bond Falls on the Ontonagon River. Many point to Tahquamenon Falls as the U.P.'s biggest, but Bond Falls is thought by many to be the peninsula's most aesthetically satisfying. About 100 feet wide at the crest, the water tumbles over 40 feet down a widening staircase of rock, gathering below in deep shady pools. A dam upstream controls the flow and maintains the waterfall's scenic quality.

The waterfall is completely accessible. A wide level path leads up to the base of the falls, and a platform extends over the river downstream. Another path climbs to the top of the falls and follows a portion of the Ontonagon above. On the road that bypasses the parking area, next to the Bond Falls Basin, there's a small gift shop that sells ice cream and souvenir T-shirts.

To get there from US 2, drive north from Watersmeet on US 45 for 10 miles. Turn right on Bond Falls Road. The parking area is fewer than 3 miles east.

when tourism was a bit hammier. In 1964, the Statue of Hiawatha, "the world's tallest Indian," was shipped to Ironwood to help the town attract traffic. Today it stands somewhat unceremoniously in a small neighborhood park overlooking the old downtown. East on US 2, in Bessemer, a rather stiff downhill skier graces the sign for Big Powderhorn Mountain.

Driving into Ironwood, you will notice a large red cap on the south side of US 2. The Stormy Kromer cap is a Yooper icon. Back in 1903, a railroad engineer and retired semiprofessional baseball player, George "Stormy" Kromer, was fed up with his caps blowing off at work. His wife, Ida, came up with a solution. Taking one of Stormy's old baseball caps, she sewed on flaps that covered the ears—thus the famed **Stormy Kromer** was born. The hat was popular with fellow railroad engineers, and soon folks from all over were looking to keep their ears warm. In 1919 Stormy founded the Kromer Cap Co. and moved the whole operation to Milwaukee.

After nearly a century in business, the company was struggling. Bob Jacquart saw an opportunity and bought the rights to produce the legendary caps at his textile plant in Ironwood, bringing the Stormy Kromer to its present home on Wall Street. You can tour the factory on weekdays. There's only one tour each day, so call ahead or check the website for an up-to-date schedule.

Many folks looking at a map can't understand why the U.P. is not, at least in some portion, part of Wisconsin. Even more baffling is the seemingly gerrymandered line that separates the two states. More than half the border, however, follows natural boundaries — the Montreal, Brule, and Menominee Rivers. The rest is a straight line drawn through the lake country.

Near Ironwood, there's a spectacular waterfall on the Montreal River, Superior Falls, with several drops that add up to 110 feet. Most of it can be observed from the edge of the gorge above — mind the fence. A visit to the falls requires a swing through Wisconsin. Drive west on US 2 to WI 122 north. The highway curves back into Michigan. About 0.5 mile past the border is the gravel road that leads to the parking area (there's a sign).

The Gabbro Falls in Bessemer is possibly the most impressive waterfall on the Black River. A short hike from the parking area, the river cuts through a dark gorge, dropping 40 feet to the bottom. It's not as developed as other falls in the area, so you are less likely to run into a crowd on the trails to the river. To get there, drive 1 mile east of Bessemer, and turn north on Prospect

Statue of Hiawatha, Ironwood

The Black River Trail follows a portion of the North Country Trail.

The Black River Crossing B&B

Road. At 1 mile farther on, turn east on Black Jack Road. The park is 1 mile down on the right. Two trails split off from the parking area. The top of the falls is on the right, and the base on the left.

The Black River Scenic Byway follows the river from Bessemer to Black River Harbor on Lake Superior. The drive itself is quite beautiful, but it's just icing on the cake. Along the way, five major waterfalls are accessible from small parking areas. In most cases the trails to the falls are relatively short, though some require a climb. If time is limited, head for the shared parking area for Gorge Falls and Potawatomi Falls. These are the two most impressive sights on the river and happen to have the shortest hike.

There are hotels and motels in the Ironwood-Bessemer area, and most are independently owned. For cheap lodging, I almost prefer the old cabin-style motels near Ontonagon with their views of Lake Superior. However, the **Black River Crossing B&B,** north of Bessemer, is a magnificent place to stay. This grand log cabin has three guest rooms, two with whirlpool tubs. There are several common areas where guests can relax after a day of hiking or snowmobiling, each with its own fireplace, and outside there's a wood-fired sauna to warm away the cold. This is not a place to bring children, and the B&B requires a minimum two-night stay.

There are few exceptional restaurants in Ironwood. **Don & GG's Food & Spirits** is one of the nicer places on US 2. The menu features Lake Superior whitefish, burgers, sandwiches, and wraps. Another is **Tacconelli's Town House,** serving great Italian and heart-stopping pork ribs.

Northeast of Ironwood and Bessemer lie the Porcupine Mountains, or the Porkies. The main entrance and visitors center for the **Porcupine Mountains Wilderness State Park** is on the east end of the wilderness area. Follow MI 28 east to MI 64 north to get there quickly. A more scenic route is to take Presque Isle Road north from Wakefield into the park, turning right on Forest Trail 117, which becomes South Boundary Road. (Just past the turn, you can continue toward Lake Superior and see Manabezho Falls and Nawadaha Falls on the Presque Isle River.) The road follows the southern edge of the park 24 miles to the main entrance. Though only 45 miles, this route will take just shy of two hours.

The Porcupine Mountains Wilderness State Park is Michigan's largest state park. In fact, with 60,000 acres, it's one of the largest remaining wilderness areas in the Midwest. More than half the park is old-growth forest. It has over 90 miles of trails, including the Lake Superior Trail, which follows 17 miles of Lake Superior shoreline from MI 107 to the Presque Isle River, and nine trails have been set aside for mountain biking.

For a short visit, drive to the western end of MI 107 and stop for a moment at the Lake of the Clouds scenic viewing area. From the parking lot, the path climbs a short rise through a pine forest. From the lookout platform, the 300-acre lake is surprisingly beautiful. The view looks down nearly 400 feet to the lake, nestled in a dark green valley. On a recent visit, a ranger pointed out an eagle's nest opposite our lookout.

Another accessible scenic spot is Summit Peak. To get to the 0.5-mile

The Presque Isle River winds along the west boundary of the Porcupine Mountains Wilderness Area.

Everyone needs to visit the Lake of the Clouds at least once.

The Adventure Mining Company allows visitors an up-close look at how copper was mined.

Houghton and Hancock are connected by this one bridge.

Summit Peak Side Trail, take South Boundary Road to Summit Peak Road. At 1,958 feet, this peak is the highest in the park. Climb the 40-foot observation tower for views that reach Wisconsin and Minnesota. From this height, you can even see the Apostle Islands out in Lake Superior. The trailhead is off South Boundary Road, 12.5 miles from MI 107.

Yurts and rustic cabins are available in the park year-round. Not for the day visitor, these lodgings are accessible only by trail, some several miles from a trailhead. Another option is the Kaug Wudjoo Lodge, which can be can be rented by the week. Featuring a fieldstone fireplace and knotty pine furniture, it was built in the 1940s as a home for the park manager.

Continuing east on MI 107, the highway follows the shore of Lake Superior. South 5 miles from Silver City is White Pine, the home of **Antonio's**. Great Italian food, the best in Michigan, is one of the graces given to the western U.P. by Italian immigrants who came here to work the mines. Antonio's has become a White Pine mainstay, serving excellent thin-crust pizza, baked pasta and cheese with Italian sausage, and their popular 1/3-pound hamburger.

In Ontonagon, MI 64 ends, and the road to Houghton and the Keweenaw Peninsula continues on MI 38 southeast for 14 miles. In Greenland, you can get your first real taste of Copper Country with an **Adventure Mining Company** tour. Signs are well posted along the highway. This mine was active from 1850 until 1920. Capturing the true spirit of mining, guests are outfitted with a hard hat and headlamp—the only light they will have underground. The tour passes through various rooms where visitors see copper still in the walls. It's pretty cold in the mine year-round, so bring a coat.

Continuing east, the road to Houghton follows MI 26 north.

The Keeweenaw Peninsula is the heart of Copper Country. While the first French explorers sat around campfires, listening intently to descriptions of copper boulders too big for a man to carry, Native Americans had been mining copper in northern Michigan for nearly seven thousand years. Remains of primitive pit mines have been found on Isle Royale and elsewhere in the U.P., and archaeological digs throughout North America have shown that Keeweenaw copper was traded rather extensively. In the 18th century, copper-mining companies relied on local Ojibwa to show them where outcroppings of the precious metal could be found.

With the explosion of copper mining on the Keeweenaw, the towns of Houghton and Hancock became the center of business and industry. The waterway that nearly severed the tip of the peninsula from the mainland was dredged and extended out to Lake Superior, creating Copper Island to the north. Ships were able to fill their holds and deliver supplies directly to the heart of the peninsula.

The **Quincy Mine** sits on the bluff overlooking the Keeweenaw Waterway. Its profile has become an icon of Houghton-Hancock, seen from nearly any vantage point in the sister cities. At one point, 10 such mines lined the ridge. The Quincy Mine tour has two parts—visitors can chose to do one or the other, or both. The surface tour takes a look at the mine equipment on the ground and includes an exciting ride down the tramway to an entrance tunnel in the side of the hill. The underground portion of the tour follows the tunnel 0.5 mile into the mine. Once underground, the temperature stays in the 40s. The complete two-part tour takes up to two hours, and be sure to save time to view the short mining video and check out the other displays.

As a college town (the home of Michigan Tech) and the center of commerce for the Keeweenaw Peninsula, Houghton has a lot of great places to eat. **The Library Restaurant & Brew Pub** waits on a side street downtown. The bar area is finished in dark woods, and books and bookshelves are a central design feature throughout. The dining room's tall windows let in views of the waterway and Hancock beyond. The menu has a variety of dishes, all done well, from the expertly charred chicken quesadilla to the hearty sandwiches. They also have pizza and a fine selection of steak and seafood.

The Library Restaurant in Houghton

A small roadside park features these falls in Lac La Belle.

Fort Wilkins has numerous exhibits displaying what life was like in the old fort.

Just across the Portage Canal Lift Bridge into Hancock, a sign outside a bright red and green building boasts ITALIAN SPECIALTIES. This is **Gemignani's,** another one of those great Italian restaurants that you find tucked in quiet corners all over the Upper Peninsula. This unpretentious family-owned restaurant serves homemade ravioli and pasta with their family-recipe meat sauce. (If you fall in love with it, you can purchase the special blend of seasonings on their website.) Sandwiches and panini make for a great lunch, and you must try the tiramisu.

Visitors looking for a hotel or motel have a lot of options in Houghton. There are a couple of Best Westerns, a Country Inn & Suites, a Budget Host Inn, and even a Holiday Inn Express and a Super 8. On the other side of the waterway, the lodging options become more interesting, with some unique B&Bs—from two mansions under the same ownership in Laurium to a lighthouse on each side of the peninsula.

From Hancock take US 41 north toward Calumet. Before the turn for the airport, turn south on Shortcut Road and follow it into Dollar Bay. From there, turn to the northeast (left) on MI 26. This will take you into Lake Linden. Taking Valley Road north, turn right on Gay Road and follow it to the world-famous **Gay Bar.**

The town was named for Joseph Gay, the director of the Mohawk and Wolverine Mining Companies. The

Mohawk Mining Company built a stamp mill in the town, and it is the mill's superintendent's home that has become the Gay Bar today. In addition to serving drinks, they sell a selection of tacky merchandise.

Leaving town on Lac La Belle Road, it's 20 scenic miles to the next stop. As the road begins to round the curve of Bete Grise Bay, it turns westward and loops around Lac La Belle. A small roadside park on the left is home to a pleasant waterfall. In Lac La Belle, you will find the **Lac La Belle Lodge.** Situated on the lake, this is the best place around for lodging, dining, and general relaxation. The restaurant is the **Bear Belly Bar & Grill** and it offers dining with a view of the water. There's also gas and a convenient store to stock up on supplies. The lodge's cabins are tucked along the wooded shore.

Lake La Belle itself is nearly 400 feet deep and has direct access to Lake Superior. The lodge store stocks bait and rents out boats to anglers looking for some time on the water.

The tip of the Keweenaw Peninsula is where the copper boom of the 19th century began. In 1841 Michigan's first geologist, Douglas Houghton, surveyed what is now Lighthouse Point and reported that copper mining there would be economically feasible. Miners soon arrived, and the nearby natural harbor near Lake Fanny Hooe was named Copper Harbor.

Fearing hostilities with the native Ojibwa, and concerned about unruly miners, the government built the stockaded **Fort Wilkins** in 1844. The troops proved not to be needed; there was little lawlessness and no friction with the Native Americans. Mining activities eventually moved south, and by 1846 the fort was abandoned. (The

The cabins outside the fort were for families.

army returned troops to Fort Wilkins for a few years after the Civil War, mainly as a place where they could serve out the remaining years of their enlistments.)

In 1848, a light tower and keeper's dwelling were built to guide the increasing number of ships in Lake Superior around the dangerous point. Poorly constructed, the tower was replaced in 1866 with the **Copper Harbor Lighthouse,** a schoolhouse-style light. Many of the original tower's whitewashed bricks were used in the foundation of the new lighthouse.

Both of these sites are part of the **Fort Wilkins Historic State Park.** The fort has been preserved and reconstructed in parts. Throughout the summer, the fort features costumed actors who reenact what life was like for soldiers in the 19th century. Buildings in the fort are open for exploring—rooms are displayed to look as they did 150 years ago.

At the lighthouse, the 1848 keeper's home serves as an orientation center for the lighthouse complex. For a unique perspective, consider taking one of the **Copper Harbor Lighthouse Tours.** Visitors are taken from the marina to Lighthouse Point in a boat very similar to an old lighthouse launch. After arriving at the lighthouse, there is a complete tour of the lighthouse and surrounding point, which includes a look at the vein of copper discovered by Houghton those many years ago.

Even without its historical focus, the park would be worth a visit. The wooded property is hemmed in by Lake Superior and Lake Fanny Hooe, and shady campgrounds east and west of the fort offer 159 campsites.

You need to sign up for a tour in order to ride out to the Copper Harbor Lighthouse.

If you happen to catch a chill or rainy bit of weather, there's nothing better than heading over to **Grandpa's Barn** to find a great book for the trip. Housed in a rustic cabin, this bookstore has a surprisingly deep selection of books, especially if you are looking for local interest titles. There are well-worn couches and a wood-fired stove, making it extra cozy.

For lodging in Copper Harbor other than camping, consider the bright red **Bella Vista Motel**. Right in the center of town and on the harbor, the motel is within walking distance of everything. Rooms share a long porch facing the water, and the landscaped grounds are a comfortable place for a picnic. The motel also rents cabins.

The most celebrated place to stay in Copper Harbor is the **Keeweenaw Mountain Lodge**. The lodge offers

Grandpa's Barn has a great selection of books—especially if you're looking for local flavor.

both motel-style rooms and guest cabins, and its dining room serves breakfast, lunch, and dinner daily. For recreation, there are tennis courts and a nine-hole golf course. The drive from Copper Harbor on US 41 passes the lodge just 1.5 miles south of town, and the portion of US 41 that runs from Copper Harbor to the small village of Central was recognized in 1995 as the state's first scenic heritage route. The rolling terrain and dense forest make for a very pleasant drive.

West of Copper Harbor, Brockway Mountain Drive breaks away from Lake Shore Drive (MI 26). At the top of the ridge there's a parking area at 1,328 feet above sea level with wide open views of Lake Superior. To the southeast, the clearing on the far hill is the Keweenaw Mountain Lodge golf course. With a gift shop and some pit toilets, it's not a bad place for a break. Coming down the mountain into Copper Harbor, there's a short pullout at a switchback in the road. Stop here for views of Copper Harbor and Fort Wilkins on Lake Fanny Hooe.

Following MI 26 down the west edge of the peninsula, between Eagle Harbor and Eagle River, near Jacob's Falls, the monks of the Holy Transfiguration Skete have a monastery as well as a shop, **The Jampot.** Inside, delicious preserves line

The view of Copper Harbor from Brockway Mountain Drive

The route back south winds along the rocky coast of Lake Superior.

For local preserves and incredibly delicious muffins, visit the monks at the Jampot.

the shelves—thimbleberry, chokeberry, strawberry-rhubarb, boysenberry. The list is seemingly endless. Thimbleberry is a regional favorite, and the Keweenaw is one of the few places in the world where these wild berries are harvested (in many places the berries are considered a weed). Each summer the monks search the wilds for berries for their exquisite jams. They also make cookies, fruitcakes, truffles, and perhaps the most wonderful muffins you'll ever try.

Though there is no good harbor in Eagle River, the number of copper mines east of the town brought ships anyway. Docks were built far out into the lake, and for a time Eagle River experienced its own little boom. The local hotel hosted dignitaries like President Garfield and Horace Greeley. A small factory that made fuses for the mines had all the business it could handle. Soon the town had not one, but two breweries. On their day off, miners would fill the town's saloons and end the night with legendary brawls.

Eagle River is much more low-key these days. When you cross the bridge into town, be sure to pull out in the parking area to take a look at the Eagle River Timber Bridge. The wooden bridge features twin timber arches pinned together with steel hinges. From the bridge you can also look upstream to view the Eagle River Falls.

Continuing south, you come to US 41 and pass through Mohawk and

Ahmeek on the way to the historic town of Calumet. The act of Congress that established the **Keweenaw National Historic Park** states that the history of copper mining on the Keweenaw is best served in the preservation of three sites: "the Village of Calumet, the former Calumet & Hecla Mining Company properties (including the Osceola #13 mine complex), and the former Quincy Mining Company properties." Calumet's historic buildings are particularly singled out because they represent "large scale corporate paternalism . . . unprecedented in American industry."

The Lake Shore Drive Bridge over the Eagle River *Kim Forster*

The Calumet and Hecla Mining Company was the biggest copper-mining operation in the northern Keweenaw Copper Range. In the 1870s the company produced half the country's supply of copper. During its heyday, Calumet and the neighboring bedroom community of Laurium were the area's social, economic, and cultural center, and the population rose to thirty thousand. Driving into Calumet, one can't help but be struck by the planning that went into creating the town: It is laid out like a metropolitan area in miniature, as was befitting for the up-and-coming city it was at the time.

To get a sense of the town's mining history, a visit to the **Coppertown Mining Museum** is a necessity. Exhibits will introduce you to the process of pulling copper from the Keweenaw Peninsula. There is a two-man drill, ore cars, and a Sheffield pump car, which was made by the Sheffield Car Company in Three Rivers (see Chapter 5 for related itinerary). The struggles of the labor movement are also documented, including artifacts from the Italian Hall tragedy.

The disaster at the Italian Hall (often called the 1913 Massacre) occurred on Christmas Eve 1913. The evening began with a Christmas party for striking miners and their families on the second floor of Calumet's Italian Hall. The event was sponsored by the Ladies Auxiliary of the Western Federation of Miners, and more than 400 people had gathered to celebrate. At some point someone yelled "Fire!" and created a stampede for the doors. In the crush of the crowd, 73 people died; more than half of them were children.

After much investigation, there were enough witness accounts to suggest the cry was first raised by an antiunion supporter. The striking miners had been off the

The Italian Hall arch marks the site of an iconic tragedy in the story of unionization.

The Calumet Theatre opened for its first production in 1900.

job for five months at this point, and tensions between labor and management were running very high. Whether the cry of "Fire!" was an ill-conceived prank or a deliberate attempt to murder striking miners and their families, it became a galvanizing moment for the labor union movement. Years later, in 1941, Woody Guthrie immortalized the event with his song, "1913 Massacre."

You can visit the **Italian Hall Site** in Calumet. The hall itself is gone, but where it once stood a brick arch marks the location. The site is located near the intersection of Seventh and Elm Streets.

Since 1920 and the decline of the copper industry, Calumet has fallen on hard times. With the exodus of people and businesses, much of the downtown has fallen into disrepair. Thanks to the efforts of the Keweenaw National Historic Park and others dedicated to the preservation of this historic district, Calumet shows signs of a rebirth. The historic **Calumet Theatre,** which opened in 1900, hosts upwards of 80 events every year, including numerous concerts and local theatrical performances. In the summer the theater offers guided tours of the building.

Another structure with an impressive history is the Vertin Building, at the corner of Sixth and Scott Streets. For a hundred years, the Vertin Brothers & Co. department store served the people of Calumet, finally closing in 1985 along with the mine. The build-

The Laurium Manor Inn was once a private residence.

ing, with its wide-open spaces, floor-to-ceiling windows, and hardwood floors, is now home to the **Vertin Gallery.** The gallery displays the work of over a hundred artists, most of whom call the U.P. home. There are other galleries in Calumet, too— Beadazed, Mishwabik, Copper Country Artisans, and the Omphale Gallery display paintings, pottery, copper crafts, and leatherwork.

A block from the Vertin Building is the **Michigan House Café & Brew Pub,** which at one time was a hotel and bar. (Now there are just two furnished apartments on the second floor available to lodgers.) The café serves sandwiches and wraps, burgers and steaks, and seafood—all reasonably priced.

Nearby in Laurium, the wealthy of Calumet built their often-palatial homes. One example is the **Laurium Manor Inn,** a 45-room mansion built in 1908 for the owner of the Calumet & Arizona Mining Company. No expense was spared to outfit this millionaire's home. Given miners' wages at the time, a person working a 40-hour week would have had to work close to a hundred years in the mines to earn the $50,000 it cost to build the home. And then another 70 years to buy the furniture! (This assumes, of course, that the miner didn't have any other expenses like food and shelter.) The inn is wonderfully preserved and has 10 guest rooms with private baths. Across the street, there are 8 more rooms in Victorian Hall. This 34-room mansion, built in 1906, was constructed of brick and sandstone. Both homes

The walk out to Canyon Falls is almost as beautiful as the falls themselves. *Kim Forster*

Michigamee has seen many businesses come and many businesses go.

Volunteers maintain this humble museum in Michigamee.

exude history and tell a mixed story of the wealth of days past.

Lighthouses conjure romance in the imagination: A tired keeper climbing the tower at night to fuel the light, which will warn passing ships of the rocky coast. Sharp rains batter the windows, but still the lonely vigil goes on. The **Sands Hill Lighthouse Inn** in Ahmeek offers guests a chance to experience a little of what lighthouse life must have been like. Standing sentinel on the peninsula's north shore, it was built in 1913. It was the last manned lighthouse on the Great Lakes—and the biggest, housing three keepers. Today this lighthouse is a unique bed & breakfast offering eight rooms with unmatched views of Lake Superior. Wood floors throughout, fine Victorian details, private balconies, and a recreation room with billiards ensure a comfortable stay no matter the weather.

If your way home crosses the Mackinac Bridge, you will most likely follow US 41 to US 2. Still on the Keweenaw in L'Anse, the **Hilltop Restaurant** serves an excellent sweet roll, which, as they say, is as big as your head! Grab a roll and check out some of the nearby waterfalls. There is a nice run of falls along the aptly named Falls River in L'Anse. To get there, take Broad Street downtown and turn left onto Main. Park next to the ceiling-tile plant; the trail begins between the fence and the river and follows the river upstream, ending near Burger King. Along the way the trail passes Upper, Lower, and Middle Falls.

South 10 miles from L'Anse, the Canyon Falls on the Sturgeon River are right off US 41. The roadside park is clearly marked. From the parking area, it's a 1-mile hike over level ground. The path passes through a thick cedar and red pine forest. A wooden platform crosses wetter ground, and unfortunately, the mosquitoes can be unbearable if the conditions are right. The river, wide and shallow at the start of the path, begins to descend into a canyon and drops 15 feet before disappearing behind a rocky wall.

The final stop on the route is the slow-paced village of Michigamme. The eponymous 95,000-acre lake nearby has its share of multi-million-dollar mansions and classic north woods log lodges, as well as humbler cottages and lake homes. Michigamme itself, however, has seen better days. With little regional industry, the younger gener-

These falls are found at the end of a trail that begins near the back of the Burger King parking lot.

ation has left. And the older generation finds it harder to get by without a grocery store and other amenities that they find when they move to Marquette. The town does have two restaurants—one that's open year-round—and a delightful museum.

Run by a handful of dedicated volunteers, the **Michigamme Historical Museum** has artifacts celebrating the town's history—from the early lumbering days to the mining boom to the short stint at celebrity when the cast and crew of *Anatomy of a Murder* came to shoot a few scenes in town. At the back of the property, one of Michigamme's oldest homes has been transplanted and restored to its 1900s condition, and the museum often brings out the original 1900 steam fire engine—the pride of the collection.

Before you head home, plan some time to enjoy Lake Michigamme. The **Van Riper State Park** rents canoes and kayaks on the lake's eastern shore. It's also a great place for a little camping.

IN THE AREA

ACCOMMODATIONS

Bella Vista Motel. Call 1-877-888-VIEW (8439). The motel is right on the harbor and rents cabins as well as motel rooms. Website: bellavistamotel.com.

Black River Crossing B&B, N11485 Hedberg Road, Bessemer. Call 906-932-2604. This bed & breakfast requires a multinight stay and does not accommodate children. Website: blackrivercrossing.com.

Keweenaw Mountain Lodge, 14252 US 41, Copper Harbor. Call 906-289-4403 or 1-888-685-6343. Just south of Copper Harbor, the lodge has a dining room, tennis courts, and a golf course. They rent rooms and cabins. Website: atthelodge.com.

La Belle Lodge, 11627 Superior Street, Lac La Belle. Call 906-289-4293. Website: laclabellelodge.com.

Laurium Manor Inn, 320 Tamarack Street, Laurium. Call 906-337-2549. This bed & breakfast includes Victorian Hall, across the street. Website: laurium.info.

Sands Hill Lighthouse Inn, Five Mile Point Road, Ahmeek. Call 906-337-1744. Website: sandhillslighthouseinn.com.

ATTRACTIONS AND RECREATION

Adventure Mining Company, Adventure Road (off MI 38), Greenland. Call 906-883-3371. Website: adventureminetours.com.

The Calumet Theatre, 340 Sixth Street, Calumet. Call 906-337-2166. Concerts and theatrical performances scheduled year-round. In summer, they offer guided tours of the historic theater. Website: calumettheatre.com.

Copper Harbor Lighthouse Tours. Call 906-289-4966. Open May through Oct. In the summer, boats leave hourly. Website: copperharborlighthouse.com.

Coppertown Mining Museum, 25815 Red Jacket Road, Calumet. Call 906-337-4354. Website: uppermichigan.com/coppertown.

Fort Wilkins Historic State Park, 15223 US 41, Copper Harbor. Call 906-289-4215. Website: michigan.gov/ftwilkins.

The Gay Bar, 925 Lake Street, Gay. Call 906-296-0951. Website: thegaybar.com.

Grandpa's Barn, 340 South Fourth Street, Copper Harbor. Call 906-289-4377. Website: facebook.com/grandpasbarn.

Italian Hall Site, 401 Seventh Street, Calumet. Website: keweenaw.info/attractions/history/297.html.

The Jampot, Holy Transfiguration Skete, 6500 MI 26, Eagle Harbor. No phone. The shop is open in the summer, Monday through Sat. Website: http://store.societystjohn.com.

Keweenaw National Historic Park, Calumet. Call 906-337-3168. Website: nps.gov/kewe.

Michigamme Historical Museum, 110 West Main Street, Michigamme. Call 906-323-6608. Website: michigammetownship.com/michigamme-museum.

Porcupine Wilderness State Park, 33303 Headquarters Road, Ontonagon. Call 906-885-5275. Website: michigan.gov/porkies.

Quincy Mine, 49750 US 41, Hancock.

Call 906-482-3101. Website: quincy mine.com.

Stormy Kromer Mercantile, 1238 Wall Street, Ironwood. Call 1-888-455-2253. The plant offers tours during the weekdays, check Website for more information. Website: stormykromer .com.

Van Riper State Park, 851 CR Ake, Champion. Call 906-339-4461. Website: michigan.gov/vanriper.

Vertin Gallery, 220 Sixth Street, Calumet. Call 906-337-2200. Located in the old Vertin Department Store, the gallery displays the work of over a hundred artists, mostly local. Website: vertingallery.com.

DINING

Antonio's, 35409 Mineral River Drive, White Pine. Call 906-885-5223. The entrance is near the rear entrance to the mall.

Bear Belly Bar & Grill, 11627 Superior Street, Lac La Belle. Call 906-289-4293. Website: laclabellelodge.com.

Don & GG's Food & Spirits, 1300 East Cloverland Drive (US 2), Ironwood. Call 906-932-2312.

Gemignani's Italian Restaurant, 512 Quincy Street, Hancock. Call 906-482-2920. West of the bridge 0.5 mile. Website: gemignani.com.

Hilltop Restaurant, 18047 US 41, L'Anse. Call 906-524-7858. Website: sweetroll.com.

The Library Restaurant & Brew Pub, 62 Isle Royale Street, Houghton. Call 906-487-5882. Website: library brewpub.com.

Michigan House Café & Brew Pub, 300 Sixth Street, Calumet. Call 906-

The sweet rolls at Hilltop are nearly as big as your head.

337-1910. Website: michiganhouse cafe.com.

Tacconelli's Town House, 215 South Suffolk Street, Ironwood. Call 906-932-2101. Website: tacconellis.com.

OTHER CONTACTS

Copper Harbor Visitors Center, US 41 and Second Street in the Grant Township building, Copper Harbor. Call 906-289-4274. Website: copper harbor.org.

Ironwood Area Chamber of Commerce, 150 North Lowell Street, Ironwood. Call 906-932-1122. Website: ironwoodchamber.org.

Keweenaw Chamber of Commerce, 902 College Avenue, Houghton. Call 906-482-5240 or 1-866-304-5722. Website: keweenaw.org.

Keweenaw Convention & Visitors Bureau, 56638 Calumet Avenue, Calumet. Call 906-337-4579 or 1-800-338-7982. The visitors center is on the right side of US 41 as you approach from the south. Website: keweenaw.info.

The cliffs of Fayette bound the east shore of the harbor.

12 Lake Michigan's Other Coast

CURTIS & THE MANISTIQUE LAKES, BLANEY PARK, MANISTIQUE, AND ESCANABA

Estimated length: 230 miles
Estimated time: 5 hours

Getting there: This trip begins on US 2 west of the Mackinac Bridge in the Upper Peninsula. When 22 miles west of Naubinway, turn right on Manistique Lakes Road to get to Curtis. The drive from Curtis to Blaney Park follows Curtis Road west, with a jog to the south on Diller and continuing west on County Highway 447. At MI 77, drive south through Blaney Park back to US 2. The rest of the route follows US 2 along the coast of Lake Michigan to Escanaba.

Highlights: Beginning on the Lake Michigan Scenic Highway, the trip begins with wide open views of Lake Michigan shoreline. All along the coast, there are sandy beaches for sunning and swimming. West of Brevort is the Cut River Bridge and Park. Farther on, the town of Curtis is tucked in between the Manistique Lakes. The area has plenty of fishing and boating in the summer, ice fishing and snowmobiling in the winter. Blaney Park, to the west, is a little community with excellent antiques shops and a bed & breakfast. Just north of Blaney Park, near Germfask, is the entrance to the Seney National Wildlife Refuge and its scenic Marshland Wildlife Drive. Returning to US 2 and Lake Michigan, tour the Seul Choix Point Lighthouse on your way to Manistique. For fishing and paddling, the Manistique River is a nice easygoing stretch of water that passes through the Seney National Wildlife Refuge and Manistique River State Forest. There are campgrounds along the way, so a canoe trip with Northland Outfitters out of Germfask can be a multiday affair. West of Manistique, there are two state parks on Indian Lake: Indian Lake State Park has camping and lake access, and the Palms Book State Park centers on Michigan's largest spring, Kitch-iti-kipi. South on the Garden Peninsula, the state maintains the ghost town of Fayette as part of Fayette State Park. A good part of a

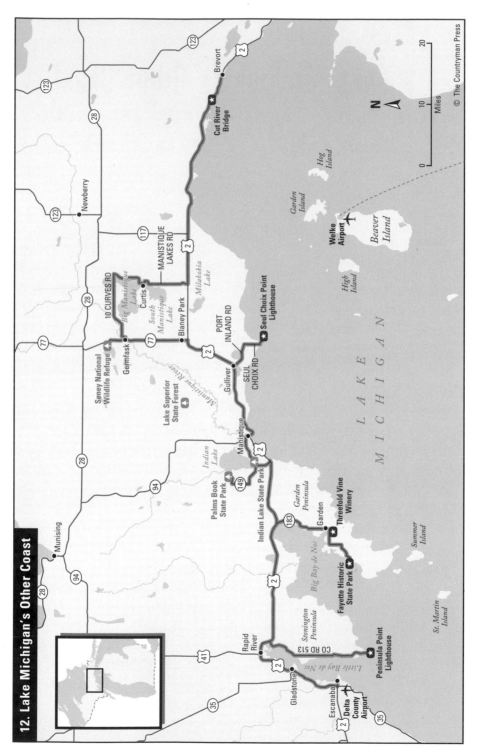

12. Lake Michigan's Other Coast

day could be spent exploring this scenic spot on Lake Michigan. To the west, at the southern tip of the Stonington Peninsula, visitors can climb the tower of Peninsula Point Lighthouse. Bring a picnic lunch so you can spend more time appreciating this secluded point on the lake. In Escanaba, the Ludington Park has a beach on Sand Island, or you can tour the Sand Point Lighthouse.

The main highway across the Upper Peninsula, US 2 begins at I-75 north of the bridge and continues through to Duluth, Minnesota. The first stretch of highway is bordered by a long sandy beach on Lake Michigan. If the beach is not part of your plans, your first stop on this trip is 4 miles west of Brevort.

Locals call it the "million-dollar bridge over a two-bit creek," but when the Michigan Department of Transportation built the Cut River Bridge in the 1940s, it was clear it was a special project. The cantilevered bridge was built during World War II, and since almost all available steel was being diverted to the war effort, it took nearly five years to complete. The bridge stretches 641 feet across the Cut River Valley, and at 147 feet above the creek below, it is the state's second tallest (Big Mac soars close to 200 feet). Incorporated into its construction are walkways that allow visitors underneath the bridge to see the structure up close, and on either end of the bridge there are roadside parks with shady picnic areas and paths that lead to the valley below. From there, it's a short walk out to Lake Michigan.

When 30 miles past the bridge, turn north on Manistique Lake Road. Between Big Manistique and South Manistique Lakes is the little town of Curtis. (North Manistique Lake is up near the town of Helmer.) This entire system of lakes drains into the Manistique River and Lake Michigan, and all three lakes are popular for fishing. Overall they are rather shallow—South Manistique is near 30 feet deep at its north end, but overall not so deep, and Big Manistique is mostly 5 to 10 feet deep.

Curtis, which began as a lumber town, became a resort area that was popular for years. Many of the old classic lodges are now private retreats, but some are still operated as lodges, and the town has become the center of activity for the flood of visitors that vacation here every year.

On a wide shady lawn, overlooking Big Manistique Lake, **Chamberlin's Ole Forest Inn** is a great restaurant and bar as well as a bed & breakfast. The inn dates back to the logging days of the late 19th century. Built near the

The grand porch at Chamberlin's Ole Forest Inn overlooks the largest of the Manistique Lakes.

train station in Curtis, the home was originally intended to serve as a hotel for railroad passengers. The structure was moved near the lake in 1924, and instead it was used as a hunting resort and lakeside lodge for various owners. In 1990, Bud Chamberlin opened the inn as a B&B, and the rest is history. Folks in the U.P. will drive an hour each way for dinner and a drink at Chamberlin's.

About 10 miles east of Curtis, close to MI 117, the **Sandtown Farmhouse Bed & Breakfast** in Engadine sits on 80 acres of field and forest. The farmhouse was built in 1920 from a Sears kit. The inn offers three guest rooms with private baths, and breakfast is cooked each morning on a classic wood-fired stove. Also, kids are welcome.

Canada geese in the Seney Wildlife Refuge *Kim Forster*

West of Curtis on MI 77 is the Seney National Wildlife Refuge near Germfask and the old lumber company town of Blaney Park. To get to Germfask, take Manistique Lakes Road north to 10 Curves Road west. At MI 77, turn north. The entrance to the **Seney National Wildlife Refuge** is 2.5 miles north on the west side of the road. This 95,000-acre preserve includes 7,000 acres of managed wetlands and 25,000 acres of wilderness. The 10,000-acre Strangmoor Bog is a national natural landmark and represents one of the most southern patterned bogs in the country. Throughout it all run miles and miles of hiking and biking trails, ski trails, and river paddling routes. This unique sanctuary is home to hundreds of different kinds of birds and a treasure trove of other wildlife.

The easiest way to experience the refuge is to take the Marshland Wildlife Drive. This 7-mile one-way loop winds its way around numerous ponds with

Sandhill cranes in the Seney Wildlife Refuge

plenty of opportunities for sightseeing and bird-watching. The optional Fishing Loop is slightly more wooded and all told only adds a scant 0.5 mile to the trip. Be sure to stop by the visitors center before you start your tour to ask about recent wildlife sightings.

Antique shops are nestled into old cottages in Blaney Park.

At 9 miles south of the refuge sits the seasonal town of Blaney Park, which began as a company town for the Wisconsin Land & Lumber Company. It was purchased by the Washington Earle family, and in the 1920s, they turned it into a hunting and fishing resort. Today the town is comprised of a bed & breakfast, a hotel, and a small row of cottages with antiques shops.

One of these shops is the **Blaney Park Antiques & Tea Shop**, where over half a dozen antiques dealers display their treasures. The tables are crowded with Depression glass and Royal Doulton figurines and mugs, old railroad lanterns, fishing creels, and antique snowshoes. It's a treasure hunter's dream. The shop also carries tins of their own custom blend of teas—always using organic and fair trade leaves. Also be sure to check out **Sadie's Antique Cottage,** which has

This small community of antique shops offers a great variety of treasures.

treasures tucked into nearly every nook and cranny, offering a surprisingly varied collection for antiques hunters.

At the north end of Blaney Park, past the rows of cottages, waits the **Celibeth House.** Built in 1895 as a private home, this bed & breakfast sits on 80 acres overlooking a small lake. Guests are encouraged to explore the property. In the winter, ungroomed trails are open to snowshoeing and cross-country skiing.

The home was once the local headquarters for the lumber company, and later it was converted into an inn for the Blaney Park resort. The inn now offers seven

The Seul Choix Point Lighthouse was built in 1885.

The lighthouse in Manistique

guest rooms, each with a private bath. Common areas include the library and living room; the latter has a nice fireplace. Unlike many B&Bs, the innkeepers at the Celibeth House welcome children.

Return to US 2 and continue west to Manistique. Between the Straits of Mackinac and the Garden Peninsula, a small point edges out into Lake Michigan. The point was named "only choice" (or *seul choix* in French) by trappers who were once forced to weather out a storm in its harbor. When the **Seul Choix Point Lighthouse** was built in 1895, the end of the point was still wilderness. Without any roads, the lighthouse was supplied by ships. Today the light is thankfully accessible by road.

The keeper's quarters from 1895 and the additional living quarters added in 1925 are maintained as a lighthouse museum, complete with period furniture, photographs of the light and its keepers, and even items owned by those who once lived here. Guests can climb the tower for a small donation. Next door to the light is a more modern building, once a private home that now houses the gift shop. The road to the light is 8 miles south of Gulliver (on US 2, 12 miles east of Manistique). The locals pronounce *seul choix* as "sis shwah."

Manistique was once a lumber and paper mill town. A string of motels along Lake Michigan and a few restaurants make this a nice place to set up camp while you explore the surrounding sites.

The Manistique River, which begins its 71.2-mile run to Lake Michigan from Manistique Lake east of Germfask, is a wide lazy river, popular with anglers and paddlers of all abilities. The river passes through the Seney National Wildlife Refuge and the Manistique River State Forest. The folks at **Northland Outfitters** in Germfask offer canoe and kayaking trips that last 2 1/2 hours to 7 days.

In 1926 the Palms Book Land Company sold 90 acres of property to the state of Michigan for 10 dollars. The sale was arranged by Jim Bellaire, who wanted the famed spring, Kitch-iti-kipi, to be preserved for the public's enjoyment. The deed required that the property forever be used for public rec-

The raft in Palms Book State Park takes visitors across the middle of Kitch-iti-kipi, the Big Spring.

reation and be named **Palms Book State Park.** When Bellaire first came across the spring, a lumber company was using the property as a dump. Enchanted by the spring's deep pool, he saw past the debris and envisioned an attraction that would delight thousands. There are many legends about the springs that are attributed to Native Americans, though it has been suggested that these stories were created as an early marketing tool.

It's hard to imagine the spring as Bellaire would have seen it. Cedar and pine trees now line the wide path that leads back to the spring. There's an observation deck on the shore, and a large raft allows visitors to cross over the middle of the pool, looking down 40 feet to the bottom. The raft is attached to a cable stretched over the water, and visitors turn a wheel to propel the raft across the pool and then back. Below, large trout swim lazily in the pool's gentle currents as nearly 20 small springs gush 10,000 gallons of water per minute. The water flows out into a wide shallow stream that empties into Indian Lake. Since the water remains 45 degrees year-round, the spring can be visited in the winter. The entrance, however, is gated in the winter, so visitors have to hike in from the road. To get to Kitch-iti-kipi from Manistique, take Deer Street (MI 94) west out of town. When MI 94 turns north at the edge of town, continue west on Deer Street (now CR 442). The road passes through Indian Lake State Park and joins with MI 149. MI 149 makes some turns north and then east, but after a few miles you will see signs for the spring.

Southwest of Manistique, the Garden Peninsula reaches a finger out into Lake Michigan, creating the Big Bay de Noc. The point is loosely linked by a chain of islands to Wisconsin's Door Peninsula, which forms Green Bay. On the south-

The preserved company town of Fayette

A view of the harbor in Fayette

Horses on the Garden Peninsula

west shore of the Garden Peninsula is the Historic Fayette Townsite. Now a ghost town maintained by the **Fayette Historic State Park,** Fayette was a company town in the 1880s. It was here that iron ore was smelted into pig iron before being shipped to steelmaking plants. The remains of the Jackson Iron Company's furnace complex and the charcoal kilns overlook the town's natural harbor.

A lot of the town's buildings remain: the Shelton Hotel, the machine shop, the company office, as well as the doctor's home on the wooded point. The superintendent's house overlooks the Snail Shell Harbor, and the limestone cliffs across the water create a wonderfully scenic backdrop. In the summer, recreational craft sidle up to the modern dock, and it's not rare to find an angler casting a line from a rowboat in the harbor.

The park has an excellent interpretive center that has a model of what the town once looked like. Overnight berths are available to boaters, and there are 63 campsites. To get to Fayette, take US 2 west of Manistique to Garden Corners and drive south on MI 183. Follow the signs to the state park.

Between Fayette and the little town of Garden, just south of 16th Road on NN Road, the family owned and operated **Threefold Vine Winery** has wine tasting and winemaking tours. Located on the Green family farm, the 4-acre vineyard was planted in 2002. The farm also grows sugar beets, pumpkins, and apples.

Returning to US 2, Escanaba is 38 miles west and south. Along the way, US 2 crosses the top of the Stonington Peninsula. County Road 513 (CR 513), about 3 miles east of Rapid River, turns south and follows the western edge of the peninsula to the **Peninsula Point Lighthouse.** The 40-foot lighthouse tower is open to the public (the keeper's home is no more), and there's a nice picnic area on the site. From the top of the tower's iron spiral staircase, you can see Little Bay de Noc to the west and as far as Washington Island off Wisconsin's Door Peninsula to the south. The 18-mile trip to the lighthouse is scenic in its rural simplicity— well worth the drive.

Most recently celebrated in Jeff Daniels's play and subsequent movie *Escanaba in da Moonlight*, Escanaba is one of the region's biggest cities, with over thirteen thousand residents. Overlooking the mouth of the Little Bay de Noc, with direct access to Chicago via Lake Michigan, the town was an important port for shipping lumber, iron ore, and copper. Iron ore is still shipped out of Escanaba, though the industry has shifted and the town's largest employer is now the NewPage paper mill.

As Escanaba is just five to six hours north of Chicago and two north of Green Bay, most tourists come from Wisconsin and Illinois. The city's big attraction is the waterfront. East of

Fayette

The Sand Point Lighthouse is part of Ludington Park in Escanaba.

Lakeshore Drive, Ludington Park incorporates a beach, the Yacht Harbor, and the **Sand Point Lighthouse.**

Built in 1868, the lighthouse served the growing number of ships that came to Escanaba's port after the town was connected to the Negaunee iron mines by railroad. In 1938, another light farther out in the bay replaced the Sand Point Light, and a year later the Coast Guard went about converting the old lighthouse into housing, removing its light and covering the brick structure with aluminum siding. Since 1986 the lighthouse has been under the care of the Delta County Historical Association. In the summer the restored lighthouse and its museum are open daily.

Downtown Escanaba has a couple of coffeehouses, some shops, and a unique steakhouse, **Hereford & Hops.** The name refers, of course, to the menu, which prominently features steak and beer. Guests cook their own meal on one of the restaurant's two open grills, or you can always have one of their chefs grill a steak for you. Seafood, pasta, and pizza are also offered, and several standard beers and seasonal brews are always on tap.

A few blocks away is the **Swedish Pantry.** Very popular for breakfast, the restaurant serves a menu of Swedish and American dishes, and their bakery has great muffins and giant cookies. Across the street and up the block is the Canterbury Book Store, a little storefront bookshop with an incredible selection of titles. They carry books in every category imaginable—from new fiction to kids' books to titles covering every aspect of Michigan.

IN THE AREA

ACCOMMODATIONS

Celibeth House, 4446 North MI 77, Blaney Park. Call 906-283-3409. Website: celibethhousebnb.com.

Chamberlin's Ole Forest Inn, N9450 Manistique Lakes Road, Curtis. Call 906-586-6000 or 1-800-292-0440. The inn is located 1 mile north of Curtis off Manistique Lake Road (also called H 33 and MI 135). Website: chamberlins inn.com.

Sandtown Farmhouse Bed and Breakfast, W14142 Sandtown Road, Engadine. Call 906-477-6163. Website: sandtownfarmhouse.com.

ATTRACTIONS AND RECREATION

Blaney Park Antiques & Tea Shop, 4370 North MI 77, Germfask. Call 906-283-1515. Open daily in the summer, weekends in the fall.

Canterbury Book Store, 908 Ludington Street, Escanaba. Call 906-786-0751. Carries a wide selection of new books.

Fayette Historic State Park, 4785 II Road, Garden. Call 906-644-2603. Website: michigan.gov/fayette.

Northland Outfitters, 8174 MI 77, Germfask. Call 906-586-9801 or 1-800-808-3FUN (386). Website: north outfitters.com.

Palms Book State Park, Manistique. Call 906-341-2355. Website: michigan .gov/palmsbook.

Peninsula Point Lighthouse, southern tip of the Stonington Peninsula.

Sadie's Antique Cottage, 4375 MI 77, Germfask. Call 906-283-0041.

Sand Point Lighthouse, 16 Water Plant Road, Escanaba. Call 906-786-3763.

Seney National Wildlife Refuge, 1674 Refuge Entrance Road, Seney. Call 906-586-9851. Website: fws.gov/ refuge/seney.

Seul Choix Point Lighthouse, 672N West Gulliver Lake Road, Gulliver. Call 906-283-3183. Website: greatlake lighthouse.com.

Threefold Vine Winery, 5856 NN Road, Garden. Call 906-644-7089.

DINING

Chamberlin's Ole Forest Inn. Call 906-586-6000 or 1-800-292-0440. The inn is located 1 mile north of Curtis off Manistique Lake Road (also called H 33 and MI 135). Website: chamberlins inn.com.

Hereford & Hops, 624 Ludington Street, Escanaba. Call 906-789-1945. The steakhouse is one of three nationwide. Open daily for lunch and dinner (dinner only on Sunday). Website: herefordandhops.com.

Swedish Pantry, 819 Ludington Street, Escanaba. Call 906-786-9606. Website: swedishpantry.com.

OTHER CONTACTS

Bays de Noc Convention and Visitors Bureau, 230 Ludington Street, Escanaba. Call 906-789-7862. Website: travelbaysdenoc.com.

Curtis Michigan Chamber of Commerce. Call 906-586-3700 or 1-800-652-8784. Website: curtischamber.com.

INDEX

A

accommodations. *See specific destinations and accommodations*
Ackroyd's Scottish Bakery (Redford), 27, 34
Ada Covered Bridge, 82
Adventure Mining Company (Greenland), 218, 230
agates, 199–200, 207
Agawa Canyon Tour Train (Sault Ste. Marie, Ontario), 187, 188
Ahmeek, 225; lodging, 228, 230
Albert East Sleeper State Park, 46, 50
Alger County Chamber of Commerce, 209
Algoma's Water Tower Inn (Sault Ste. Marie, Ontario), 186, 188
Allen, 64–65
Allen Antique Barn, 65, 72
Alpena, 161–62; dining, 162, 169; information, 169; lodging, 162–63, 167
Alpena Michigan Convention and Visitors Bureau, 169
ALTRAN Bus Service (Alger County Transit), 203, 207
American Coney Island (Detroit), 21, 35
Amway Grand Plaza Hotel (Grand Rapids), 86, 89
Ann Arbor, 69–71; dining, 70–71, 73; information, 73; lodging, 71; traveling to, 53
Ann Arbor Area Convention and Visitors Bureau, 73
antiques: Allen, 64–65; Bay City, 47, 50; Blaney Park, 237, 242; Holly, 29, 34; Lowell, 81, 89
Antlers, The (Sault Ste. Marie), 186, 189
Antonio's (White Pine), 218, 231
Appledore IV, 47
apples, 99, 141, 143, 164
Applesauce Inn (Bellaire), 141–42, 151
Archives Book Shop (East Lansing), 79, 89
Ark, The (Ann Arbor), 70, 72
Arnold Mackinac Island Ferry, 175–76, 189
art galleries: Calumet, 227, 231; Charlevoix, 143, 144, 151–52, 152; Elk Rapids, 139–40, 152; Grand Marais, 200, 207;

Hessel, 183–84, 188; Marquette, 206, 208; Northport, 127, 132; Suttons Bay, 128, 132
ArtPrize (Grand Rapids), 85–86, 89
Arts & Crafts Show (Harrisville), 161, 167
Arts and Crafts movement, in Detroit, 20–22
Astoria Pastry Shop (Detroit), 23–24, 35
Atwood, 143
Au Sable Point Light Station, 199
Au Sable River, 157, 158–60; cruises, 159, 167; fishing, 159–60; paddling, 158–59
Au Train: dining, 203, 209
AuSable River Canoe Marathon, 158, 167
AuSable River Queen, 159, 167
automobile industry, 11–12, 19–20, 22, 25–26. *See also* Car Country

B

Bad Dog Deli (Traverse City), 130, 133
Badger, 120, 132
Bald Mountain State Recreation Area, 32, 34
Bank 1884 Food & Spirits (Port Austin), 45, 51
Barb's Bakery (Northport), 127, 133
Bark Chapel (Mackinac Island), 177
Baroda: winery, 99, 112
Bavarian Inn (Frankenmuth), 48–49, 51
Bay City, 47
Bay City Antiques Center, 47, 50
Bay Mills-Brimley Historical Research Society, 193–94
Bay Sail (Bay City), 47, 50
Bay View (town), 149–50
Bay View Association, 149, 153
Bays de Noc Convention and Visitors Bureau (Escanaba), 243
Bayside Inn (Saugatuck), 110, 111
Bear Belly Bar & Grill (Lac La Belle), 221, 231
Beaumont (Dr. William) Museum (Mackinac Island), 177
Beaver Island, 146–47; information, 153; transportation, 147, 153
Beaver Island Boat Company, 147, 153
Beaver Island Chamber of Commerce, 153
Beaver Island Lighthouse, 146
Beaver Island Lodge, 147, 153

Beaver Island Marina, 147, 151
Beaver Islander, 147
Beechwood Manor Inn & Cottage (Saugatuck), 111
Bella Vista Motel (Copper Harbor), 223, 230
Bellaire, 141; lodging, 141–42, 151
Bellaire, Lake, 141
Bellaire Chamber of Commerce, 153
Bell's Beer Bayview Mackinac Race, 40
Beltline Bar (Grand Rapids), 86, 91
Benton Harbor, 99
Bernida, 40
Berrien Springs, 104; winery, 99, 112
Bessemer, 213, 215–16
Betsie Lake, 123
Betsie River, 123
Betsie Valley Trail, 123
Bicycle Street Inn & Suites (Mackinac Island), 179, 186
Biddle House (Mackinac Island), 176–77
Bier Art Gallery (Charlevoix), 143, 151–52
Big Bay (town), 208
Big Bay de Noc, 239–40
Big Bay Point Lighthouse B&B, 207, 208
Big Dipper Ice Cream Parlour (Cheboygan), 165, 167
Big Sable Point Lighthouse (Ludington), 118, 121, 132
Big Sable River, 121
Bird Hills Nature Area (Ann Arbor), 69
bird-watching, 28, 56–57, 141, 236–37
Bishop's Bog Preserve (Portage), 95–96, 112
Black River, 105, 106, 215–16
Black River Books (South Haven), 106–7, 112
Black River Bridge, 40
Black River Crossing B&B (Bessemer), 216, 230
Black River Scenic Byway, 211, 213, 216
Black Star Farms (Suttons Bay), 129, 131, 132
Blaney Park, 233, 237–38; lodging, 237–38, 242
Blaney Park Antiques & Tea Shop, 237, 242
Blue Nile (Ann Arbor), 70, 73
Blue Star Highway, 93, 105, 108; map, 94
Blue Water Area Convention & Visitors Bureau (Port Huron), 51
Blue Water Bridge, 40
Blue Water region, 37–51; highlights, 37;
listings, 50–51; map, 38; traveling to, 37
Blueberry Festival (South Haven), 105, 112
Blueberry Store (South Haven), 105, 112
Bluewater Inn and Suites (Grand Haven), 88, 89
boat cruises, 159, 162–63, 167, 202, 208. *See also* ferries
boating. *See* paddling
Bogan Lane Inn (Mackinac Island), 181, 187
Bois Blanc Island, 166
Bois Blanc Island Ferry, 166, 169
Bond Falls, 214
bookstores: Charlevoix, 145, 152; Detroit, 22, 34; East Lansing, 79, 89; Escanaba, 242; Mackinac Island, 179, 187; Marquette, 205, 209; Northport, 127, 132; Petoskey, 149, 152; South Haven, 106–7, 112; Traverse City, 129, 132
Boone Docks (Glen Arbor), 125, 133
Boulevard Market (Tecumseh), 60, 72
Boyden House (Grand Haven), 88, 89
Boyne City, 148
Brevort, 235
bridges, covered, 81, 82, 95, 112
Brimley, 194
British Tea Garden and Rooftop Café (Tecumseh), 60, 72
Brockway Mountain Drive, 223
Brockwell Chambers B&B (Sault Ste. Marie, Ontario), 187, 188
Bronner's CHRISTmas Wonderland (Frankenmuth), 49, 50
Brooklyn: information, 73; lodging, 64, 71
Brooklyn-Irish Hills Chamber of Commerce, 73
Brown's Fish House (Paradise), 197, 209
Brownstone Inn (Au Train), 203, 209
Brownwood Acres (Central Lake), 140–41, 152
Burdickville: dining, 125, 133
Burnt Toast Inn (Ann Arbor), 71

C
Calumet, 220, 225–27; dining, 227, 231; information, 231
Calumet Theatre, 226, 230
Cambridge, 62
Cambridge Junction, 64
Campbell Street Gallery (Grand Marais), 200, 207
Camper's Cove Campground & Canoe Livery (Alpena), 162, 167

canoeing. *See* paddling
Canterbury Book Store (Escanaba), 242
Canyon Falls, 229
Capitol Building (Lansing), 80, 90–91
Captain's Quarter's Inn (Lexington), 43, 50
Car Country, 17–35; highlights, 17, 19; listings, 34–35; map, 18; traveling to, 17
carriage tours, of Mackinac Island, 178, 188
Carroll House B&B (Lexington), 43, 50
Cartier Mansion Bed & Breakfast (Ludington), 121–22, 131
Caseville, 46–47; dining, 47, 51; information, 51
Caseville Chamber of Commerce, 51
Caseville County Park, 46, 50
Caulkins, Horace, 20–22
Cedarville, 182–83
Celibeth House (Blaney Park), 237–38, 242
Central Lake, 141, 142; dining, 142, 153; information, 153
Central Lake Chamber of Commerce, 153
Chain Ferry (Saugatuck), 109
Chain of Lakes, 131, 138, 141
Chamberlin's Ole Forest Inn (Curtis), 235–36, 242, 243
Charles H. Moore Public Library (Lexington), 42, 50
Charlevoix, 143–45; information, 153
Charlevoix, Lake, 145, 148; ferries, 145, 148
Charlevoix Chamber of Commerce, 153
Charlevoix City Beach, 144
Cheboygan, 165–66; lodging, 166, 169
Cheboygan River, 165–66
Cheeseburger in Caseville, 46–47, 50
Chelsea, 68–69
Chelsea Milling Company, 69, 72
cherries, 117, 129, 132, 143
Cherry Coast, 115–33; highlights, 115, 117; listings, 131–33; map, 116; traveling to, 115
Chicago Pike Inn & Spa (Coldwater), 65, 71
Chicago Road, 56, 61–63; map, 54
Chocolate Garden (Coloma), 98, 112
Christmas shop, in Frankenmuth, 49, 50
cider mills, 32, 34, 35
City of Milwaukee (Manistee), 123, 132
Clarkston, 31; dining, 31, 35; lodging, 31, 34

Clarkston Union, 31, 35
Classic Pizza (Central Lake), 142, 153
Clementine's (South Haven), 107, 113
climate, 14–15
Clinton, 60
Clyde's Drive-In (Sault Ste. Marie), 185–86, 189
Coldwater, 65; dining, 65, 73; lodging, 65, 71
Coloma, 98–99
Colonial Michilimackinac, 174
Coney Island restaurants, 21, 33, 35
Conor O'Neill's (Ann Arbor), 70, 73
Cook's Farm Dairy (Ortonville), 30, 35
Copper Harbor, 222–23; information, 231; lodging, 223, 230
Copper Harbor Lighthouse, 222, 230
Copper Harbor Visitors Center, 231
Coppertown Mining Museum (Calumet), 225, 230
Corner Bar (Rockford), 86, 91
Cornwell's Turkeyville USA (Marshall), 68, 73
Cove Restaurant (Leland), 126, 133
covered bridges, 81, 82, 95, 112
Crooked Lake, 165
Crooked Tree Arts Center (Petoskey), 149, 152
Cross Village, 150–51; dining, 151, 153
Crystal Lake, 123
Curious Book Shop (East Lansing), 79, 89
Curtis, 235–36; information, 243
Curtis Michigan Chamber of Commerce, 243
Custer, George Armstrong, 57–58
Cut River Bridge, 235

D
Dalwhinnie Bakery and Deli (Beaver Island), 147, 153
Dam Store (Oscoda), 159–60, 167
Darrow's Family Restaurant (Mackinaw City), 175, 189
De Tour Reef Lighthouse, 186–87
De Tour Village, 186–87
Dearborn, 25–26
Delhi Metropark (Ann Arbor), 69
Detroit, 17–27; dining, 21, 23–24, 35; history of, 11–12, 19; information, 35; listings, 34–35; lodging, 24–25, 34; map, 18; sights/activities, 20–27, 34–35; traveling to, 17
Detroit Convention and Visitors Bureau, 35
Detroit Institute of Arts, 12–13

Detroit Marriott, 24
Detroit Riots of 1967, 12, 19
DeVries & Co. (Detroit), 23, 34
Dewey Lake Manor (Brooklyn), 64, 71
Dexter, 69
dining. *See specific destinations and establishments*
Dog Ears Books (Northport), 127, 132
Dog House Restaurant (Tecumseh), 60, 73
Dogpatch Restaurant (Munising), 203, 209
Don & GG's Food & Spirits (Ironwood), 216, 231
Donckers (Marquette), 205, 209
Dougherty House (Traverse City), 130
Dovetail Antiques (Lowell), 81, 89
Drummond Island, 186–87
Dundee, 59
dune buggy rides, 118, 132
Dutch elm disease, 12, 19–20

E
Eagle River, 224
Eagle River Falls, 224
Eagle River Timber Bridge, 224
East Channel Lighthouse, 202
East Lansing, 79; folk festival, 79, 90; lodging, 79, 89
East Tawas, 155
Eastern Market (Detroit), 22–23, 34
Eaton Rapids, 77–78; lodging, 78, 89
Edison (Thomas) Depot Museum (Port Huron), 41, 50
Edmund Fitzgerald, 185, 195, 196
Elberta, 123
Elderly Instruments (Lansing), 80, 89–90
Elk Lake, 139, 140
Elk Rapids, 135, 139–40; dining, 139, 153; information, 153
Elk Rapids Chamber of Commerce, 153
Elk Rapids District Library, 139
Elk River, 139
Ellsworth, 142; lodging, 142, 151
Empire: lodging, 124, 131–32
Engadine: lodging, 236, 242
English Inn (Eaton Rapids), 78, 89, 91
Erie, Lake, 53, 55, 56; beaches, 57
Erie and Kalamazoo Railroad Company, 59–60
Escanaba, 241–42; dining, 242, 243; information, 243
Escanaba in da Moonlight (movie), 241

F
Fair Lane (Dearborn), 26, 34
Fallasburg Covered Bridge, 81
Fallasburg Historic Village (Lowell), 81–82, 90
Fallasburg Park (Lowell), 81, 90
Falls River, 228–29
Fanny Hooe Lake, 222
Farm Restaurant (Port Austin), 45, 51
farmer's markets. *See* markets
Farmington Hills, 28
Fayette, 240
Fayette Historic State Park, 240, 242
ferries, 181; Beaver Island, 147; Bois Blanc Island, 166, 169; Charlevoix, Lake, 145, 148; Drummond Island, 186; Grand Island, 203, 207; Mackinac Island, 175–76, 189; Michigan, Lake, 120, 132
Fireside Inn Resort (Presque Isle), 163–64, 167
First Street Garden Inn (Ann Arbor), 71
Fitzgerald Park (Grand Ledge), 81, 90
Flat River, 81
Flat River Grill (Lowell), 82, 91
flea market, in Paw Paw, 98, 112
Ford, Henry, 11–12, 22, 25–26; Estate (Fair Lane; Dearborn), 26, 34
Ford Motor Company, 11–12, 19–20, 22, 25–26
Ford (Gerald R.) Museum (Grand Rapids), 85, 90
Ford Road, 26
Forgotten Highways, 53–73; highlights, 53, 55; listings, 71–73; map, 54; traveling to, 53
Fort Gratiot Lighthouse, 41, 50
Fort Mackinac (Mackinac Island), 174, 177–78, 187
Fort Wilkins Historic State Park, 221–22, 230
Fox Barn Agricultural Marketplace and Winery (Shelby), 117, 132
Fox River, 198–99
Francisco Morazan, 125–26
Frankenmuth, 47–49; dining, 48–49
Frankenmuth Brewery, 49, 51
Frankfort, 123
Fred Meijer White Pine Trail State Park, 87, 90
Frederik Meijer Gardens & Sculpture Park (Grand Rapids), 83, 90
Free Run Cellars (Berrien Springs), 99, 112

Fresh Air Aviation, 147, 153
Friends Good Will, 106
Friske's Farm Market (Atwood), 143, 152
fudge, 43, 50, 144, 176, 179

G
Gabbro Falls, 215–16
Garden: winery, 240–41, 243
Garden Grove Bed and Breakfast (Union Pier), 103, 111
Garden Peninsula, 239–41
Gay, 220–21
Gay Bar & Grill, 220–21, 230
Gemignani's Italian Restaurant (Hancock), 220, 231
Gerald R. Ford Museum (Grand Rapids), 85, 90
Germfask, 236
Gitche Gumee Agate & History Museum (Grand Marais), 200, 207
Glen Arbor, 124–25; dining, 125, 133; lodging, 125, 132
Glen Arbor Bed & Breakfast, 125, 131
Glen Haven, 123, 124
Golden Brown Bakery (South Haven), 108, 113
Golden Harvest (Lansing), 79–80, 91
Good Hart, 150
Good Hart & Soul Tea Room, 150, 152
Good Hart General Store, 150, 152
Goodells County Park, 39, 50
Goodison Cider Mill (Rochester), 32, 34
Gorge Falls, 216
Governor's Mansion Museum (Marshall), 65–66, 72
Grand Haven, 87–88; dining, 88, 91; information, 91; lodging, 88, 89
Grand Haven Area Convention & Visitors Bureau, 91
Grand Haven Lighthouse, 87
Grand Haven State Park, 87, 90
Grand Hotel (Mackinac Island), 179–80, 187
Grand Island, 202–3
Grand Island Ferry, 203, 207
Grand Island National Recreation Area, 209
Grand Lake, 163–64
Grand Lake Road, 163
Grand Ledge, 80–81
Grand Marais, 199–201; dining, 201, 209; information, 209
Grand Marais Chamber of Commerce, 209
Grand Marais Truck Trail, 199

Grand Mere State Park, 101–2, 112
Grand Rapids, 77, 82–87; dining, 86, 91; events, 85–86, 89; information, 91; lodging, 85, 86, 89; traveling to, 75
Grand Rapids Convention and Visitors Bureau, 91
Grand River, 26, 75, 77–79, 81, 82–83, 87–88; highlights, 75, 77; map, 76
Grand River Avenue, 75, 77, 78, 80, 81; map, 76
Grand Traverse Bay, 135, 137, 142–43; map, 136
Grand Traverse Lighthouse, 127, 132
Grandpa Tiny's Farm (Frankenmuth), 49, 50
Grandpa's Barn (Copper Harbor), 223, 230
Grange Hall Road, 29–30
Grape Coast, 93–113; highlights, 93–95; listings, 111–13; map, 94; traveling to, 93
Grass River Nature Area, 141, 152
Grayling, 159
Great Lakes Folk Festival (East Lansing), 79, 90
Great Lakes Maritime Heritage Center (Alpena), 162, 167
Great Lakes Shipwreck Museum (Paradise), 195–96, 207
Great Lakes Visitors Center (Ludington State Park), 121
Great Northwest, 135–53; highlights, 135; listings, 151–53; map, 136; traveling to, 135
Great Thumb Fire of 1881, 39
Great Wolf Lodge (Traverse City), 129, 131
Greater Lansing Convention Center, 91
Greater South Haven Chamber of Commerce, 113
Greektown (Detroit), 23–24
Greenfield Village (Dearborn), 25–26, 34
Griffin, 40–41

H
Hack-Ma-Tack Inn & Restaurant (Cheboygan), 166, 169
Hagadorn, 78
Hamlin Lake, 121
Hancock, 219, 220
Harbor Country, 99–111; highlights, 93–95; listings, 111–13; map, 94
Harbor Country Chamber of Commerce, 113
Harbor Grand (New Buffalo), 103–4, 111

Harbor Trolley (Grand Haven), 88, 90
Harrisville, 161; events, 161, 167
Harrisville Arts & Crafts Show, 161, 167
Harrisville State Park, 161, 167
Hart, 117
Hartford, 98
Hartwick Pines State Park, 166–67
Hayes State Park, 61, 72–73
Heart of Michigan, 75–91; highlights, 75, 77; listings, 89–91; map, 76; traveling to, 75
Hemingway, Ernest, 137, 148, 166, 198–99
Henry Ford, The (Dearborn), 25–26, 34, 35
Henry Ford Museum (Dearborn), 25–26, 34
Hereford & Hops (Escanaba), 242, 243
Heritage Hill (Grand Rapids), 83–85
Heritage Hill Neighborhood Association (Grand Rapids), 84, 90
Hessel, 182–84; dining, 184, 189
Hessel Bay Inn, 184, 189
Hessler Log Home (Traverse City), 131
Hiawatha National Forest, 194, 202–3
Hiawatha Riverboat (Soo Junction), 198
Hiawatha statue (Ironwood), 214
Hidden Lake Gardens (Tipton), 60–61, 72
Hill Auditorium (Ann Arbor), 70
Hillsdale, 64
Hilltop Restaurant (L'Anse), 228, 231
Historic Holly Hotel, 29, 35
Historic Mill Creek Discovery Park, 175, 187
Historic White Horse Inn (Metamora), 31–32, 35
Historic White Pine Village (Ludington), 119, 132
History Center at Courthouse Square (Berrien Springs), 104, 112
Hoeft State Park, 164, 169
Holdridge Lakes Mountain Bike Area, 30
Holly, 29; lodging, 29, 35
Holly State Recreation Area, 30, 34
Holly Wilderness Trail, 30
Holly's Main Street Antiques, 29, 34
Holy Transfiguration Skete (Eagle Harbor), 223–24
Horizon Books (Traverse City), 129, 132
Horton Bay, 148
Hostel Detroit, 25, 34
Hotel Iroquois on the Beach (Mackinac Island), 180–81, 187
hotels. See specific destinations and hotels

Houghton, 219; dining, 219, 231; information, 231
House of Flavors Restaurant (Ludington), 122, 133
House on the Hill Bed & Breakfast (Ellsworth), 142, 151
Hudson Mills Metropark (Dexter), 69, 72
Hurley, 213
Huron, Lake, 37–39, 155, 157, 161–63, 171–72, 182–83; beaches, 46, 158, 164; maps, 38, 156, 172; paddling, 45–46; sailing, 47, 50. See also Straits of Mackinac; Sunrise Coast; Thumb's Blue Water region
Huron City Museums (Port Austin), 44–45, 50
Huron County Visitors Bureau (Bad Axe), 51
Huron House B&B (Oscoda), 160, 167
Huron Lightship Museum (Port Huron), 41, 50
Huron National Forest, 160; Visitors Center, 160, 168
Huron River, 28
Huron River Parkway, 28
Huron Sunrise Trail, 164
Hurricane River Campground, 199
Hush Puppy Shoes, 86

I
Iargo Springs, 168
Indian Lake State Park, 239
Indian River, 165
Indian River Marina, 165, 167
Inn at 97 Winder (Detroit), 25, 34
Inn at Black Star Farms (Suttons Bay), 129, 131
Inn at Ludington, 122, 131
Inn at Union Pier, 103, 111
Inn on Ferry Street (Detroit), 24–25, 34
Inn the Garden B&B (Lexington), 42–43, 50
Insel Haus Bed & Breakfast (Bois Blanc), 166, 167
Irish Hills, 60–61
Irish Hills Towers, 61–62
Ironton Ferry, 145, 148
Ironwood, 213–15; dining, 216, 231; information, 231
Ironwood Area Chamber of Commerce, 231
Island Airways, 147, 153
Island Bookstore (Mackinac Island), 179, 187
Italian Hall (Calumet), 225–26, 230

J

Jampot, The (Eagle Harbor), 223–24, 230
Jilbert Dairy (Marquette), 205–6, 209
John A. Lau Saloon (Alpena), 162, 169
John Ball Zoo (Grand Rapids), 85, 90
John K. King Books (Detroit), 22, 34
Jollay Orchards (Coloma), 99, 112
Jonesville, 64; lodging, 64, 71–72

K

Kalamazoo, 96; lodging, 96, 111
Kalamazoo House B&B, 96, 111
Kalamazoo Lake, 109
Kalamazoo River, 59, 109
Kaug Wudjoo Lodge (Porcupine Mountains), 218
kayaking. *See* paddling
Keewatin Maritime Museum (Saugatuck), 108–9, 112
Kensington Metropark (Milford), 28, 34
Kewadin Sault Casino (Sault Ste. Marie), 185
Keweenaw Chamber of Commerce (Houghton), 231
Keweenaw Convention & Visitors Bureau (Calumet), 231
Keweenaw Mountain Lodge (Copper Harbor), 223, 230
Keweenaw National Historic Park, 225, 230
Keweenaw Peninsula, 211, 213, 218–29; map, 212
Killmaster Soapworks Natural Soap Co., 161, 167
King Books (Detroit), 22, 34
King Orchards (Central Lake), 141, 152
Kitch-iti-kipi, 239
Knaebe's Mmmunchy Krunchy Apple Farm and Cider Mill (Rogers City), 164, 167–68
Korner Kottage Bed & Breakfast (Suttons Bay), 128–29, 131
Krazy Jim's Blimpy Burger (Ann Arbor), 71, 73

L

L. Mawby (Suttons Bay), 239
L. Mawby Vineyards (Suttons Bay), 129, 132
La Bécasse (Maple City), 125, 133
La Belle Lake, 221
La Belle Lodge (Lac La Belle), 221, 230
La Cantina Restaurant (Paw Paw), 97, 113

Lac La Belle, 221; dining, 221, 231; lodging, 221, 230
Lafayette Coney Island (Detroit), 21, 35
lakes. *See specific lakes*
Lake Michigan Beach (town), 105
Lake Michigan Carferry (Ludington), 120, 132
Lake Michigan Scenic Highway, 233; map, 234
Lake Michigan Shore AVA, 96–97, 99, 113
Lake Michigan Shore Wine Trail, 113
Lake of the Clouds, 217
Lake Superior Brewing Co. (Grand Marais), 201, 209
Lake Superior Trail, 217
Lakenenland, 203–4, 207
Lakesports & Paradise Bay Gifts (Beaver Island), 147, 152
Landmark Inn (Marquette), 206, 207
Langley Covered Bridge, 95, 112
L'Anse, 228–29; dining, 228, 231
Lansing, 77, 79–80; dining, 79–80, 91; information, 91
Laughing Whitefish Falls, 203–4
Laurium, 225, 227; lodging, 227–28, 230
Laurium Manor Inn, 227–28, 230
Lawrence, 98
Leelanau Peninsula, 115, 117, 124–28; map, 116
Leelanau Peninsula Chamber of Commerce, 133
Leelanau Peninsula Wine Trail, 133
Leelanau State Park, 127
Lefty's Diner & Drive-In (Caseville), 47, 51
Legs Inn (Cross Village), 151, 153
Leland, 126; dining, 126, 133; lodging, 126, 131
Les Cheneaux Historical Museum (Cedarville), 183, 187–88
Les Cheneaux Islands, 172, 182–84; map, 172; paddling, 182, 183, 189
Les Cheneaux Islands Art Gallery (Hessel), 183–84, 188
Les Cheneaux Islands Chamber of Commerce (Cedarville), 189
Les Cheneaux Maritime Museum (Cedarville), 183, 188
Lexington, 42–43; lodging, 42–43, 50
Library Restaurant & Brew Pub (Houghton), 219, 231
lighthouses. *See specific lighthouses*

Lipuma's Coney Island (Rochester), 33, 35
Little River Railroad (Coldwater), 65, 72
Little Sable Point Lighthouse, 118
Little Traverse Bay, 148–49
Los Tequilas (Coldwater), 65, 73
Lowell, 81–82, 90; dining, 82, 91
Lower Trout Lake, 32
Ludington, 119–22; dining, 122, 133; information, 133; lodging, 121–22, 122, 131
Ludington Area Convention and Visitors Bureau, 133
Ludington House Bed & Breakfast, 122, 131
Ludington State Park, 121, 132
lumber industry, 11, 39, 99, 137, 160
Lumberjack Tavern (Big Bay), 208
Lumberman's Monument (Oscoda), 160, 168

M

Mac Wood's Dune Rides (Mears), 118, 132
McGinnis Lake, 30
McGulpin House (Mackinac Island), 177
Mackinac Bridge, 171, 181–82, 228
Mackinac Bridge Museum, 182, 188
Mackinac Bridge Walk, 182
Mackinac Island, 176–81; dining, 179, 189; ferries, 175–76, 189; information, 189; lodging, 179–81, 186–87; map, 172
Mackinac Island Carriage Tours, 178–79, 188
Mackinac Island State Park, 178–79, 188
Mackinac Island Tourism Bureau, 189
Mackinaw City, 173–75; dining, 175; information, 189
Mackinaw City Chamber of Tourism, 189
McLean & Eakin Booksellers (Petoskey), 149, 152
MacLeod House Bed & Breakfast (Newberry), 198, 207
Manabezho Falls, 216
Manistee, 123
Manistee Lake, 123
Manistee River, 159
Manistique, 238–39
Manistique Lake Road, 235
Manistique Lakes, 233, 235–36; map, 234
Manistique River, 238–39; paddling, 239
Manistique River State Forest, 239
Manitou Island Transit, 126, 132
Manitou Outfitters (Leland), 126
Maple City: dining, 125, 133

maritime museums, 106, 108–9, 112, 162, 167, 183, 185, 188, 193–94, 195, 207, 208
markets: Detroit, 22–23, 34; Hart, 117, 132; Paw Paw, 98, 112; Port Austin, 45, 50; Shelby, 117, 132
Marquette, 204–6; dining, 205–6, 209; information, 209; lodging, 206, 207
Marquette, Jacques, 119
Marquette County Convention & Visitors Bureau, 209
Marshall, 65–68; dining, 67–68; information, 73; lodging, 66–67, 72
Marshall Area Chamber of Commerce, 73
Marshall Historical Society, 66, 72
Martha Barker Country Store (Monroe), 58–59
Martha's Leelanau Table (Suttons Bay), 128, 133
Marvin's Marvelous Mechanical Museum (Farmington Hills), 28, 34
Mason County Courthouse (Ludington), 119
Meadow Brook Hall & Gardens (Rochester), 33–35
Mears, 117–18
Meijer (Frederik) Gardens & Sculpture Park (Grand Rapids), 83, 90
Meijer White Pine Trail State Park, 87, 90
Mermaid Bar & Grill (Saugatuck), 110, 113
Metamora, 30–32; lodging, 31–32
Mexicantown (Detroit), 24, 35
MexicanTown Bakery (Detroit), 24, 35
Meyer May House (Grand Rapids), 84, 90
MGM Grand Detroit, 24
Michigamme, 229
Michigamme, Lake, 229; paddling, 229
Michigamme Historical Museum, 229, 230
Michigan, Lake, 77, 87, 95, 99–102, 109, 117, 127, 150–51; beaches, 87, 100, 101–2, 106, 121, 123–24, 144, 235; ferry, 120, 132; fishing, 87; maps, 76, 94, 116, 136, 234; paddling, 59. *See also* Cherry Coast; Grape Coast; Great Northwest
Michigan Artists Gallery (Suttons Bay), 128, 132
Michigan Avenue, 17, 26, 56
Michigan House Café & Brew Pub (Calumet), 227, 231

Michigan Maritime Museum (South Haven), 106, 112
Michigan State Capitol (Lansing), 80, 90–91
Michigan State University (East Lansing), 78–79
Michigan Sugar Company, 39
Michilimackinac State Park, 174, 188
Middle Island, 162–63
Middle Island Boat Tours, 162–63, 168
Middle Island Keepers' Lodge (Alpena), 162–63, 167
Middle Island Lighthouse, 162
Milford, 28
Milford Road, 28–29
Mill Creek, 174–75
Mill Pond Inn (Clarkston), 31, 34
Mill Race Village (Northville), 27–28, 35
Millennium Park (Grand Rapids), 86
Miners Falls, 201
mining, 10–11, 218–21, 224, 225–26, 230–31
Mio, 159
missionaries, 10, 139, 148, 185
Model T Automotive Heritage Complex (Detroit), 22, 35
Mohawk, 224–25
Moka (Bellaire), 142, 153
Monocle Lake, 194
Monocle Lake Campground, 194, 207
Monroe, 57–59
Monroe County Historical Museums and Archives (Monroe), 58, 72
Montreal River, 215
Moore Public Library (Lexington), 42, 50
Mount Baldhead, 109
Muldoon's Pasties (Munising), 203, 209
Mullet Lake, 166
Munising, 201–2; dining, 203, 209; information, 209
Munising Falls, 201
Munising Visitors Bureau, 209
Munro House B&B (Jonesville), 64, 71–72
Museum Ship *Valley Camp* (Sault Ste. Marie), 185, 188
Muskallonge Lake State Park, 199, 207

N
National Blueberry Festival (South Haven), 105, 112
National Cherry Festival (Traverse City), 117, 132
National House Inn (Marshall), 66–67, 72
Native Americans, 10, 38, 146, 165, 184–85, 219, 221–22

Nature Gems Rock Shop (Northport), 127, 132
Nawadaha Falls, 216
Neahtawanta Inn (Traverse City), 131
New Buffalo, 99, 102–3; dining, 102–3, 113; information, 113; lodging, 103–4, 111
New Buffalo Beach Park, 100
New Presque Isle Lighthouse, 163, 168
Newberry, 198–99; information, 209; lodging, 198, 199, 207
Newberry Area Tourism Association, 209
North Country Grill & Pub (Suttons Bay), 128, 133
North Country Trail, 200–201
North Huron Shore Drive, 171, 182
North Manitou Island, 125–26
North Seas Gallery (Charlevoix), 144, 152
North Star Brick Oven Bakery (Newberry), 197–98, 207–8
Northland Outfitters (Germfask), 239, 242
Northport, 126–27; dining, 127, 133
Northville Road, 27–28

O
Oakland Township, 32
Oakland University (Rochester), 33–34
Ocqueoc Falls, 164–65
Ocqueoc Falls State Forest, 165
Ocqueoc River, 164–65
Oh! Fudge Shoppe (Lexington), 43, 50
Ojibwa Indians, 10, 193, 221–22
Old Hamlin Restaurant (Ludington), 122, 133
Old Mackinac Point Lighthouse, 175, 189
Old Mill Museum (Dundee), 59, 72
Old Mission General Store (Traverse City), 130, 132
Old Mission Point, 129–31
Old Mission Point Lighthouse, 130–31
Old Presque Isle Lighthouse and Museum, 163, 168
Old State Highway 21, 39–40
Old Town (Lansing), 79–80
Ontonagon, 218
Ontonagon River, 214
Opera House (Cheboygan), 165, 168
Orion, Lake, 19, 32
Orion Road, 19, 32
Ortonville, 30
Oscoda, 159–60; dining, 160–61, 169; information, 169; lodging, 160, 167
Oscoda Area Convention and Visitors Bureau, 169

Oscoda Canoe Rental, 159, 168–69
Oval Beach (Saugatuck), 109

P

Pablo's Panaderia (Lansing), 80, 91
paddling: Au Sable River, 158–59; Chain of Lakes, 138; Huron Lake, 45–46; Les Cheneaux Islands, 182, 183, 189; Manistique River, 239; Michigamme Lake, 229; Michigan Lake, 59; River Raisin, 59; Seven Mile Pond, 162, 167
Paint Creek Cider Mill (Oakland Township), 32, 35
Paint Creek Trail, 32, 35
Painted Horse Gallery (Northport), 127, 132
Palms Book State Park, 239, 243
Palm's Krystal Bar and Restaurant (Port Huron), 42, 51
Paradise, 194, 195; dining, 197, 209; information, 209
Paradise Chamber of Commerce, 209
Paw Paw, 97–98; dining, 97, 113; wineries, 97, 112–13
Paw Paw Wine and Harvest Festival, 97, 112
Peaches Bed & Breakfast (Grand Rapids), 85, 89
Pearl's New Orleans Kitchen (Elk Rapids), 139, 153
Pegasus Taverna (Detroit), 23, 35
Peninsula Grill (Traverse City), 130, 133
Peninsula Point Lighthouse, 241, 243
Pentamere Winery (Tecumseh), 60, 72
Pentwater, 119
Pere Marquette Highway, 115, 119
Petoskey, 145–46, 148–50; information, 153; lodging, 149–50, 151
Petoskey Regional Chamber of Commerce, 153
Petoskey Stones, 152
Petoskey United Methodist Church, 149
Pewabic Pottery (Detroit), 21–22, 35
Phelps, William Lyon, 44–45
P.H. Hoeft State Park, 164, 169
Phoenix Hose Company #1 Firehouse (Ludington), 119
Pickerel Lake, 165
Pictured Rocks, 200–201
Pictured Rocks Cruises (Munising), 202, 208
Pictured Rocks National Lakeshore, 199, 200–202, 208
Pierce Stocking Scenic Drive, 124

Pigeon River Country State Forest Area, 166, 169
Pinckney State Recreation Area, 69, 72
Piquette Plant (Detroit), 22
P.M. Steamers (Ludington), 122, 133
Point Iroquois Lighthouse & Maritime Museum, 193–94, 208
Pointe aux Barques, 44
Pointe aux Barques Lighthouse, 44, 50
Pointe Mouillee State Game Area, 56
Polly Ann Trail, 30, 32
Porcupine Mountains (Porkies), 213, 216–18; map, 212
Porcupine Mountains Wilderness State Park, 213, 216–18, 230
Port Austin, 44–46; dining, 45, 51; information, 51
Port Austin Chamber of Commerce, 51
Port Austin Farmer's Market, 45, 50
Port Austin Kayak, 45–46, 50
Port Huron, 40–42; dining, 41–42, 51; information, 51
Port Huron Fire of 1871, 39
Port Huron Museum, 41, 50
Port Huron to Mackinac Sailboat Race, 40
Port Sanilac, 43–44; dining, 44, 51
Port Sanilac Lighthouse, 44, 50
Portage, 95–96
Portage Canal Lift Bridge, 220
Potawatomi Falls, 216
Potawatomi Trail, 69
Presque Isle, 163–64; lodging, 163–64, 167
Presque Isle Park, 206, 208
Presque Isle River, 216, 217
Preston's Antique Gaslight Village (Allen), 65, 72
Primitive Images (Good Hart), 150, 152
Pumpernickel's Eatery (Saugatuck), 110, 113

Q

Quincy Mine (Hancock), 219, 230–31

R

rails-to-trails, 32, 111
Rainbow Lodge (Newberry), 199, 207
Raven Café (Port Huron), 41–42, 51
Red Arrow Highway, 93, 96–105; map, 94
Red Arrow Roadhouse (Union Pier), 102, 113
Red Cedar River, 78–79
Red Knapp's Dairy Bar (Rochester), 32, 35

Redamak's (New Buffalo), 102–3, 113
Redford, 27
Redford Theatre (Detroit), 27, 35
Reflections Art Gallery (Leland), 126
Reits Flea Market (Paw Paw), 98, 112
Rennhack Orchards Market (Hart), 117, 132
restaurants. *See specific destinations and restaurants*
Rifle River, 157
Risak Pottery & Gallery (Marquette), 206, 208
River Raisin, 55, 57, 59; paddling, 59
River Raisin National Battlefield Park, 57, 72
River Road Scenic Byway, 155, 159–60, 160, 168; map, 156
Riverside Inn (Leland), 126, 131, 133
Riverside Marina (Bellaire), 141, 152
Riverwalk Grill (Elk Rapids), 139, 153
Robert East Lee, 81
Rochester, 32–34, 34; cider mills, 32, 34, 35; dining, 32–33
Rochester Road, 32–33
Rockford, 86; dining, 86, 91
Rockford Footwear Depot, 86, 91
Rogers City, 164; information, 169
Rogers City Chamber of Commerce, 169
Rose Hill Inn (Marshall), 67, 72
Rouge River Park (Belmont), 26
Round Barn Winery (Baroda), 99, 112
Round Island Passage Light, 177
Round Lake, 61, 145
Round Lake Books (Charlevoix), 145, 152
Rowe Inn Restaurant (Ellsworth), 142
Royal Farms (Ellsworth), 143, 152

S
Sadie's Antique Cottage (Germfask), 237, 243
Saginaw River, 47
S. Ignace Visitors Bureau, 189
S. Joseph, 99, 104; dining, 104, 113
S. Joseph River, 95
S. Joseph's Church and Shrine (Cambridge), 62, 72
S. Julian Winery (Paw Paw), 97, 112
S. Laurent Brothers (Bay City), 47, 50
S. Mary's Islands, 186–87
S. Mary's River, 171, 184–85; map, 172
St. Clair Chamber of Commerce, 51
St. Clair County Farm Museum (Wales), 39
St. Clair River, 37, 40–41, 56
Sand Point Lighthouse, 242, 243

sandhill cranes, 28, 141
Sands Hill Lighthouse Inn (Ahmeek), 228, 230
Sandtown Farmhouse Bed & Breakfast (Engadine), 236, 242
Sanilac County Historic Village and Museum (Port Sanilac), 43, 50
Sarnia, 40
Saugatuck, 108–11; dining, 110, 113; information, 113; lodging, 110–11
Saugatuck and Douglas Visitors and Conventions Bureau, 113
Saugatuck Dune Rides, 110, 112
Saugatuck Dunes State Park, 109–10, 112
Sauk Trail, 55
Sault Ste. Marie, 184–85; dining, 185; information, 189
Sault Ste. Marie, Ontario, 188; lodging, 186, 187, 188
Sault Ste. Marie Chamber of Commerce, 189
Schoolcraft, Henry Rowe, 30–31, 55–56, 129, 173–74, 193
Schrier Park (Portage), 95–96
Schuler's Restaurant & Pub (Marshall), 67–68, 73
Seaberg Pontoon Rentals (Munising), 202, 208
seasons, 14–15
Seney, 201
Seney National Wildlife Refuge, 236–37, 243
Seul Choix Point Lighthouse, 238, 243
Seven Mile Pond: paddling, 162, 167
Seymour Lake Road, 30
Sheffield Car Company, 95
Shelby, 117
Shepler's Mackinac Island Ferry, 175–76, 189
Shipwreck Tours (Munising), 202, 208–9
Silliman House & Blacksmith Shop (Three Rivers), 95, 112
Silver Beach Pizza (S. Joseph), 104, 113
Silver Lake, 117–18
Silver Lake Buggies (Mears), 118, 132
Silver Lake Sand Dunes Area Chamber of Commerce, 133
Silver Lake State Park, 118, 132
Six Mile Lake, 141
Skyline Trail, 121
Sleeping Bear Bed & Breakfast (Empire), 124, 131–32
Sleeping Bear Dunes National Lakeshore, 123–24, 125–26, 132

Sleeping Bear Dunes Visitors Center, 123, 132
Snowbound Books (Marquette), 205, 209
Snug Harbor (Grand Haven), 88, 91
Somewhere in Time (movie), 180
Song of Hiawatha (Longfellow), 193
Soo Junction, 198
Soo Locks Park (Sault Ste. Marie), 185, 189
South Dune Highway, 123–24
South Haven, 104–8; dining, 107–8, 113; information, 113; lodging, 108, 111
South Manitou Island, 125–26
Southern Michigan Railroad Society (Clinton), 60, 72
Stafford's Perry Hotel (Petoskey), 149–50, 151
Star Line Mackinac Island Hydro-Jet Ferry, 175–76, 189
State Capitol (Lansing), 80, 90–91
Sterling State Park, 57, 73
Stone, Nancy, 137
Stone House Bread Café (Leland), 126, 133
Stoney Beach Farm (Traverse City), 129–30, 132–33
Stony Creek, 17
Stormy Kromer Mercantile (Ironwood), 214–15, 231
Straits of Mackinac, 171–89; highlights, 171–73; listings, 186–89; map, 172; traveling to, 171
Strang, James Jesse, 146–47
Strangmoor Bog, 236
Stratton, Mary Chase Perry, 20–22
Sturgeon Point Lighthouse, 161, 169
Sturgeon Point Scenic Site, 161
Sturgeon River, 229
Sue Silliman House & Blacksmith Shop (Three Rivers), 95, 112
sugar beets, 39, 240–41
Sukhothai (Rochester Hills), 33, 35
Summit Peak, 217–18
Summit Peak Side Trail, 218
Sunrise Coast, 155–69; highlights, 155, 157; listings, 167–69; map, 156; traveling to, 155
Superior, Lake, 191, 193; beaches, 201, 203; maps, 192, 212. *See also* Superior Lake shoreline
Superior Falls, 215
Superior Lake shoreline, 191–209; highlights, 191, 193; listings, 207; map, 192
Supino Pizzeria (Detroit), 23, 35

Suttons Bay, 127–29; dining, 128, 133; lodging, 128–29, 131
Swedish Pantry (Escanaba), 242, 243
Sweet Water Café (Marquette), 205, 209
Sylvan Inn (Glen Arbor), 125, 132

T
Tacconelli's Town House (Ironwood), 216, 231
Tahquamenon Falls, 197
Tahquamenon Falls Brewery & Pub (Paradise), 197, 209
Tahquamenon Falls Riverboat, 198
Tahquamenon Falls State Park, 197, 209
Tahquamenon Falls Wilderness Excursion (Soo Junction), 198, 209
Tahquamenon Logging Museum (near Newberry), 198, 209
Tahquamenon River, 194, 196–97; cruises, 198
Taquería Mi Pueblo (Detroit), 24, 35
Tawas, 155, 158; information, 169
Tawas Bay Tourist and Convention Bureau, 169
Tawas Point Lighthouse, 158
Tawas Point State Park, 158, 169
Tawas Point-Sand Hook Nature Trail, 158
Tecumseh, 60; dining, 60, 73; winery, 60, 72
Ten Pound Fiddle (East Lansing), 79, 91
Terrace Inn, The (Petoskey), 150, 151
Territorial Road, 55, 56, 65–66; map, 54
Thirsty Perch Watering Hole & Grille (South Haven), 107, 113
Thomas Edison Depot Museum (Port Huron), 41, 50
Thornapple River, 82
Three Oaks, 99
Three Rivers, 95
Threefold Vine Winery (Garden), 240–41, 243
Thumb Area Tourism Council, 51
Thumb's Blue Water region, 37–51; highlights, 37; listings, 50–51; map, 38; traveling to, 37
Thunder Bay National Marine Sanctuary and Underwater Preserve, 161–62, 169
Thunder Bay River, 157, 161–62
Tipton, 60–61
Torch Lake, 140–41
Tower of History (Sault Ste. Marie), 185, 189
Train Depot Museum (Grand Haven), 87, 91

Trapper's Alley (Detroit), 23
Trattoria Funistrada (Burdickville), 125, 133
Traverse City, 129–31; dining, 130, 133; festival, 117, 132; lodging, 129, 131
Tunnel of Trees, 150–51
Turnip Rock, 45–46
Twisted Fish Gallery (Elk Rapids), 139–40, 152
Two Hearted River, 191, 199
Two Lads Winery (Traverse City), 130, 133

U

Union Pier, 102–3; dining, 102, 113; lodging, 103, 111
Union Woodshop (Clarkston), 31, 35
University of Michigan (Ann Arbor), 70

V

Valley Camp Museum Ship (Sault Ste. Marie), 185, 188
Van Buren State Park, 111, 112
Van Buren Trail State Park, 111, 112
Van Camp House (Port Sanilac), 44, 51
Van Riper State Park, 229, 231
Vertin Gallery (Calumet), 227, 231
Village Inn (Mackinac Island), 179, 189
vineyards. *See* wineries
Voigt House (Grand Rapids), 84, 91

W

Wales, 39
Walker Tavern Historic Site (Onsted), 62–63, 72
Walter J. Hayes State Park, 61, 72–73
War of 1812, 57, 106, 177
Warner Vineyards Winery (Paw Paw), 97, 112–13
Warren Dunes State Park, 100–101, 113
Warren Woods State Park, 102, 113
Watervliet, 98
weather, 14–15
Weathervane Restaurant (Charlevoix), 145
West Bay, 199
West Monroe Road, 119
West Pier Drive-In (Sault Ste. Marie), 186, 189
West Shelby Road, 115
Wheels of History Museum (Brimley), 194
White Horse Inn (Metamora), 31–32, 35
White Pine, 218; dining, 218, 231
White Pine Trail, 87, 90
White Pine Trail State Park, 87, 90

White Pine Village (Ludington), 119, 132
Whitefish Bay, 193–94
Whitefish Point Lighthouse (Paradise), 194–96
Wild Goose Inn (East Lansing), 79, 89
Wilderness State Park, 151, 152
Wiltse's Brew Pub & Family Restaurant (Oscoda), 160–61, 169
Windermere Doghouse (Mackinac Island), 179, 189
Wine Country, 93–113; highlights, 93–95; listings, 111–13; map, 94; traveling to, 93
wineries, 96–97; Garden, 240–41, 243; Lake Michigan Shore AVA, 96–97, 99, 112–13; Shelby, 117, 132; Suttons Bay, 129, 132; Tecumseh, 60, 72; Traverse City, 130, 133
Wings of Mackinac Butterfly Conservatory, 178, 189
Wm. C. Sterling State Park, 57, 73
Woods & Water Ecotours (Hessel), 183, 189
Woodward Dream Cruise (Detroit), 19, 35
Wright, Frank Lloyd, 84

Y

Yates Cider Mill (Rochester), 32, 35
Yelton Manor Bed & Breakfast (South Haven), 108, 111
Young, Earl, 144–45

Z

Zehnder's of Frankenmuth, 48–49, 51
Zingerman's Bakehouse (Ann Arbor), 71, 73
Zingerman's Delicatessen (Ann Arbor), 70–71, 73
Zingerman's Roadhouse (Ann Arbor), 71, 73